S0-ASH-468

How to Use

MICROSOFT
EXCEL 97 FOR
WINDOWS

James J. Palermo
74 Emily Lane
Northampton MA
01060
413-584-0702

How to Use
MICROSOFT
EXCEL 97 FOR
WINDOWS

DEBORAH CRAIG

SPECIAL VALUE

Original Price
$24.99 BUS
$5.98
076559189-8

N 0701 MDC HT USE MS EXCEL 97

ZD PRESS

Ziff-Davis Press
An imprint of Macmillan Computer Publishing USA
Emeryville, California

Publisher	Stacy Hiquet
Acquisitions Editor	Lysa Lewallen
Copy Editor	Dusty Bernard
Technical Reviewer	Mark Hall
Production Editor	Madhu Prasher
Proofreader	Laurie K. Stewart
Book Design	Dennis Gallagher/Visual Strategies, San Francisco
Page Layout	M.D. Barrera and Janet Piercy
Indexer	Julie Kawabata

Ziff-Davis Press, ZD Press, and the Ziff-Davis Press logo are trademarks or registered trademarks of, and are licensed to Macmillan Computer Publishing USA by Ziff-Davis Publishing Company, New York, New York.

Ziff-Davis Press imprint books are produced on a Macintosh computer system with the following applications: FrameMaker®, Microsoft® Word, QuarkXPress®, Adobe Illustrator®, Adobe Photoshop®, Adobe Streamline™, MacLink® *Plus*, Aldus® FreeHand™, Collage Plus™.

Ziff-Davis Press, an imprint of
Macmillan Computer Publishing USA
5903 Christie Avenue
Emeryville, CA 94608

Copyright © 1996 by Macmillan Computer Publishing USA. All rights reserved.
PART OF A CONTINUING SERIES

All other product names and services identified throughout this book are trademarks or registered trademarks of their respective companies. They are used throughout this book in editorial fashion only and for the benefit of such companies. No such uses, or the use of any trade name, is intended to convey endorsement or other affiliation with the book.

No part of this publication may be reproduced in any form, or stored in a database or retrieval system, or transmitted or distributed in any form by any means, electronic, mechanical photocopying, recording, or otherwise, without the prior written permission of Macmillan Computer Publishing USA, except as permitted by the Copyright Act of 1976, and except that program listings may be entered, stored, and executed in a computer system.

THE INFORMATION AND MATERIAL CONTAINED IN THIS BOOK ARE PROVIDED "AS IS," WITHOUT WARRANTY OF ANY KIND, EXPRESS OR IMPLIED, INCLUDING WITHOUT LIMITATION ANY WARRANTY CONCERNING THE ACCURACY, ADEQUACY, OR COMPLETENESS OF SUCH INFORMATION OR MATERIAL OR THE RESULTS TO BE OBTAINED FROM USING SUCH INFORMATION OR MATERIAL. NEITHER MACMILLAN COMPUTER PUBLISHING USA NOR THE AUTHOR SHALL BE RESPONSIBLE FOR ANY CLAIMS ATTRIBUTABLE TO ERRORS, OMISSIONS, OR OTHER INACCURACIES IN THE INFORMATION OR MATERIAL CONTAINED IN THIS BOOK, AND IN NO EVENT SHALL MACMILLAN COMPUTER PUBLISHING USA OR THE AUTHOR BE LIABLE FOR DIRECT, INDIRECT, SPECIAL, INCIDENTAL, OR CONSEQUENTIAL DAMAGES ARISING OUT OF THE USE OF SUCH INFORMATION OR MATERIAL.

ISBN 1-56276-469-1

Manufactured in the United States of America
10 9 8 7 6 5 4

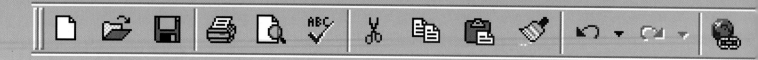

TABLE OF CONTENTS

ACKNOWLEDGMENTS

 I somehow sandwiched this latest writing project in between school, music, running, and a ragtag assortment of other extracurricular activities. I wouldn't have made it to the end of the book without the help of a long list of people.

My appreciation to all the experts at Ziff-Davis Press who smoothed the path and kept my spirits up. Thanks to Lysa Lewallen for getting this project on the road and keeping it there with the fewest possible swerves and side trips. Extra special thanks to Madhu Prasher for supreme competence, outstanding commitment to quality, general hilarity and hilariousness, and near unruffle-ability. It's a rare pleasure to work with someone who has the same delight in off-kilter humor, dog tales, and the all-round silliness of life. Thanks also to M. D. Barrera, Janet Piercy, and Laurie Stewart. These people are not just routinely proficient but are a treat to work with.

Thanks to Mark Hall for his careful technical review of the manuscript, his timeliness, and his astonishingly good humor throughout.

Immeasurable thanks to Dusty Bernard, one of the best copy editors in the business. Dusty has a wonderful sense of the language and a true dedication to getting the meaning just right. It was a thrill to have an editor who didn't simply stick commas in the proper places and trade this's for that's.

Many people contributed to the project even though they weren't formally "on board." Heidi Steele, friend and cohort, fielded questions throughout and answered most of them patiently and knowledgeably, despite being buried under a writing project of her own. (Time to send me a tech support bill, girl!) Johanna Clark extended considerable sympathy and helpful guidance at both on and off hours. Thanks also to Rebecca Black for occasional but invaluable phone support and special insights.

The infamous "Monday Night Band" chipped in with their typical quirky blend of inharmonious sounds and improbable humor. Thanks to Greg, Joe, Terry, and Dino (when they let him in the Palace door) for good-natured cacophony and acerbic nurturing.

My parents supported me unflinchingly in my decision to return to art school, even though it's one of the most far-fetched ideas I've dreamed up in a decade or so.

And thanks as ever to Lisa Biow, for sharing life and love and all the things in between that don't fit into words.

INTRODUCTION

 The book you have in your hands is for beginners. It doesn't assume that you know the slightest thing about the Excel spreadsheet program. It also doesn't bandy about special computer code words or mysterious acronyms. At the same time, this book doesn't presuppose that you need to be talked down to or that you can proceed, at best, at the intellectual equivalent of a slow crawl. (If you have absolutely no knowledge of Windows basics, such as how to use a mouse or a menu, you'd be better off consulting a beginning Windows book before you begin.)

What this book does assume is that you're a reasonably intelligent beginner. It starts at the beginning, explaining what Excel is and what it can do in a straightforward and no-frills manner. Once you've read this book, you'll have a firm grasp of the fundamentals. What's more, you'll be comfortable enough with Excel concepts and vocabulary to tackle its documentation, work your way through other, more advanced books on the topic, and even talk to Excel experts, including the support personnel at Microsoft Corporation. In short, this book aims to make you as self-sufficient as possible, supplying you with both the skills and the self-confidence to go out and explore the world of spreadsheet programs on your own. (And don't worry if you're not quite clear what a spreadsheet program really is. Chapter 1 will quickly clear up any lingering questions on this score.)

As you've probably noticed by now, this book is a bit different from other computer books you may have had to wrestle with. Rather than being organized around text, with pictures thrown in periodically to illustrate a point, it's organized around the pictures themselves. Each section consists of two pages covering a single topic. This way you get information in bite-sized pieces. Each of these two-page spreads is arranged in a series of easy-to-follow numbered steps that revolve around a central graphic; the imagery should make concepts both easier to grasp and easier to retain.

While the numbered steps explain the basics of carrying out each task, Tip Sheets in every section furnish somewhat more specialized information. They include valuable shortcuts, insights that may help you out in a pinch, and interesting or even entertaining asides.

In addition to its 18 chapters, this book contains three strategically located Try It sections to help you put your skills to the test. If you haven't been experimenting as you go along (and even if you have), you should try out these exercises. There is absolutely no better way to learn a computer program—or anything else, for that matter—than by doing things yourself, doing them again, and then doing them some more. Who knows? You may even have fun while you're at it.

CHAPTER 1

Introducing Excel

 A computer program that lets you manage financial data on your computer is called a *spreadsheet program,* and the data it manages is called a *spreadsheet.* Spreadsheets make it simple to track sales data, generate expense reports, and more. Best of all, spreadsheets perform all the calculations for you, even magically recalculating totals if any of your numbers change. This chapter first supplies an overview of what you can do with the Excel spreadsheet. Then it maps out the Excel landscape so you won't be in foreign territory when you go to work in Chapter 2.

When you start Excel, you're greeted with the electronic equivalent of a blank sheet of ledger paper. But the screen is far from empty. Instead it contains a whole assortment of tools you can use in your work. Some of these tools are common to most Windows-based programs and should seem familiar. (If not, consult a beginning book on Windows.) Others are specific to Excel. Try not to be overwhelmed by what may seem like a parade of foreign objects. Most of the tools you'll use are straightforward and easy to master. Many of the rest are so specialized that you can learn about them as needed, or happily ignore them.

Worksheets and workbooks are a critical piece of the Excel environment. The term *worksheet* means a basic spreadsheet; it's like a single page from a ledger pad. A *workbook* is like the ledger book itself—a set of worksheets stored in a single file. (Even if you're working with just a single worksheet, it's contained within a workbook file that can potentially contain a whole slew of worksheets.) Workbooks are convenient for organizing related spreadsheets into the same file; you could keep the sales data for each quarter on a separate worksheet within a single workbook, for instance.

What Can Excel Do?

Spreadsheets such as Excel can help you manage, analyze, and present data like that shown here. As you can see, Excel lets you organize numerical data into easy-to-follow columns and rows. It can nimbly carry out several other functions, which are described next.

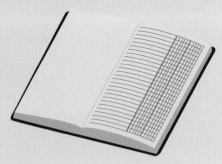

▶ ① Like all spreadsheet programs, Excel supplies an onscreen grid of columns and rows—an electronic ledger—into which you can enter data. Each box in the grid (the intersection of a row and a column) is called a *cell.* Usually you put numbers in cells, but you can also enter descriptive text, such as column and row headings.

TIP SHEET

▶ **If you've used a spreadsheet program other than Excel, many of the concepts presented in this book should seem familiar, although the exact commands and procedures may differ from those you're used to. But even if you know nothing about spreadsheets, you'll have no trouble following this book, which spells out spreadsheet basics in plain English instead of computerese.**

▶ **Not quite sure what a computer program is? (Programs may also variously be called *software, applications, software applications,* and any number of other things.) A program is simply a group of instructions that tell your computer what to do. Computers need programs to do any useful work.**

▶ **Often you need to install programs before you can use them, although these days more and more computers come with wads of programs already installed and ready to go. If Excel is not installed on your computer, you'll need to install it before using this book. (Don't read without having the program running!) Follow the instructions that came with Excel to do so. And don't worry: Installing software was once a somewhat cryptic process, but now it's typically a matter of following simple instructions in your documentation and/or on your screen.**

2nd Qtr Totals > $5,000	
Dept.	**Total**
R & D	$8,094
Sales	$14,257

⑥ Excel makes it easy to find just the data you need. For instance, you can say you want the name of every department that spent more than $5,000 in the second quarter, and Excel will track down this information for you speedily.

2 Excel can perform calculations and display the results. Any cell can contain the results of a calculation performed on any other cells in the spreadsheet.

3 You can easily change the contents of any cell. And the best part is that if you change a number that is used in a calculation elsewhere in the spreadsheet, the result of that calculation changes automatically.

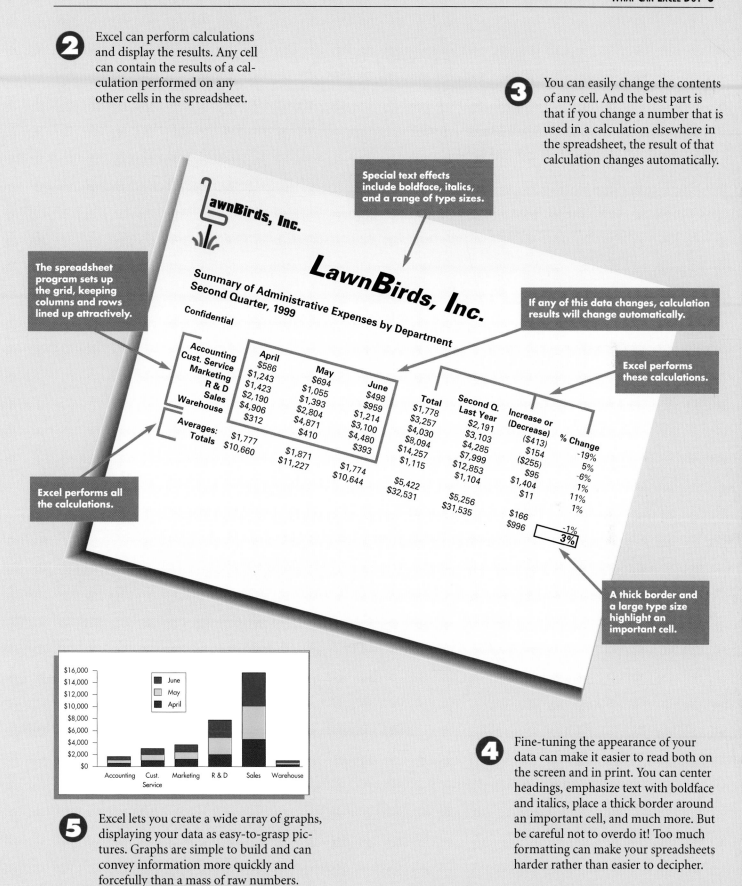

Special text effects include boldface, italics, and a range of type sizes.

The spreadsheet program sets up the grid, keeping columns and rows lined up attractively.

If any of this data changes, calculation results will change automatically.

Excel performs these calculations.

Excel performs all the calculations.

A thick border and a large type size highlight an important cell.

LawnBirds, Inc.

LawnBirds, Inc.

Summary of Administrative Expenses by Department
Second Quarter, 1999
Confidential

	April	May	June	Total	Second Q. Last Year	Increase or (Decrease)	% Change
Accounting	$586	$694	$498	$1,778	$2,191	($413)	-19%
Cust. Service	$1,243	$1,055	$959	$3,257	$3,103	$154	5%
Marketing	$1,423	$1,393	$1,214	$4,030	$4,285	($255)	-6%
R & D	$2,190	$2,804	$3,100	$8,094	$7,999	$95	1%
Sales	$4,906	$4,871	$4,480	$14,257	$12,853	$1,404	11%
Warehouse	$312	$410	$393	$1,115	$1,104	$11	1%
Averages:	$1,777	$1,871	$1,774	$5,422	$5,256	$166	-1%
Totals	$10,660	$11,227	$10,644	$32,531	$31,535	$996	**3%**

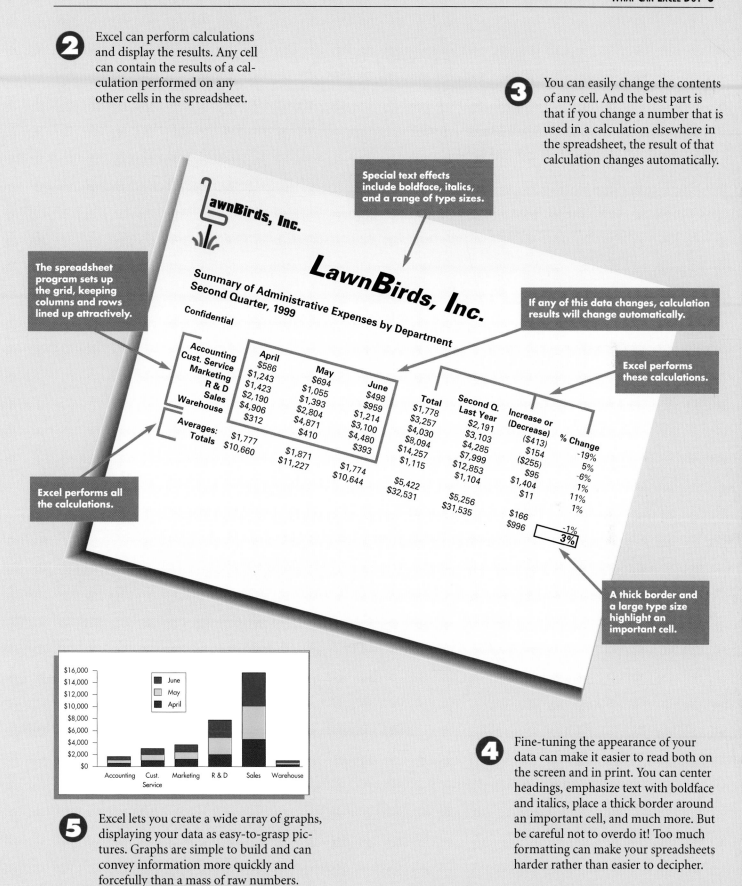

5 Excel lets you create a wide array of graphs, displaying your data as easy-to-grasp pictures. Graphs are simple to build and can convey information more quickly and forcefully than a mass of raw numbers.

4 Fine-tuning the appearance of your data can make it easier to read both on the screen and in print. You can center headings, emphasize text with boldface and italics, place a thick border around an important cell, and much more. But be careful not to overdo it! Too much formatting can make your spreadsheets harder rather than easier to decipher.

What's on Your Screen

When you start Excel, you see a screen similar to the one shown here. (Excel is nice enough to open a new workbook for you.) Before you get started, you should familiarize yourself with what's on this screen, much as you would consult a road map before setting off on a voyage. Once again, try not to be intimidated: Excel has far less clutter than many spreadsheet programs, and soon these tools will come to seem like old friends.

TIP SHEET

▸ **Don't feel compelled to memorize every bit of information that sails your way. In Chapter 6 you'll learn how to use Excel's Office Assistant and help system, which you can always call upon if you have a memory lapse or need to be bailed out of a bad situation.**

▸ **Because Windows-based programs are customizable, your screens may not look exactly like the ones shown in this book. If your screens seem to be missing an important piece, try pulling down the View menu. If the Formula Bar command has no check mark to its left, click it to introduce one. The same goes for the Status Bar command. If you can't find the toolbars mentioned here, click Toolbars in the View menu and then click Standard and Formatting. (Notice that Excel provides a whole slew of other toolbars; you'll learn about some of these in your travels.)**

▸ **When you start Excel, you see only the upper-left corner of the worksheet. An Excel worksheet contains 256 columns and 65,536 rows! After Z, Excel uses the column headings AA, AB, and so on, through IV. Although you're extremely unlikely to use the entire available grid, many worksheets are large enough that you have to scroll to track down the data you need.**

▶ **1** If Excel isn't already started, start it now by choosing Programs from the Start menu and choosing Microsoft Excel. (If you're lucky, you may be able to start Excel just by double-clicking on a desktop shortcut labeled "Shortcut to Excel" or something similar.)

8 The status bar at the bottom of the screen supplies helpful hints about what's going on with Excel. Now it says *Ready,* meaning that Excel is ready for you to enter data. It also displays the names of keys such as Caps Lock and Num Lock when they are in use. Finally, and most handily, it displays the sum of any numbers you select.

7 The mouse pointer takes on the shape of a plus sign when it's over a cell. But it may take on other shapes if you are pointing to different areas of the screen. The meanings of different mouse pointer shapes are explained as they come up in this book.

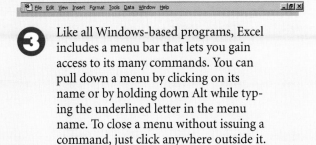

2 The title bar lists the name of the application plus the name of the workbook file you're currently using. (The names will be on two separate title bars if the document window isn't maximized.) When you start Excel, the program opens a blank workbook and calls it Book1. Excel uses this temporary name until you name and save the workbook, as described in Chapter 3.

3 Like all Windows-based programs, Excel includes a menu bar that lets you gain access to its many commands. You can pull down a menu by clicking on its name or by holding down Alt while typing the underlined letter in the menu name. To close a menu without issuing a command, just click anywhere outside it.

4 The Standard and Formatting toolbars contain mouse shortcuts for a whole range of Excel commands. These shortcuts can save you time and trouble; for example, you can click the B button to boldface your data. If you're not sure what a particular button is for, place your mouse pointer over it. In a moment, Excel displays the button's name as a *ScreenTip* immediately underneath the button.

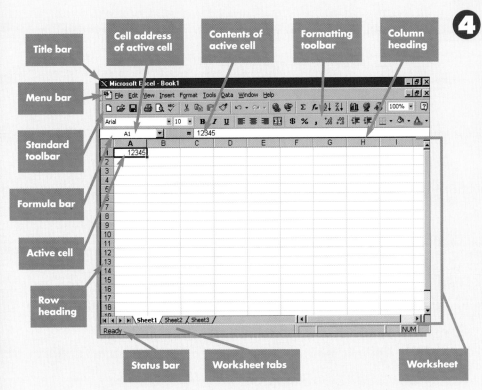

Title bar | Menu bar | Standard toolbar | Formula bar | Active cell | Row heading
Cell address of active cell | Contents of active cell | Formatting toolbar | Column heading
Status bar | Worksheet tabs | Worksheet

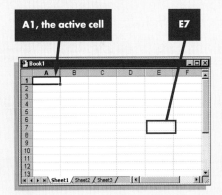

A1, the active cell | E7

5 In this worksheet, the highlighted *worksheet tab* indicates that you're in Sheet1, the first worksheet in the workbook. (It's like the first page in a ledger book.) Excel labels each column with a letter and each row with a number. This way, you can identify each cell by its *cell address*—the column letter and row number combination. For example, the cell where column E and row 7 intersect is called cell E7. The *active cell*, the cell affected by actions you take, is enclosed within a thick border.

6 The *formula bar* (below the toolbar) displays the contents of the active cell. The left part of the formula bar lists the address of the active cell. The right portion shows the contents of the active cell. Here the right side of the formula bar is empty because there's nothing in the active cell. As you'll discover in Chapter 2, what you see in the worksheet may differ from the cell's contents as displayed in the formula bar.

CHAPTER 2

Setting Up a Worksheet

Now that you've learned a bit about Excel's topography, you're probably eager to start entering and making sense of some data. This chapter explains the basics of inputting data and doing rudimentary arithmetic—the main skills you'll need to set up a simple worksheet. (Chapter 3 explains how to save your data so you can come back to it later or close your workbook without saving it.)

Before you start typing merrily away, however, it's wise to stop and consider how best to present your data. There's nothing mysterious about organizing a spreadsheet; you can probably get by with your own personal quota of common sense. For starters, it's a good idea to include a title that plainly identifies the worksheet's purpose. You should also supply column and row headings to make it clear what the numbers stand for. And you need to spend some time thinking about what types of calculations you want to perform. A well-thought-out worksheet saves you time and aggravation in two ways. It makes data easy to find and work with—both for you and for others. It also keeps you from having to overhaul your work later on down the line.

Although your worksheet has to be easy to understand, you don't need to obsess about getting everything "just right" the first time. Chapter 4 introduces some editing skills for correcting your mistakes, Chapter 6 describes some easy techniques for fixing errors, and Chapter 7 explains how to restructure the worksheet if necessary. Chapter 8 then reveals some secrets for improving your worksheet's appearance so you can produce worksheets that are not only accurate but also look great.

How to Enter Data

Whenever you see the word *Ready* in the status bar, you can enter data into your worksheet. Entering data actually takes three steps: First, you need to activate the desired cell; second, you have to type your data; and third, you need to finalize that data entry, typically by pressing Enter, Tab, or one of the arrow keys. The steps are the same whether you're entering text—such as column headings—or numbers.

TIP SHEET

▸ **Finalizing data entry with the Enter button doesn't move you from the active cell. Pressing the Enter key finalizes your data entry and moves you down one cell (making it easy to enter a column of data), Tab moves you right one cell, and each arrow key moves you one cell in the direction of the arrow. With these methods, you can keep your hands on the keyboard and are less likely to accidentally overwrite the data you just typed. You can also finalize data entry and activate any other cell by clicking that cell.**

▸ **If pressing the Enter key doesn't select the cell immediately below, choose Tools, Options, click the Edit tab, make sure Move Selection After Enter is selected, and choose the desired Direction setting.**

▸ **Excel lets you enter data that is too wide for the cell, but it may not display the data in full. Wide text entries spill over into the adjacent cells if they're empty; otherwise, these entries are cut off at the cell's edge. (Excel considers any combination of numbers, spaces, and nonnumeric characters to be text.) Numbers that are too wide for their cells are displayed either in scientific notation (something like 1.23E+12) or as a series of pound signs (#). Even if your data doesn't show up completely, it's still stored in full in Excel and used in calculations. Also, both text entries and numbers show up if you widen the column sufficiently (see Chapter 7).**

▸ **If you're fuzzy about any of the mouse, keyboard, or menu techniques mentioned here, consult a basic book on Windows.**

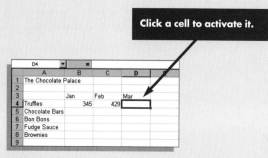

Click a cell to activate it.

1 Locate the cell in which you need to enter data. If you can't see the cell you want, use the scroll bars to bring it into view. Click the desired cell to make it the active cell. It takes on a dark border and its column and row headings look raised so it's easy to see the cell address.

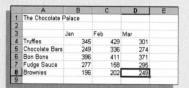

 5 Repeat the steps you just learned to enter the rest of your data.

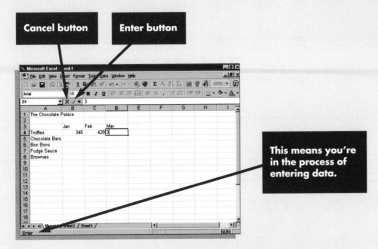

Cancel button

Enter button

This means you're in the process of entering data.

2 Type your data in the active cell. Whatever you type appears in both the active cell and the formula bar. Two buttons also show up in the formula bar when you start typing: the Enter button and the Cancel button. Notice that the status bar reads *Enter* to indicate that you're in the process of entering data.

3 Click the Enter button to indicate that you are done typing the data. You can also press the Enter key, the Tab key, or one of the arrow keys to finalize your data entry. What's the difference between all these keys and buttons? Check the Tip Sheet for details.

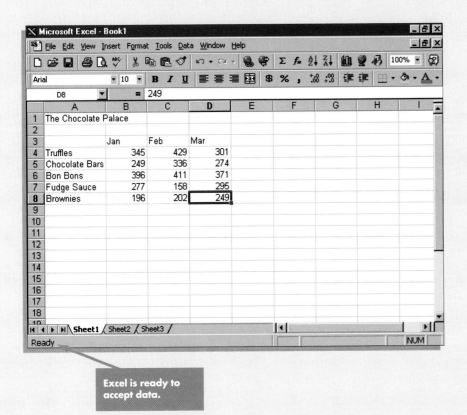

Excel is ready to accept data.

Press Backspace to delete the character to the left of the insertion point.

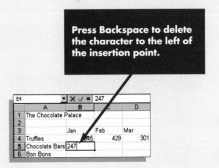

4 If you make a mistake before you've finalized your data entry, press the Backspace key to delete the character to the left of the insertion point (it's the blinking vertical line). To erase everything you've typed and start over, click the Cancel button or press the Escape (Esc) key. (Chapter 4 explains some techniques for editing data after you've already entered it.)

How to Enter a Formula

O ne of the magical things about electronic spreadsheets is that cells don't have to contain fixed data. Instead, they can contain formulas—sets of instructions that perform calculations and display the results. A formula can be as simple as =2+2 (in Excel you need to start all formulas with an equal sign). But it's far more useful for formulas to use cell references rather than numbers. *Cell references* are just cell addresses that tell Excel to perform its calculations using the data currently in the designated cells. If you then edit the data being referred to, the formula results change automatically. (This is sometimes called *automatic recalculation.*)

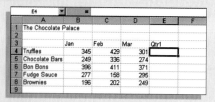

> **1** Click the cell where you want to place the formula, making it the active cell.

TIP SHEET

▶ **You can't tell by looking at a worksheet whether a cell contains a fixed number or the result of a formula. To find out, activate the cell and then look at the formula bar, which always shows a cell's underlying contents.**

▶ **When you type an equal sign or click the Edit Formula (=) button on the formula bar, Excel displays a list of functions on the left end of the formula bar. (Click the drop-down arrow to see and select these functions.) Functions are tools that help simplify calculations. You'll learn about a basic function, the SUM function, on the next page. You'll also learn more about functions in Chapters 9 and 16.**

▶ **You can type cell references in either uppercase or lowercase. Excel converts the letters to uppercase when you enter the formula. Also, you needn't type spaces around the mathematical operators, but you can if you like.**

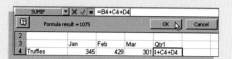

> **6** You can also enter formulas by first clicking the Edit Formula (=) button on the formula bar. (You may be greeted by your Office Assistant. You'll learn more about this handy and friendly creature in Chapter 6.) When you use this method, you can see the results of your formula as you go along. If you're satisfied with the results, click OK; if not, click Cancel.

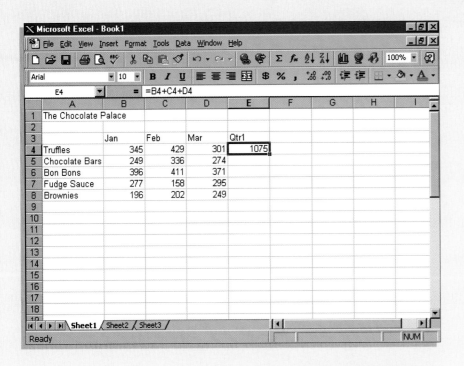

2 Type an equal sign (=). You need to start formulas with an equal sign so Excel doesn't read them as text entries. If you forget the =, Excel won't perform any calculations and instead just displays exactly what you typed.

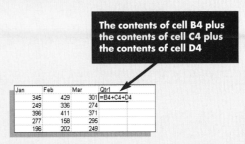

The contents of cell B4 plus the contents of cell C4 plus the contents of cell D4

3 Type your formula, if possible using cell references instead of numbers. This way, if you change any of the numbers being referred to, Excel updates the calculation results automatically based on the new numbers. The mathematical operators you can use in formulas include + for addition, – for subtraction, * for multiplication, / for division, and ^ for exponentiation. The formula shown here will add the January, February, and March sales figures for truffles to produce the first-quarter total.

4 Enter the formula by clicking the Enter button or by pressing Enter, Tab, or any of the arrow keys.

The formula itself shows up in the formula bar.

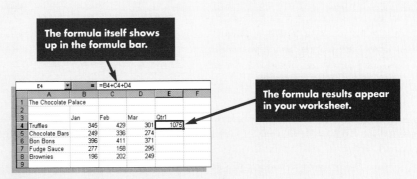

The formula results appear in your worksheet.

5 As you can see, the cell now contains the results of the calculation—the first-quarter truffle sales. Whenever the cell is active, however, the formula bar displays the underlying formula.

How to Sum Numbers

A moment ago you saw how to add two or more numbers by building a formula in which the cells being added together are separated by plus signs. When you have to add many numbers—12 monthly totals, for example—this approach can be pretty cumbersome. Luckily, Excel offers the SUM function, a built-in formula that produces the same result with a great deal less effort. The SUM function is especially convenient when the numbers you're adding are in adjacent cells, either along a row or down a column.

TIP SHEET

▶ **SUM is just one of literally hundreds of Excel functions. (Don't worry! You don't have to learn all of them, or even very many of them.) Among other things, these functions can help you perform statistical, financial, and database calculations. Chapter 9 covers several additional functions and Chapter 16 delves into some more advanced functions.**

▶ **The Sum= indicator in the status bar shows the sum of selected numbers and is a handy way to quickly see what a set of numbers adds up to. (Chapter 4 explains selecting.)**

▶ **Common mistakes when typing SUM and other functions include forgetting the equal sign and forgetting the opening parenthesis. (Don't worry about forgetting the closing parenthesis; Excel supplies it for you if you do.) Chapter 4 explains how to edit cell contents and correct mistakes like these.**

▶ **When you used the SUM function—and when you created a formula on the previous page—you simply typed in any cell references. You can speed up the process, often considerably, by selecting cell references with the mouse. For example, to sum the numbers in the range B4:B8, you could type =sum(, drag across the cells B4 through B8, type), and press Enter.**

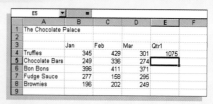

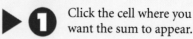

▶ **1** Click the cell where you want the sum to appear.

2 Type **=sum(** using either lowercase or uppercase. (Excel converts the letters to uppercase automatically. Feel free to type in lowercase so you don't have to bother with the Caps Lock key.)

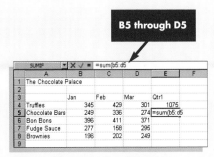

B5 through D5

3 If you're adding adjacent cells, type the first cell reference, followed by a colon (:), followed by the last cell reference. If the cells are not adjacent, just list their cell references, separated by commas. (Any rectangular group of adjacent cells is called a *range*, which you specify by typing the address of the upper-left cell, a colon, and the address of the lower-right cell. For example, the range B2:C4 includes the cells B2, B3, B4, C2, C3, and C4.)

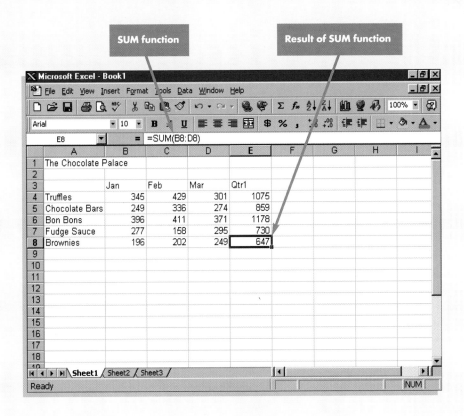

SUM function

Result of SUM function

4 Type a closing parenthesis,), and then click the Enter button, or press Enter, Tab, or one of the arrow keys. Note that the elements of the function between parentheses are often called the function's *arguments*. Most functions need at least one argument; some need more.

6 You can calculate quarterly totals for the remaining sale items using the same strategy. This particular SUM function isn't any briefer than a formula that uses plus signs, but if you're adding a group of ten cells—or 100 cells—instead of three, using SUM will greatly simplify your life. The next page also explains some strategies for summing numbers even more quickly, and Chapter 9 describes a handy shortcut for generating similar formulas and functions.

5 As you can see, the cell now displays the sum of the numbers from the specified cells, while the formula bar displays the SUM function when the cell is active. If you edit the data in any of the cells in the designated range, Excel immediately recalculates the results.

How to Sum Numbers Automatically

When you're adding numbers, typing the SUM function instead of building formulas with plus signs can speed up your work considerably. Under the right set of circumstances, Excel can go one better: When summing rows or columns of contiguous numbers, you can use the AutoSum toolbar button to have Excel generate one or more SUM functions for you.

TIP SHEET

▶ **The AutoSum toolbar button works best when you're adding adjacent cells. If you want to sum a series of nonadjacent cells, you can type in a SUM function, entering cell references separated by commas. (Don't forget that you can enter cell references by clicking or dragging across cells.) For example, to add the contents of A1, B2, and C3, you would enter the function =SUM(A1,B2,C3).**

▶ **You can sum columns and rows at the same time. To do this, you select the numbers to be summed, plus an extra column to the right and an extra row below to hold the totals, and then click the AutoSum toolbar button. Check the next chapter for the details about selecting ranges.**

▶ **You can also sum numbers by choosing SUM from the function drop-down list that appears on the formula bar when you type = or press the Edit Formula (=) button. You'll see a dialog box for creating formulas. Check whether Excel has selected the correct numbers. If so, click OK; if not, click the button to the right of the Number1 box, click or drag across the cells to be summed, press Enter, and then choose OK. As you can see, AutoSum is easier when you're adding columns and/or rows of adjacent numbers!**

▶ **If Excel suggests the wrong range of cells when you use the AutoSum button, you can enter a different range just by dragging across it. This technique won't work if you generate several SUM functions at once, however.**

	A	B	C	D	E	F
1	The Chocolate Palace					
2						
3		Jan	Feb	Mar	Qtr1	
4	Truffles	345	429	301	1075	
5	Chocolate Bars	249	336	274	859	
6	Bon Bons	396	411	371	1178	
7	Fudge Sauce	277	158	295	730	
8	Brownies	196	202	249	647	
9	Totals					
10						

▶ **1** This worksheet doesn't yet include monthly totals. See if you can figure out which SUM function you would use to add up these totals (but don't type it in). Also notice that the monthly data is arranged in columns that don't contain any empty cells.

E9		=	=SUM(E4:E8)			
	A	B	C	D	E	F
1	The Chocolate Palace					
2						
3		Jan	Feb	Mar	Qtr1	
4	Truffles	345	429	301	1075	
5	Chocolate Bars	249	336	274	859	
6	Bon Bons	396	411	371	1178	
7	Fudge Sauce	277	158	295	730	
8	Brownies	196	202	249	647	
9	Totals	1463	1536	1490	4489	
10						

 If you click in the various cells containing the new SUM functions, you'll notice that they all add up the numbers just above or just to the left of the active cell.

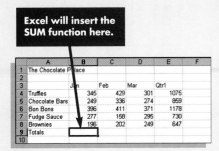

Excel will insert the SUM function here.

② Activate the cell that will contain the results of the SUM function. You need to select a cell either beneath a column of contiguous numbers or to the right of a row of contiguous numbers.

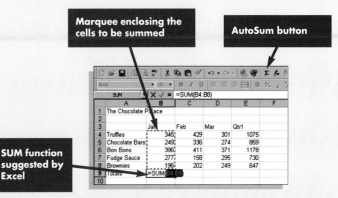

Marquee enclosing the cells to be summed

AutoSum button

SUM function suggested by Excel

③ Click the AutoSum toolbar button. Excel displays a SUM function that will add the numbers above or to the left of the active cell. (Does this formula match the one you thought of in step 1?) A flashing marquee (dashed line) also encloses the cells to be summed.

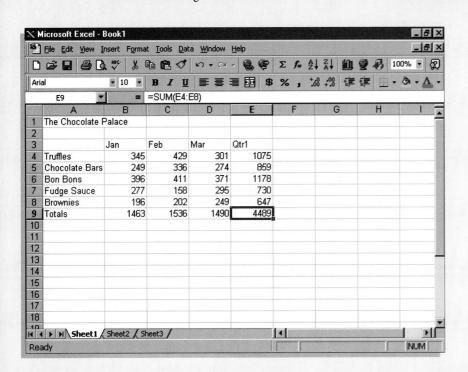

④ Click the Enter button or press the Enter key to accept the formula.

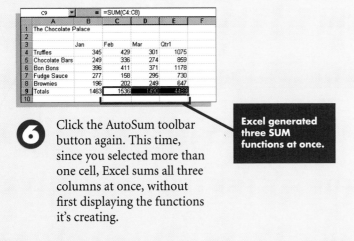

Excel generated three SUM functions at once.

⑥ Click the AutoSum toolbar button again. This time, since you selected more than one cell, Excel sums all three columns at once, without first displaying the functions it's creating.

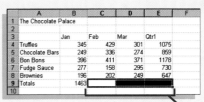

These cells are selected.

⑤ You can also enter several SUM functions at once by dragging across the cells that are to hold the functions. This selects the cells, enclosing them within a border. Selected cells are black except for the active cell, which is white. (You'll learn more about selecting cells in Chapter 4.)

How to Enter Data Automatically

At the beginning of this chapter, you got a lesson in basic data entry. Excel provides a few neat tricks for speeding up the entry of data series. For example, if you're creating labels for the months of the year, you don't have to type in each month individually. Instead, you can type just the first month and use Excel's fill handle to produce the remaining month names automatically. You can also use the fill handle to generate series of numbers separated by regular intervals.

Fill handle

▶ **1** The first step in creating a series of labels is to enter the initial label. For instance, if you want to enter the days of the week, enter the name of the day you want to start with. (You can start with any day of the week; there's no law that says you have to start with Monday. In addition, you can use the spelling you like best. Both *Monday* and *Mon* are just fine, for example. Excel takes its cue from the spelling you use and generates either complete labels—*Tuesday, Wednesday,* and so on—or abbreviated labels—*Tues, Wed,* and so on—accordingly.) Make sure the cell containing the initial label is the active cell, and notice the fill handle in its lower-right corner.

TIP SHEET

▶ **When creating a series of numbers, don't enter the first two numbers and then drag across them. (This just selects the numbers.) Also don't enter the first two numbers and drag on the fill handle of the second one. (You'll just make copies of the second number!)**

▶ **You can use the fill handle to copy formulas as well as to create data series (see Chapter 9).**

▶ **You may have noticed Excel entering information automatically when you typed columns of labels. This feature is called *autocompletion,* and here's how it works: When you enter a label in a cell directly underneath a column of one or more existing labels, Excel guesses what you want to enter based upon the data already in that column. For example, if you've already typed Truffles and then you type T, Excel typically assumes that you want to enter Truffles again and fills it in for you. You can also right-click the cell directly below a column of labels, choose Pick From List from the menu, and choose from a list of all labels in the column. To turn it off, choose Tools, Options, click the Edit tab, and deselect the check box Enable AutoComplete for Cell Values.**

Because the first two times were one hour apart, Excel generates additional times separated by one hour.

7 As before, drag the fill handle across the cells you want to fill with data. When you release the mouse button, Excel fills in your data, like a charm.

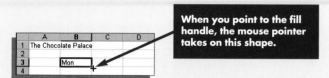

When you point to the fill handle, the mouse pointer takes on this shape.

2 Place the mouse pointer over the fill handle; it changes into a plus sign.

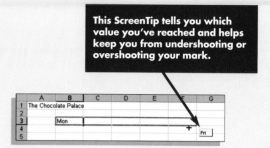

This ScreenTip tells you which value you've reached and helps keep you from undershooting or overshooting your mark.

3 Now drag across the cells that are to contain the additional labels in the series. Notice that as you drag, Excel displays a ScreenTip telling you which label will displayed in the cell you're dragging over.

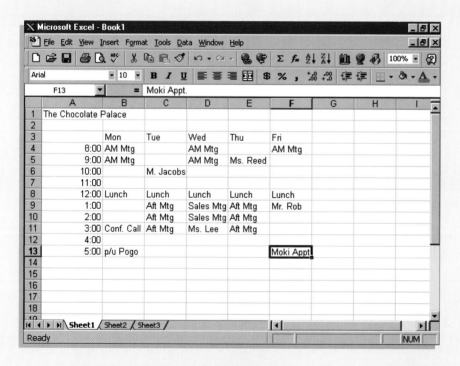

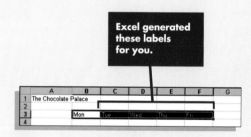

Excel generated these labels for you.

4 When you release the mouse button, Excel inserts the rest of your labels automatically. You can use this technique to enter not only months and days of the week, but also series of labels such as Quarter1, Quarter2, and so forth.

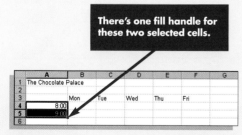

There's one fill handle for these two selected cells.

6 Once you've entered the initial two numbers, drag across them to select them. You'll see a fill handle in the rightmost or bottom cell you selected.

5 You can use a similar approach to produce a series of numbers. In this case, you start by entering the first *two* numbers in the series. Excel uses the interval between these two numbers to determine which numbers should follow. If you start with 1 and 2, for example, Excel will continue with 3, 4, and so on. If you start with 110 and 120, Excel will continue with 130, 140, and so forth. You get the picture.

CHAPTER 3

Managing Your Workbooks

At times you'll want to do the electronic equivalent of crumpling up your workbook and pitching it in the trash. (Remember, even if you're working with a single worksheet, it's contained within a workbook file.) Very often, however, you'll need to preserve your workbooks so you can return to them later—to finish them, to edit them, or to print them. Other skills you'll want to know are how to start with a fresh workbook and how to exit from Excel when you're done for the day. Once you've stored a workbook in a safe place, you'll also need to know how to open it, bringing it back up on your computer screen so you can work with it again.

This chapter covers an array of features. It explains how to save a workbook, remove it from the screen, and close Excel. It also shows you how to start a brand-new workbook, how to retrieve a workbook you've saved, and how to use different worksheets within a workbook. These techniques are among the most fundamental you'll learn in this book, and many of the concepts behind them apply to almost any Windows program you'll ever use.

How to Save and Close a Workbook

When you first create a workbook in Excel, it is stored temporarily in your computer's memory (RAM). But that memory is like a slate that is wiped clean each time the computer goes off. If you turn off your computer or there's a power outage, all your hard work is instantly vaporized. Unless you've saved it, that is. Saving a workbook just means recording it on disk—either a hard disk or a floppy—so you can come back to it later.

TIP SHEET

▶ You can also use the Close command to remove a workbook from the screen without saving it or saving any new changes you've made to it. To do this, just respond No when asked whether you want to save the changes you've made.

▶ You use the Save command to name and save a file initially or to save the newest version of a file without changing the file's name. (The Save command overwrites the old version of the file with the new.) If you instead want to save an extra copy of your file with a different name and/or in a different location, you should use the Save As command on the File menu. This brings up the Save As dialog box, and from here you can rename your file and/or choose a new location for it, as described on these pages.

▶ If you see a Properties dialog box when you save a file, you can enter or not enter information—such as a title and subject—about the workbook, as you see fit. When you're done, click OK.

▶ If your computer misbehaves, you may lose whatever is in memory. Even so, if you've saved regularly you should have all or most of your data on disk. After restarting your computer, you can open the workbook from disk and continue working on it, as described later in this chapter.

1 After you've invested a fair amount of time on a workbook, choose Save from the File menu or click the Save toolbar button. (It looks like a little floppy disk.) Be sure to save before it becomes impossible—or at least unpleasant—to reconstruct your workbook from scratch.

8 If you continue working on a workbook, you should save it at regular intervals using the Save command. After you've saved a file initially, invoking the Save command doesn't bring up a dialog box. Instead it just saves the new version of your workbook with the same name and in the same location.

7 Your workbook is now stored safely on disk, but it also stays on screen so you can continue to work with it. Notice that the file name you entered shows up in the title bar. If you are done working on this workbook for now, close it by choosing Close from the File menu.

6 Click the Save button to save your workbook under the specified name and in the specified location. If you change your mind, click Cancel or press Esc to close the dialog box without saving your workbook.

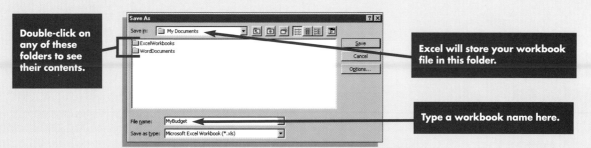

Double-click on any of these folders to see their contents.

Excel will store your workbook file in this folder.

Type a workbook name here.

2 You'll see the Save As dialog box. Type a name for your workbook in the File Name text box. Workbook names can contain up to 255 characters, including spaces, but cannot include any of these characters: ? * / \ | : < > ". They can also include an optional three-character extension, but depending on your Windows 95 setup, these extensions may not be displayed.

3 The entry to the right of "Save in" (here it reads *My Documents*) tells you which folder your workbook will be stored in. (A *folder* is a place for stashing a group of files on disk; folders used to be called *directories*.) If the listed folder seems okay, you can skip the next two steps.

4 To store the workbook on a different drive (such as a floppy disk), click the arrow to the right of the "Save in" entry and click on a new drive in the list that appears.

Up One Level button

Create New Folder button

5 To store the workbook in a different folder, double-click on that folder in the list of folders. This also displays the contents of the selected folder. If you can't see the folder you want, pull down the "Save in" list and click on any folder to display its contents in the dialog box. You can create a new folder by clicking the Create New Folder button. You can move up one level in the directory structure by clicking the Up One Level button or pressing Backspace.

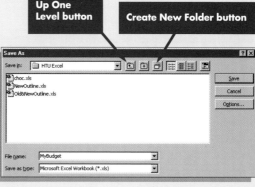

How to Start a New Workbook

When you start Excel, the program is courteous enough to open a new, blank workbook for you. As you work, however, you may need to start new workbooks—much as you'd have to pull out a fresh pad of ledger paper to start a new project on paper. You can start a new workbook anytime Excel is running, even if you haven't saved and closed the workbook you are working on. (When you open one workbook without closing another, the one that was already open disappears from view but remains in memory.) You can also open (redisplay) a workbook you have saved on disk rather than start a new one, as described a bit later in this chapter.

TIP SHEET

▶ Although you don't need to save or close your current workbook before starting a new one, it's a good idea to at least save the current one, using any of the methods described on the previous two pages. This way, you know that any workbook that is open but not visible is safely stored on disk in case adversity strikes. You should also get into the habit of closing workbook files you're no longer using, to cut down on clutter if nothing else.

▶ If you close all open workbook files, you'll see a mostly blank screen and a mostly grayed-out toolbar. Don't panic. Most of the toolbar is unavailable because there is no workbook for Excel to operate on. But you can still start a new workbook or open a workbook that you've saved.

▶ If you hold down the Shift key while pulling down the File menu, the Close command appears as Close All, which lets you close all open files at once.

▶ **1** An easy way to start a new workbook is to click the New toolbar button. (Don't try using the New command on the File menu just yet. It works a bit differently than the toolbar button, as described in Chapter 17.)

6 You edit formulas in the same way: Double-click on the cell in question. (When you do this, any cell references in the formula are shown in a different color, and the cells they refer to in the worksheet are enclosed within a colored border.) Then make any needed changes and press Enter. Excel recalculates a formula as soon as you edit it and displays the new result in the cell.

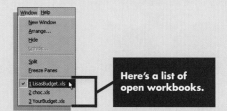

Here's a list of open workbooks.

5 Remember, you can have other workbooks open—even though you may not be able to see them. To switch back to another open workbook, click on its window if you can see any part of it. Otherwise, open the Window menu and then click on the name of the workbook you want.

2 At this point you'll see a blank screen that's probably identical to the one you saw when you started Excel for the day. From here you can start a new worksheet, putting into practice the skills you have acquired so far.

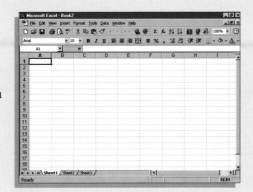

Excel gives new workbooks the titles Book1, Book2, and so on.

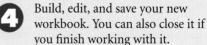

3 Take a look at the title bar of your new workbook. It may be named Book2, Book3, or may have an even higher number. As you start new workbooks throughout a work session, Excel bumps up the number in this temporary name. When you save your workbook (as described on the preceding two pages), the name you supply replaces this temporary name.

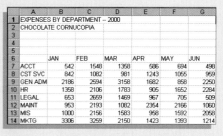

	A	B	C	D	E	F	G
1	EXPENSES BY DEPARTMENT – 2000						
2	CHOCOLATE CORNUCOPIA						
3							
4							
5							
6		JAN	FEB	MAR	APR	MAY	JUN
7	ACCT	542	1548	1358	586	694	498
8	CST SVC	842	1082	981	1243	1055	959
9	GEN ADM	2186	2594	3158	1682	858	2250
10	HR	1358	2106	1783	905	1652	2284
11	LEGAL	653	2659	1469	967	705	509
12	MAINT	953	2193	1082	2354	2166	1060
13	MIS	1000	2156	1583	958	1592	2058
14	MKTG	3306	3259	2150	1423	1393	1214

4 Build, edit, and save your new workbook. You can also close it if you finish working with it.

How to Exit and Restart Excel

It's a good idea to shut down Excel when you're done using it—unless you'll be returning to it again very soon or you plan to use it in tandem with another program. Technically, you don't need to close one program before using another. But your computer runs more efficiently—and your desktop will be more manageable—if you exit from programs you're not working with at the moment.

TIP SHEET

▸ **You don't need to exit Excel to use another Windows program. If the program you want to switch to is already open, just click on the program's application window (if you can see it) or click the taskbar button representing the program in question. If the program you want to switch to is not already open, you can start it as usual from the Start menu.**

▸ **If closing Excel places you in another program rather than Excel, you can return to the Windows desktop by right-clicking on a blank area of the taskbar and choosing Minimize All Windows from the menu that appears.**

▸ **If you don't have a shortcut to Excel on your desktop, you can create one pretty easily: Use My Computer or Explorer to find the Excel icon. (It's probably in the Program Files/Microsoft Office folder.) Then right-drag the icon onto the desktop (hold down the right mouse button instead of the left while dragging) and choose Create Shortcut(s) Here. If you're mystified by any of these instructions, a beginning book on Windows should help you get on track.**

▸ **1** Save and close any open workbooks, as just described. Don't worry too much if you forget this part. If your workbooks include any unsaved changes and you try to leave the program, Excel demands to know whether you want to save the changes.

6 You can restart Excel at any time by choosing Programs from the Start menu and clicking on Microsoft Excel or by clicking on your Excel desktop shortcut, if you're lucky enough to have one.

5 If you click Yes and the workbook has never been saved before, the Save As dialog box appears. From here you can name and save the workbook as described earlier in this chapter.

2 Choose Exit from the File menu or click Excel's Close button (the *X* in the right corner of the Excel title bar).

3 If you have no unsaved workbooks, Excel closes and you return immediately to your Windows desktop, or perhaps to some other program you happen to have open.

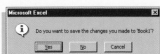

4 If you have an unsaved workbook or a workbook containing unsaved changes, Excel asks whether you want to save it. Click Yes to save it or No to discard it. You can also click Cancel to return to your workbook instead of exiting from the program.

How to Open a Workbook from Disk

The whole point of saving workbook files on disk is so you can come back to them later—either to review or to rework them. If you want to retrieve a workbook that you created earlier, you need to open it. Opening a workbook displays it in the state it was in when you last saved it. Once you open a file, you can keep working on it as before. Although Excel doesn't limit the number of workbooks you can open, you may run into trouble if you open too many for your computer's memory to handle. If this happens, just close one or more of your open workbooks and try again.

1 Choose Open from the File menu or click the Open toolbar button. (It's the second-from-the-left button on the Standard toolbar—the one that looks like an open folder.)

TIP SHEET

▶ If you modify a workbook that you've opened, make sure to save your changes with the Save command on the File menu or the Save toolbar button.

▶ There's a handy shortcut for reopening one of the four workbooks you opened most recently. Just choose File from the menu bar and then choose the name of your workbook file from the list at the bottom of the menu.

▶ Sometimes it's useful to open a workbook, change it, and save it under a new name. That way you still have the original workbook available on disk under the original name. To do this, use the Save As command on the File menu, as described earlier in this chapter.

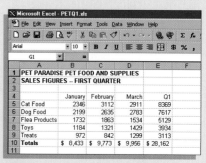

6 The workbook appears on your screen, and its name is displayed on the title bar. You can now add data to the workbook, edit existing data, or both.

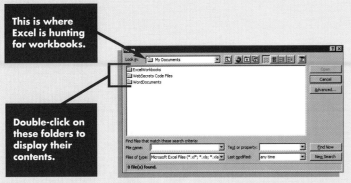

This is where Excel is hunting for workbooks.

Double-click on these folders to display their contents.

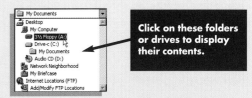

Click on these folders or drives to display their contents.

2 In the Open dialog box that appears, look at the entry to the right of "Look in." This tells you which folder Excel is searching for workbooks. If the workbook you're looking for is in the folder listed here, you can bypass the next two steps.

3 If the workbook you want to open is on a drive other than the default, click the arrow to the right of the "Look in" entry, and click on the drive containing the workbook. For example, if the workbook is on your floppy drive, click on it. (Here it's labeled 3½ Floppy (A:).)

The contents of the current folder—files and other folders

Double-click on workbooks to open them.

4 To open a workbook from a different folder, track down that folder and double-click on it to display its contents (folders and/or files). If you don't see the folder you want, try pulling down the "Look in" list again. Here you can click on any folder to list its contents. You can also click the Up One Level button to look for folders higher up in the folder structure.

5 In the list of the contents of the selected folder, find the workbook you want to open and double-click on it.

How to Work with Worksheets

Remember, a workbook is like a binder containing multiple worksheets. So far you've only used a single worksheet, but sometimes it's convenient to place several related worksheets (also called *sheets*) within a single workbook. This way it's easy to flip through your data, and you can perform calculations using numbers from any and all of the sheets. (Chapter 15 provides more details on working with multiple worksheets.) For example, a sales workbook might contain separate sheets for each quarter of the year. You could determine the totals for the individual quarters and also build a separate sheet for calculating the yearly totals.

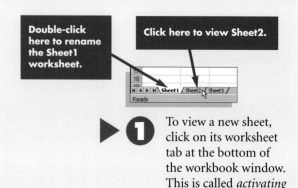

Double-click here to rename the Sheet1 worksheet.

Click here to view Sheet2.

1 To view a new sheet, click on its worksheet tab at the bottom of the workbook window. This is called *activating* the worksheet.

TIP SHEET

▸ Like the scroll bars, the tab scrolling buttons change the displayed worksheet tabs but don't change the active worksheet. To activate a new worksheet, click on its tab after bringing the tab into view. In addition, if your workbook only contains three or four worksheets, the tab scrolling buttons may have no effect: There may simply be nothing to scroll into and out of view.

▸ Chapter 15 goes into detail on working with multiple worksheets. There you'll learn how to copy and move data between worksheets, how to set up formulas that combine numbers from various worksheets, and more.

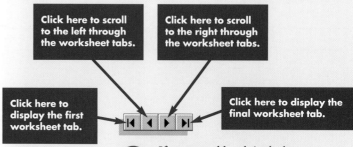

Click here to scroll to the left through the worksheet tabs.

Click here to scroll to the right through the worksheet tabs.

Click here to display the first worksheet tab.

Click here to display the final worksheet tab.

6 If your workbook includes many tabs and you can't see the tab for the sheet you want to move to, click the *tab scrolling buttons* to the left of the worksheet tabs. The plain arrows scroll one tab at a time in the direction of the arrow. The arrows with lines scroll to the last or first tab in the workbook.

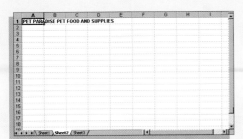

2 Once you've activated a new sheet, you have a clean slate to work with—just like a new page in a paper ledger book. From here you can enter and edit data, formulas, and functions as you normally would.

Descriptive sheet names make it easier to find your data.

3 Initially, Excel names worksheets Sheet1, Sheet2, and so on, as you can see on the worksheet tabs. It's best to rename sheets to reflect their contents so you can track down your data quickly. To do this, just double-click on the worksheet tab you want to rename, type a descriptive name of up to 31 characters, and press Enter. Worksheet names can include letters, numbers, and most other characters, but cannot include the characters * \ / and ?.

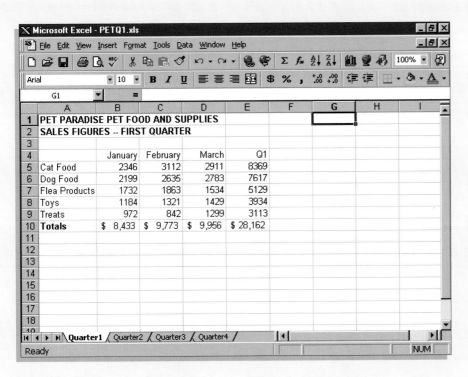

4 New workbooks you open will most likely include three worksheets for starters. If you need more, you can add them with the Worksheet command on the Insert menu, which adds and activates a new worksheet. (The new worksheet's tab appears to the left of the one for the previously active worksheet.) The number of sheets you can have in any one workbook is limited only by your computer's available memory.

5 To delete a worksheet, right-click on the sheet tab and choose Delete from the shortcut menu that appears. (You can instead choose Delete Sheet from the Edit menu if you prefer.) You'll be asked to confirm the deletion. Click OK to do so.

CHAPTER 4

Working with Worksheets

So far you've discovered how to set up simple worksheets by entering data and formulas. But it's not enough to know how to enter data. You also need to know how to modify your worksheet—to fix those unavoidable typing mistakes, to update your facts and figures when they change, and to project the impact of possible future data, among other things.

Anyone who uses an electronic spreadsheet needs certain worksheet maintenance skills. This chapter covers the most basic of those skills. You learn how to find your way around a large worksheet, how to edit data, how to project future results (what-if analysis), and how to select a group of cells so that you can make changes that affect them all. In later chapters you'll find out more about fine-tuning the structure and appearance of your worksheets.

Once you get the knack of using these important tools, you can rework spreadsheets as needed to keep them up-to-the-minute. No longer will your worksheets be static batches of figures. Instead, they'll become invaluable tools for helping you understand your business data, forecast the future, and make reasoned decisions.

How to Move through a Worksheet

Most worksheets are too large to fit on the screen all at once. Many Excel worksheets sprawl across dozens of columns and hundreds of rows. For example, a personnel worksheet may contain pay and benefits information for hundreds of employees. A worksheet with a company's financial figures may cover every month in the year. You already know that you can scroll any part of the worksheet into view and then click on any cell to activate it, or simply move onto a cell using the arrow keys. Here are some easier, more efficient ways to move around in a large worksheet.

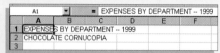

1 To move to cell A1, press Ctrl+Home. This handy keystroke combination moves you straight back to the upper-left corner of your worksheet—whether B10 or ZZ10000 is the active cell. You can press Ctrl+Home to find your way "home" when you've wandered to the far reaches of your worksheet.

TIP SHEET

▶ Scrolling changes your view of the worksheet but doesn't change the active cell. (To change the active cell, scroll it into view and click on it.) Because of this, the active cell may be out of view. Even so, the formula bar will indicate which cell is active.

▶ You can press Ctrl+G (or F5) to go directly to the Go To dialog box, without passing through the menu system.

▶ Excel keeps a record of the last several cells or groups of cells you moved to with the Go To command. To return to one of these locations, open the Go To dialog box and double-click on the desired cell reference under "Go to."

▶ The techniques in steps 2 and 4 may not work as described if you entered and then deleted data farther down and/or to the right in the worksheet.

7 Finally, a quick way to move up, down, left, or right through columns and rows is to double-click on the appropriate border of the active cell. For instance, if the active cell is within a column of numbers and you click on the bottom border of that cell, Excel activates the last number in that column. Similarly, if a cell within a row is active and you double-click on the cell's left border, Excel activates the leftmost cell containing data in that row. (If there are blank cells in the row or column, Excel activates the cell immediately before the blank cell.)

6 Next, in the Reference text box of the Go To dialog box, type the address of the cell you want to move to and click the OK button. The specified cell becomes the active cell.

2 Press Ctrl+End to move to the lower-right cell in the active area of the worksheet. This cell is the intersection of the last nonblank row and the last nonblank column in the worksheet. For instance, if column F is the last column in your worksheet containing data, and row 10 is the last row containing data, pressing Ctrl+End activates cell F10, regardless of whether that cell contains any data itself.

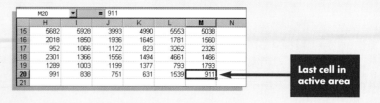

Last cell in active area

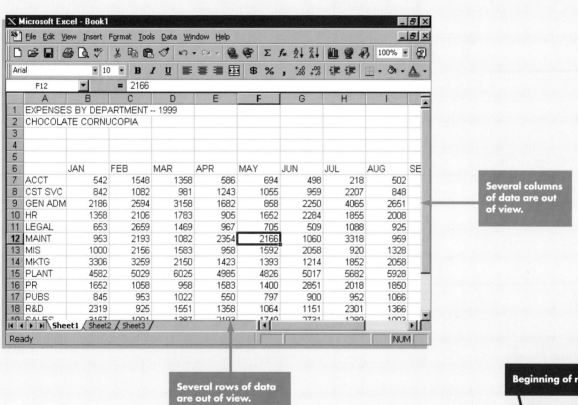

Several columns of data are out of view.

Several rows of data are out of view.

5 To move to a specific cell, first choose Edit in the menu bar and choose the Go To command.

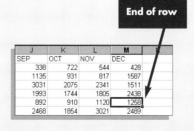

End of row

4 To move to the last nonblank cell in the current row, press End and then press Enter.

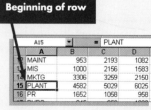

Beginning of row

3 To move to the beginning of the current row, press Home.

How to Edit the Contents of Your Worksheet

There are many reasons to modify the contents of a worksheet: to correct a misspelling, to revise data, to fix a formula you entered incorrectly, and so on. Editing cell contents is pretty much the same whether the cell contains text, a number, a formula, or a function such as SUM. These pages cover several editing basics; in addition, Chapter 6 describes some convenient techniques for undoing actions and fixing your spelling.

M9		=	3197		
	J	K	L	**M**	N
5					
6	SEP	OCT	NOV	DEC	
7	338	722	544	428	
8	1135	931	817	1587	
9	3031	2075	2341	3197	
10	1993	1744	1805	2438	

▶ ❶ Activate the cell you want to edit by clicking on it, using the arrow keys, or using any of the other techniques described on the previous two pages.

TIP SHEET

▶ Editing means changing the contents of the worksheet, not changing its appearance. You'll learn all about improving the appearance of your worksheets in Chapter 8.

▶ To completely erase a cell's contents, simply activate the cell and press the Del key. See Chapter 7 for more information.

▶ You can also edit in the formula bar. To do so, activate the cell to be edited and then click in the formula bar to place the insertion point where you click. (Don't double-click unless you want to select part or all of the entry.) Now you can edit the cell as described in steps 4 and 5 on these pages.

2 To completely replace the contents of a cell, simply type the new contents and then press Enter, Tab, or any of the arrow keys, or click the Enter button. This overwrites the previous contents of the cell. When you edit data, any formulas or functions relying on that data are recalculated automatically.

A14		▼ X ✓ =	992	
	K	L	M	N
5				
6	OCT	NOV	DEC	
7	722	544	428	
8	931	817	1587	
9	2075	2341	992	
10	1744	1805	2438	

A14		▼ X ✓ =	TOTALL			
	K	L	M	N	O	P
4						
5						
6	OCT	NOV	DEC		TOTALL	LAST YR
7	722	544	428		3250	8225

3 To modify rather than replace the contents of a cell, double-click on the cell or press F2. (Don't double-click on the cell's border, or you'll move the active cell!) A flashing insertion point tells you that the cell is ready for editing, and the status bar displays the word *Edit.* If the cell contains formula or function results, the formula or function now appears.

Incorrect formula

Misspelling

X Microsoft Excel - Book1

File Edit View Insert Format Tools Data Window Help

Arial ▼ 10 ▼ **B** *I* <u>U</u> ≡ ≡ ≡ ⊞ $ % , .00 .00 ⊞ ▼ ♦ ▼ **A** ▼

O7		=	=SUM(G7:M7)					
	K	L	M	N	O	P	Q	R	S
4									
5									
6	OCT	NOV	DEC		TOTALL	LAST YR	DIFF		
7	722	544	428		3250	8225	-4975		
8	931	817	1587		13687	12004	1683		
9	2075	2341	3197		30088	29321	767		
10	1744	1805	2438		21931	18447	3484		
11	910	1120	1258		13155	14568	-1413		
12	1854	3021	2489		23917	20031	3886		
13	1627	1524	2476		19154	19155	-1		
14	2163	1902	1398		23957	24123	-166		
15	4990	5553	5038		61648	55027	6621		
16	1645	1781	1560		20292	22349	-2057		
17	823	3262	2326		14618	19827	-5209		
18	1494	4661	1466		21212	24003	-2791		
19	1377	793	1793		19682	18720	962		
20	631	1539	911		11051	9003	2048		
21									

◄ ► ►► \Sheet1 / Sheet2 / Sheet3 /

Ready — NUM

Data entry error

A14		▼ X ✓ =	TOTAL			
	K	L	M	N	O	P
4						
5						
6	OCT	NOV	DEC		TOTAL	LAST YR
7	722	544	428		3250	8225

4 Next, type and delete characters as needed to modify the cell contents. You can use the arrow keys to reposition the insertion point. Then you can type in new text or press Del or Backspace to remove text. The Backspace key deletes characters to the left of the insertion point; Del deletes characters to the right of the insertion point.

O7		=	=SUM(B7:M7)		
	K	L	M	N	O	P
4						
5						
6	OCT	NOV	DEC		TOTAL	LAST YR
7	722	544	428		7978	8225
8	931	817	1587		13687	12004

Recalculated formula

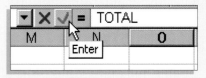

▼ X ✓ = TOTAL

M	N	O
Enter		

5 Finally, press Enter or Tab or click the Enter button to finalize your edit.

6 You edit formulas in the same way: Double-click on the cell in question. (When you do this, any cell references in the formula are shown in a different color, and the cells they refer to in the worksheet are enclosed within a colored border.) Then make any needed changes and press Enter. Excel recalculates a formula as soon as you edit it and displays the new result in the cell.

How to Ask "What If?"

What-if analysis is a fancy word for plugging in different numbers to see how they affect your results. What if the bank reduces the loan rate by 1 percent? What if your utility bills go up by $4000 next quarter? What if the new salesperson brings in $2 million in new business next year? What-if analysis in Excel instantly reveals the results of scenarios like these. All you have to do is insert your estimated data in a worksheet and let Excel's automatic recalculation feature do its thing.

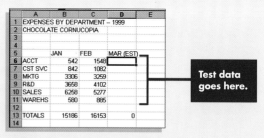

Test data goes here.

1 Set up an Excel worksheet, leaving room for the data you want to test. Here, cell D13 contains a formula similar to the one in cells C13 and B13, but the result is 0 because there isn't any data in column D yet.

TIP SHEET

▶ **Instead of inserting and replacing your sample values to test their impact, you can set up several sections in your worksheet, each section identical except for different sample data. Then you can view the results of different data sets simultaneously. Setting up similar sections in a worksheet is easier once you know how to copy data, as explained in Chapter 7.**

▶ **Setting up what-if scenarios may involve adding new columns and rows to your worksheet. You'll learn how to do this in Chapter 7.**

▶ **You can change as many or as few of the values involved in any calculation as you like. Although the examples on these pages show completely new sets of data, you could also see what happened if you changed just the R&D values, for instance.**

2 Insert the sample data the same way you insert any data in an Excel worksheet.

MAR (EST)
650
1150
1400

	JAN	FEB	MAR (EST)	TOTAL	LAST YR	DIFF
ACCT	542	1548	650	2740	3804	-1064
CST SVC	842	1082	1150	3074	2598	476
MKTG	3306	3259	1400	7965	8770	-805
R&D	3658	4102	2500	10260	3222	7038
SALES	6258	5277	4890	16425	14419	2006
WAREHS	580	885	350	1815	1989	-174
						0
TOTALS	15186	16153	10940	42279	34802	7477

3 Notice the results in cells that contain formulas that refer to the sample data. You might want to write down or print the results (see Chapter 5) so you can compare them with the results from other sets of sample data.

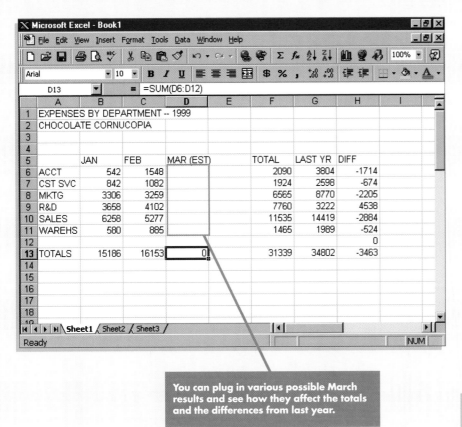

	A	B	C	D	E	F	G	H	I
	Microsoft Excel - Book1								
	File Edit View Insert Format Tools Data Window Help								
	D13			=SUM(D6:D12)					
1	EXPENSES BY DEPARTMENT -- 1999								
2	CHOCOLATE CORNUCOPIA								
3									
4									
5		JAN	FEB	MAR (EST)		TOTAL	LAST YR	DIFF	
6	ACCT	542	1548			2090	3804	-1714	
7	CST SVC	842	1082			1924	2598	-674	
8	MKTG	3306	3259			6565	8770	-2205	
9	R&D	3658	4102			7760	3222	4538	
10	SALES	6258	5277			11535	14419	-2884	
11	WAREHS	580	885			1465	1989	-524	
12								0	
13	TOTALS	15186	16153	0		31339	34802	-3463	
14									

Sheet1 / Sheet2 / Sheet3 /

Ready — NUM

You can plug in various possible March results and see how they affect the totals and the differences from last year.

4 Replace the sample data with new data. (If you need to refresh your memory about how to edit cells, flip back to the preceding pages.)

MAR (EST)
800
1400
1450
2750
5550
350
12300

	JAN	FEB	MAR (EST)	TOTAL	LAST YR	DIFF
ACCT	542	1548	800	2890	3804	-914
CST SVC	842	1082	1400	3324	2598	726
MKTG	3306	3259	1450	8015	8770	-755
R&D	3658	4102	2750	10510	3222	7288
SALES	6258	5277	5550	17085	14419	2666
WAREHS	580	885	350	1815	1989	-174
						0
TOTALS	15186	16153	12300	43639	34802	8837

6 Repeat steps 4 and 5 until you have tested as many sample values as you need.

5 Again check the results, comparing them with the results you obtained a moment ago. As you can see, the formula that calculates March figures totals the values currently in the cells above; when any of those values change, the total is recalculated automatically.

How to Select Portions of Your Worksheet

In Excel, you often need to select a group of cells so you can operate on them all at once. Selected cells appear highlighted, with light text on a dark background. (The exception is the active cell, which has dark text on a light background.) You can select any rectangular range of cells, as well as entire columns, rows, or the whole worksheet. You can even create ranges of nonadjacent cells.

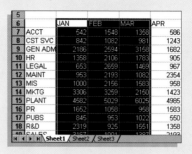

1 As you saw in Chapter 2, you can select cells by dragging over them. Don't worry if part of the range you want to select is out of view. Excel scrolls the display automatically when you drag to the edge of the window.

TIP SHEET

▶ To select a range using just the keyboard, activate one corner of the range, hold down the Shift key, use the arrow keys to move to the opposite corner of the range, and release the Shift key.

▶ You can Shift-click to change the size of a selected range. Note where the active cell is and Shift-click to establish a rectangular range between the active cell and the cell you click on.

▶ You can also select multiple adjacent columns or rows by Shift-clicking: Click on the row number or column letter of the first row or column to select, hold down Shift, and click on the row number or column letter of the final row or column to select.

▶ If you've already selected one or more columns or rows, you can select additional columns or rows by Ctrl-clicking or Ctrl-dragging across their column letters or row numbers. You can use this technique to select nonadjacent columns or rows.

 To "deselect" any selected cells, click anywhere within the worksheet or press any of the cursor movement keys (the arrow keys, Home, End, and so on). If you want to see a different portion of the worksheet without deselecting the selected cells, you can use the scroll bars.

When entire rows or columns are selected, their row numbers and column letters are highlighted.

2 You can select an entire row by clicking on its row number. (Make sure the mouse pointer is in the shape of a plus sign, not an arrow or a double-headed arrow with a bar through it.) This selects every single cell in the row, not just the cells you can see at the moment. (To select several adjacent rows, drag across their row numbers.)

3 In much the same way, you can select an entire column by clicking on its column letter. (Again, make sure the mouse pointer looks like a plus sign.) This selects every single cell in the column, from top to bottom. (To select several adjacent columns, drag across their column letters.)

The active cell is part of the selection.

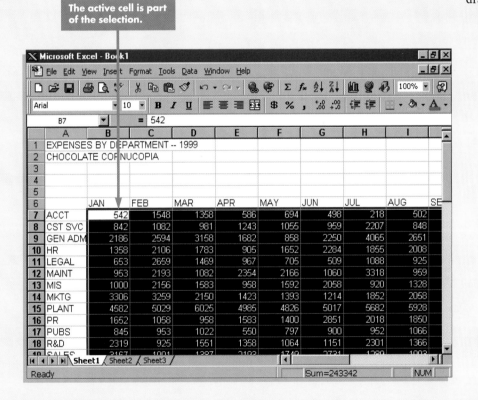

Click here to select the entire worksheet.

4 To select the entire worksheet, click the Select All button—it's immediately above row 1 and just to the left of column A—or press Ctrl+A.

5 Another quick way to select a range of cells is to activate the first cell in the range and then hold down Shift while clicking on the opposite corner of the range. This technique—sometimes called Shift-clicking—works well when you're selecting large ranges and is usually easier and more accurate than dragging over a long distance.

6 To select an additional cell or range without deselecting the currently selected one, you can hold down the Ctrl key while clicking or dragging. (These techniques are sometimes called Ctrl-clicking and Ctrl-dragging.)

CHAPTER 5

Printing

 Despite all the hoopla about the paperless office that's supposedly coming our way, people still tend to rely on printed documents as their primary way to share information. (The Internet is beginning to make a dent in this practice; see Chapter 18 for the details on using Excel with the Internet.) Excel makes printing a hassle-free process. You can print your entire workbook, the active worksheet, or specific cells that you select.

Excel automatically adds certain niceties to your printouts. For example, it automatically applies appropriate margins. But you also have a lot of leeway to customize printouts to meet your needs. That's what this chapter is all about.

You will learn several strategies for fitting data on a specified number of pages. For example, if your worksheet spills over onto a second page, you might be able to fit it on one page by printing in landscape orientation (horizontally) rather than in the default portrait orientation (vertically). Or you can have Excel squeeze the worksheet onto one page by shrinking the text. You can also move or insert page breaks to tell Excel precisely how to divide up your data, and you can modify Excel's default margins to fit less or more information on the page.

Finally, you will learn how to add headers, footers, and column and row titles to your worksheets. These features let you easily identify information on pages after the first one in multiple-page printouts.

How to Preview Your Printouts

B efore you print, it's a good idea to check what your printouts will look like. Excel lets you display print previews so you can see an accurate approximation of your printed work-sheet on the screen. Print previews give you a sense of how your data will be laid out on the page. They also let you see features—such as headers and footers—that appear on the print-out but don't show up in the worksheet itself. Make a habit of previewing worksheets before you print. More often than not, you'll spot some glitch or omission and can then return to the worksheet, make the needed changes, quickly preview your printout again, and print the perfect worksheet.

TIP SHEET

▸ **You can carry out many operations directly from within the print preview screen—including printing (the Print button), changing margins (the Margins button), and changing various things about the page setup (the Setup button). You'll learn the details about many of these features in the following pages.**

▸ **Keep in mind that you can view but can't edit your data in the print pre-view screen. To modify your data, first choose the Close button to return to the worksheet.**

▸ **Some of the things you can see in the print preview screen that you typically can't see in the worksheet window are headers and footers, page breaks, gridlines, column and row titles, page orientation, and print scaling, among others. Keep reading to get the scoop on most of these features.**

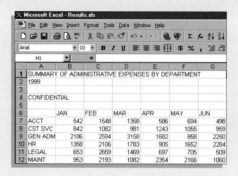

1 Open the workbook you want to preview, if it's not already open. If necessary, switch to the worksheet you want to preview.

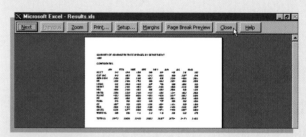

7 When you're done inspecting the print pre-view, click the Close button (or press Esc) to return to your worksheet. If anything seemed amiss in the preview, now is your chance to fix it before you go ahead and print.

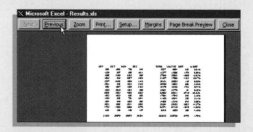

6 If your worksheet will take up multiple printed pages, you can look at pages after the first one by clicking the Next button, and you can go back to previous pages by clicking the Previous button. (If you prefer the keyboard, you can use the PgDn and PgUp keys to ac-complish the same thing.)

2 Choose Print Preview from the File menu. If you like, you can use the Print Preview toolbar button instead; it looks like a little piece of paper and a teeny magnifying glass.

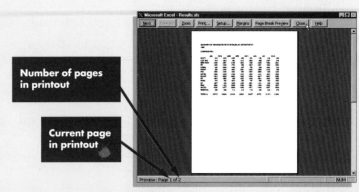

Number of pages in printout

Current page in printout

3 You'll see a print preview screen like the one shown here. The status bar at the bottom of the preview screen tells you which page is displayed—initially you'll see the first page—and how many pages your worksheet will take up when printed.

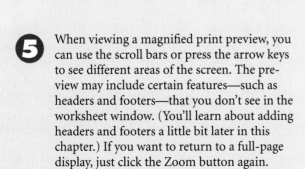

5 When viewing a magnified print preview, you can use the scroll bars or press the arrow keys to see different areas of the screen. The preview may include certain features—such as headers and footers—that you don't see in the worksheet window. (You'll learn about adding headers and footers a little bit later in this chapter.) If you want to return to a full-page display, just click the Zoom button again.

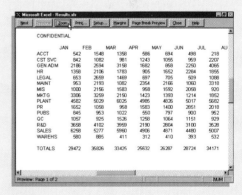

4 By default, the print preview screen shows an entire page at a time. This display gives you a good sense of the page layout but doesn't permit you to read your data because it has been reduced in size to fit on the screen. To get a close-up view of the page, click the Zoom button.

How to Print All or Part of the Worksheet

Once you've previewed your worksheet to check that everything's just right, you can go ahead and print. By default, Excel prints the active worksheet, but you can also print the entire workbook (that is, all its worksheets that contain any information) or just a selected range of cells. While you're at it, you can decide how many copies to print and which pages to print, in case you don't need to print all pages in a worksheet.

TIP SHEET

▶ **Despite what you might expect, the Print toolbar button (it looks like a little printer) doesn't lead to the Print dialog box. Instead it prints your worksheet using the current settings—without giving you any input into the matter. In other words, use this shortcut only when you're sure the print settings are already to your liking.**

▶ **Suppose you want to print only certain pages of your worksheet but aren't sure where Excel will break for a new page. One option is to go to the print preview screen, which indicates where the pages will break. (You can go directly from the Print dialog box to the print preview screen by clicking the Preview button.) A better strategy, however, is to switch to page break preview, which is described in detail in a few pages.**

▶ **In case you're wondering, when you print a worksheet or workbook, Excel prints only the portion containing data. It doesn't print the vast empty spaces at the bottom and right of most worksheets.**

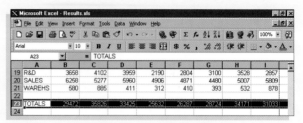

▶ **❶** If you don't want to print the whole worksheet or workbook, select the cells to be printed.

❼ Excel tells you that it's sending a copy of the workbook, worksheet, or selection to your printer. If you change your mind about printing the data, click the Cancel button.

❻ Once you've made all your selections in the Print dialog box, check that your printer is turned on and online (ready to print). And check the paper supply! Then click the OK button.

2 Choose Print from the File menu. If you don't feel like grabbing for your mouse, you can use the Ctrl+P keyboard shortcut. (Don't click the Print toolbar button, however. Check the Tip Sheet to find out why.)

These options let you decide which portion of your workbook to print.

3 Under Print What in the Print dialog box, choose Selection to print the selected cells, choose Active Sheet(s) to print the active worksheet (the default), or choose Entire Workbook to print all worksheets in your notebook that contain data.

SUMMARY OF ADMINISTRATIVE EXPENSES BY DEPARTMENT
First Quarter, 1999

CONFIDENTIAL

	JAN	FEB	MAR	TOTAL	LAST YR	DIFF	% DIFF
ACCT	542	1548	1358	3448	2201	1247	56.66
CST SVC	842	1082	981	2905	3025	-120	-3.97
GEN ADM	2186	2594	3158	7938	7260	678	9.34
HR	1358	2106	1783	5247	4203	1044	24.84
LEGAL	653	2659	1469	4781	5000	-219	-4.38
MAINT	953	2193	1082	4228	4880	-652	-13.36
MIS	1000	2156	1583	4739	4114	625	15.19
MKTG	3306	3259	2150	8715	5570	3145	56.46
PLANT	4582	5029	6025	15636	17296	-1660	-9.60
PR	1652	1058	958	3668	4125	-457	-11.08
PUBS	845	953	1022	2820	2540	280	11.02
QC	1057	925	1526	3508	3311	197	5.95
R&D	3658	4102	3959	11719	7590	4129	54.40
SALES	6258	5277	5960	17495	16299	1196	7.34
WAREHS	580	885	411	1876	1506	370	24.57
TOTALS	29472	35826	33425	98723	88920	9803	11.02

4 If you want to print more than a single copy of your data, choose the number of copies you want from the Number of Copies text box.

5 If your printout will take up more than a single page, you can choose which pages to print by selecting from the Print Range options. All, the default command, prints all pages. To print selected pages only, choose the Page(s) option button and then specify a beginning (From) and ending (To) page number. To print a single page, enter its number in both From and To.

How to Change Page Orientation and Print Scaling

Sometimes you'll have printouts that don't quite fit on one page but come pretty close. In this situation, there are several tactics for squeezing the data onto a single page—including printing across the length of the paper rather than the width and shrinking the size of the data. You can use the same approach to fit your data on a specified number of pages. And if you're printing a small amount of data, you may want to increase its size so it better fills up the page instead of confining itself to the upper-left corner.

TIP SHEET

▶ **Your print settings stay in effect indefinitely for the active worksheet. To change the settings, repeat these steps but make different selections.**

▶ **Print settings affect the active worksheet only. Other worksheets in the same workbook—as well as other workbooks—are printed the same as before unless you change their print settings, too.**

▶ **The Fit To setting (step 5) can produce very small text. If you change your mind and decide to print in standard size, get back into the Page Setup dialog box, select the Adjust To option button, and specify 100 percent of normal size in the Adjust To text box.**

▶ **These pages explain some methods of improving the way Excel prints your text. There are also several ways to improve the appearance of the text itself. For example, you can boldface text, and you can align column headings with the data below them. See Chapter 8 for details.**

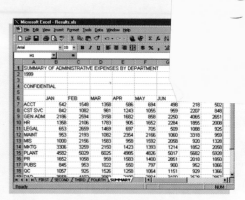

1 Open the workbook and activate the worksheet for which you want to change the print settings.

7 When you're done changing the print settings, click the OK button to put the changes into place without printing your worksheet. Or click the Print button to display the Print dialog box so you can go ahead and print.

6 If you want to change the size of your data by a specified amount, select the Adjust To option button and specify a percentage. For example, to increase the data to one and a half times its current size so it does a better job of filling up the page, you would select Adjust To and specify a percentage of 150. You can shrink or enlarge your data anywhere from 10 percent to 400 percent of its original size.

2 Choose Page Setup from the File menu. If you happen to be in the print preview screen, just click the Setup button; there's no need to exit from the preview.

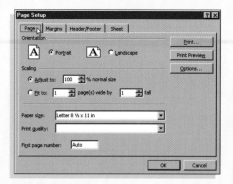

3 If the Page tab is not already active, click on Page at the top of the Page Setup dialog box.

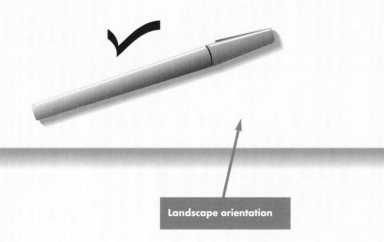

Landscape orientation

4 If you want, change the orientation of the page by clicking on either Landscape or Portrait. Often switching from portrait (the default, vertical) orientation to landscape (horizontal) orientation is all it takes to fit a wide worksheet onto a single page.

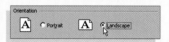

5 To shrink the text just enough to fit your worksheet on a single page, select the Fit To option button. (This changes the size of your data on the printout but not in the worksheet itself.) You can also use this option to fit the worksheet on a specified number of pages other than on one page. For instance, if your worksheet will take up seven pages, the last one of which includes only a smidgen of data, you can squeeze the printout onto six pages by choosing Fit To and specifying two pages wide by three pages tall.

How to Use Page Break Preview

When your worksheet contains too much data to fit on a single page, Excel automatically breaks the material into several printed pages. Normally, Excel—not you—decides where to divide the material. To see at a glance where your page breaks will fall, and also to move and add page breaks easily, you can work in page break preview.

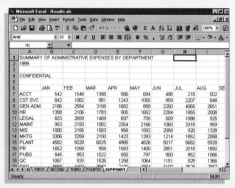

1 If it isn't open already, open the worksheet for which you want to view or edit the page breaks.

TIP SHEET

▶ **The lines indicating page breaks are for your information only. They don't show up on the printout. If you do want to insert lines into your printout, you can use gridlines (see the Sheet tab of the Page Setup dialog box), or you can use the Border feature in the Format Cells dialog box (choose Cells from the Format menu), which is covered under "How to Add Borders and Shading" in Chapter 8.**

▶ **If you set the print scaling to have Excel print a specified number of pages, that setting may override both automatic and manual page breaks.**

▶ **You can get rid of individual page breaks that you've inserted manually instead of reversing all page break changes with the Reset All Page Breaks command. To remove a page break in page break preview, drag the line representing the page break outside the print area. You can also use the menu system from either normal view or page break preview: To get rid of a horizontal page break, first select a cell immediately below the page break line; to remove a vertical page break, select a cell just to the right of the page break line. Then choose Remove Page Break from the Insert menu.**

8 Finally, to get out of page break preview, just choose Normal from the View menu.

7 If you decide to reverse any changes you've made, restoring the original page breaks and getting rid of page breaks you've inserted manually, simply right-click within the page break preview screen and choose Reset All Page Breaks from the menu that appears.

2 Choose Page Break Preview from the View menu.

3 You'll see this Welcome to Page Break Preview dialog box, which tells you a little bit about working in page break preview. (If your Office Assistant is on, you'll see a slightly different "balloon" instead of this dialog box. Chapter 6 gives you the scoop on the Office Assistant.) Click OK to remove the dialog box from view. If you don't want to see it again, click the Do Not Show This Dialog Again check box before clicking OK.

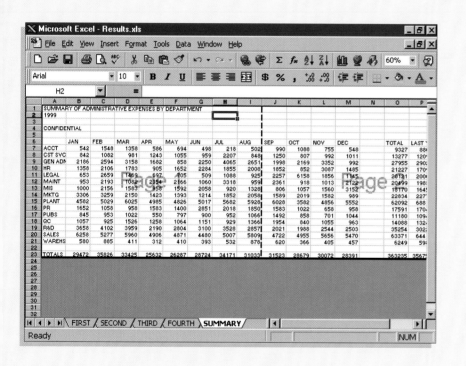

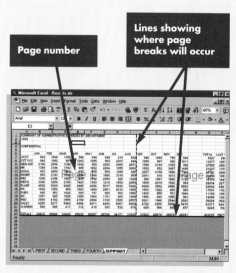

Page number

Lines showing where page breaks will occur

4 Now you're in page break preview. As you can see, this is a reduced view of your worksheet that includes lines showing where the page breaks will fall. You can drag any of these lines to move the page breaks. Notice that page numbers are also indicated in large gray characters.

6 To insert a vertical page break, select the column to the left of which you want to insert the page break (or select any cell in the column) and choose Page Break from the Insert menu.

5 You can also add additional page breaks, instead of just relocating the existing ones. To insert a horizontal page break, select the row above which you want to insert the page break and then choose Page Break from the Insert menu. (You can do this from normal view or from page break preview.) Excel inserts a line into your worksheet to indicate where the page break will occur.

How to Adjust Margins

You've already seen how to rearrange the data on printed pages by changing the page orientation, altering print scaling, and moving and inserting page breaks. Another way to go is to change margins—modifying the amount of space between the edge of the page and your printed data. In Excel, you can change margins by entering new settings in the Page Setup dialog box or by dragging margins in the print preview screen. The dragging method is more intuitive—you can see the effects of the change right away—but can be a touch less accurate. The Page Setup dialog box also includes a handy feature for centering your data on the page.

TIP SHEET

▶ **You probably noticed the extra set of horizontal lines at the top and bottom of the print preview screen. These lines let you change the position of headers and footers, which appear within the margins. You'll learn more about creating headers and footers on the next set of pages. The series of marks across the top of the screen let you change column widths by dragging. You'll probably have better luck changing column widths using the techniques described in Chapter 7.**

▶ **Like the page orientation and print scaling options you learned about earlier, margin settings affect only the current worksheet. If you want to apply certain margins to a different worksheet in the same workbook, or to a different workbook altogether, you need to repeat the steps outlined here. You can also select several worksheets to affect them all at once, as described in Chapter 15.**

▶ **❶** Get into the worksheet for which you want to modify the margins and choose Page Setup from the File menu. (If you're already in the print preview screen, just click the Setup button.)

❼ To change a margin, drag the dotted line that represents it until the line (margin) is where you want it. As you drag, the left side of the status bar lists the current size of the margin that you're changing. When you're done, you can remove the margin lines from view by clicking the Margins button a second time.

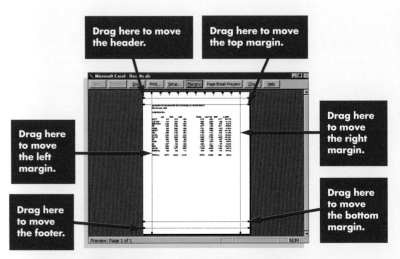

Drag here to move the header.

Drag here to move the top margin.

Drag here to move the left margin.

Drag here to move the right margin.

Drag here to move the footer.

Drag here to move the bottom margin.

❻ To change margins by dragging, first click the Margins button from within the print preview screen. You'll see a set of lines representing the current margins.

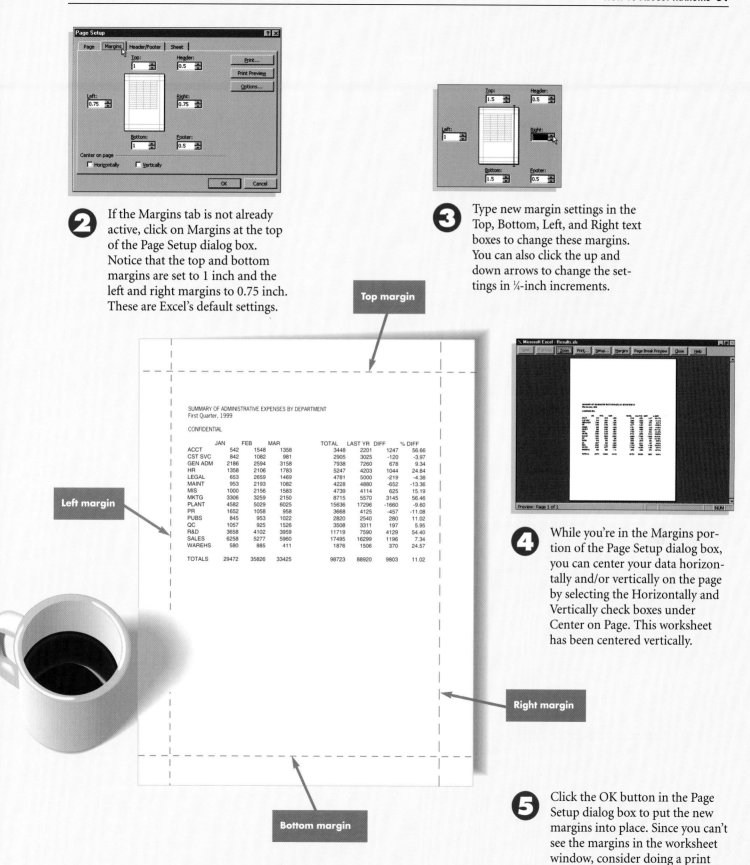

2 If the Margins tab is not already active, click on Margins at the top of the Page Setup dialog box. Notice that the top and bottom margins are set to 1 inch and the left and right margins to 0.75 inch. These are Excel's default settings.

3 Type new margin settings in the Top, Bottom, Left, and Right text boxes to change these margins. You can also click the up and down arrows to change the settings in ¼-inch increments.

Top margin

Left margin

Right margin

Bottom margin

SUMMARY OF ADMINISTRATIVE EXPENSES BY DEPARTMENT
First Quarter, 1999

CONFIDENTIAL

	JAN	FEB	MAR	TOTAL	LAST YR	DIFF	% DIFF
ACCT	542	1548	1358	3448	2201	1247	56.66
CST SVC	842	1082	981	2905	3025	-120	-3.97
GEN ADM	2186	2594	3158	7938	7260	678	9.34
HR	1358	2106	1783	5247	4203	1044	24.84
LEGAL	653	2659	1469	4781	5000	-219	-4.38
MAINT	953	2193	1082	4228	4880	-652	-13.36
MIS	1000	2156	1583	4739	4114	625	15.19
MKTG	3306	3259	2150	8715	5570	3145	56.46
PLANT	4582	5029	6025	15636	17296	-1660	-9.60
PR	1652	1058	958	3668	4125	-457	-11.08
PUBS	845	953	1022	2820	2540	280	11.02
QC	1057	925	1526	3508	3311	197	5.95
R&D	3658	4102	3959	11719	7590	4129	54.40
SALES	6258	5277	5960	17495	16299	1196	7.34
WAREHS	580	885	411	1876	1506	370	24.57
TOTALS	29472	35826	33425	98723	88920	9803	11.02

4 While you're in the Margins portion of the Page Setup dialog box, you can center your data horizontally and/or vertically on the page by selecting the Horizontally and Vertically check boxes under Center on Page. This worksheet has been centered vertically.

5 Click the OK button in the Page Setup dialog box to put the new margins into place. Since you can't see the margins in the worksheet window, consider doing a print preview to check that they're okay.

How to Print Headers and Footers

Headers and footers consist of repeating text that appears at the top and bottom of each printed page. Particularly if you're printing multiple-page worksheets, headers and footers can help identify and make sense of your data. You can devise your own headers and footers, or you can choose from among a list of ready-made headers and footers that Excel provides.

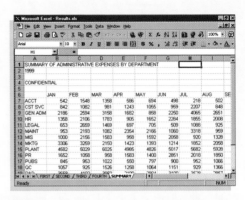

 Open the workbook and activate the worksheet for which you want to change the headers and footers.

TIP SHEET

▶ **When creating headers and footers, you can easily and fruitfully combine text and codes. (Remember, Excel inserts codes for you when you click the buttons in the Header or Footer dialog box.) For example, you could type the text Today's Date: and then click the Date button (it looks like a miniature calendar) to produce a header or footer such as this: "Today's Date: 2/5/99." In this case Excel will insert the current date, based upon your computer's calendar.**

▶ **By default, headers and footers appear a half inch from the edge of the paper. If you want to change that distance for whatever reason, enter new Header and/or Footer settings in the Margins tab of the Page Setup dialog box. Or, in the print preview screen, drag the horizontal lines above the top margin and below the bottom margin.**

8 When you're done in the Header or Footer dialog box, click OK to return to Page Setup dialog box, where you'll see your new-and-improved headers and footers. Click OK again to return to your worksheet, or to the print preview screen, if that's where you started from. It's a good idea to look over a print preview of your headers and footers since you can't see them in the worksheet window.

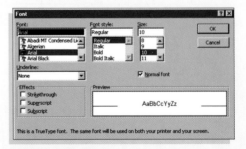

7 If you like, click the *A* button to display the Font dialog box, which lets you change a whole array of font characteristics for the header or footer. (See Chapter 8 for more information about the various font characteristics.) Note that you have to change font characteristics for the three sections (Left, Center, and Right) individually. Click OK when you're finished.

2 Choose Page Setup from the File menu. If you're in the print preview screen, just click the Setup button.

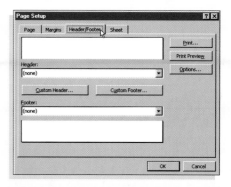

3 Click on Header/Footer at the top of the Page Setup dialog box if the Header/Footer tab is not already active.

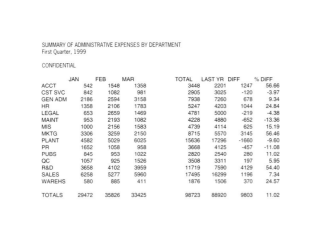

SUMMARY OF ADMINISTRATIVE EXPENSES BY DEPARTMENT
First Quarter, 1999

CONFIDENTIAL

	JAN	FEB	MAR	TOTAL	LAST YR	DIFF	% DIFF
ACCT	542	1548	1358	3448	2201	1247	56.66
CST SVC	842	1082	981	2905	3025	-120	-3.97
GEN ADM	2186	2594	3158	7938	7260	678	9.34
HR	1358	2106	1783	5247	4203	1044	24.84
LEGAL	653	2659	1469	4781	5000	-219	-4.38
MAINT	953	2193	1082	4228	4880	-652	-13.36
MIS	1000	2156	1583	4739	4114	625	15.19
MKTG	3306	3259	2150	8715	5570	3145	56.46
PLANT	4582	5029	6025	15636	17296	-1660	-9.60
PR	1652	1058	958	3668	4125	-457	-11.08
PUBS	845	953	1022	2820	2540	280	11.02
QC	1057	925	1526	3508	3311	197	5.95
R&D	3658	4102	3959	11719	7590	4129	54.40
SALES	6258	5277	5960	17495	16299	1196	7.34
WAREHS	580	885	411	1876	1506	370	24.57
TOTALS	29472	35826	33425	98723	88920	9803	11.02

4 If you like, display the Header or Footer drop-down list to choose from among several predefined headers and footers. For example, there's a header/footer that lists the page number, one that lists the sheet name, and another that includes the workbook name—to name just a few.

Change font characteristics.

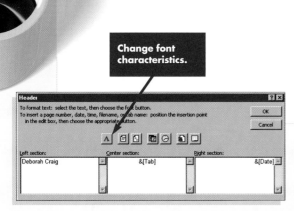

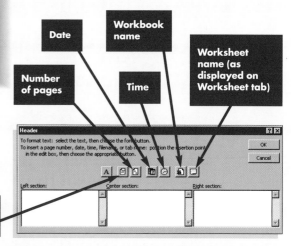

6 Enter header or footer text in the Left Section, Center Section, and/or Right Section text boxes; the text in each section will be left-aligned, centered, or right-aligned in the header or footer. Besides typing text, you can click buttons to insert codes for the current page number, the total number of pages, the current date, the current time, the workbook name, and the worksheet name.

5 To create your very own header or footer, click the Custom Header or Custom Footer button. You'll see a Header or Footer dialog box like this one.

How to Print Column and Row Titles

Like headers and footers, column and row titles can make the data on multiple-page printouts easier to read. All worksheets include not just numbers but identifying column and row titles—month names, sales categories, department names, and the like—that tell you what the numbers are all about. When your printouts extend to multiple pages, those titles don't automatically show up on pages after the first one. You can add column and row titles to ensure that this essential identifying information appears on every page.

TIP SHEET

▶ Don't confuse row and column titles with row and column headings, which you can also select in the Sheet portion of the Page Setup dialog box. You use row and column titles to repeat identifying rows and columns of information (such as month names) that already appear in your worksheet. In contrast, when you select the Row and Column Headings check box, Excel prints the column headings (A, B, C, and so on) and row headings (1, 2, 3, and so on) that appear in the worksheet window.

▶ Gridlines make your printouts more closely resemble the worksheet screen. To turn on gridlines, select the Gridlines check box in the Sheet tab of the Page Setup dialog box. Excel will place lines between every row and column in your worksheet. Another way to insert lines into your worksheet is to use the Border feature (see Chapter 8).

▶ If a row or column you select for titles includes entries that extend beyond cell boundaries, you may get unpredictable results, such as some truncated entries. If this happens, get back into your worksheet and widen the columns in question.

▶ **1** If necessary, open the workbook and activate the worksheet to which you want to add row and/or column titles.

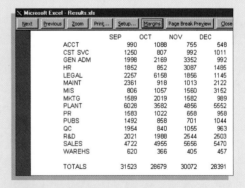

7 Click the Print Preview button in the Page Setup dialog box to put your changes into place and confirm that the titles are working as planned. (You might need to zoom in to get a good glimpse of them.) Here, for example, the department names show up on the second page, so you can tell which department the various numbers belong to without having to flip back to page 1.

2 Choose Page Setup from the File menu.

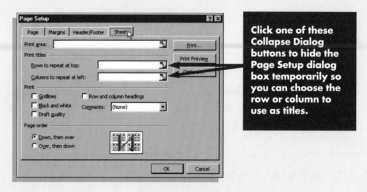

Click one of these Collapse Dialog buttons to hide the Page Setup dialog box temporarily so you can choose the row or column to use as titles.

3 Click on Sheet at the top of the Page Setup dialog box if the Sheet tab is not already active.

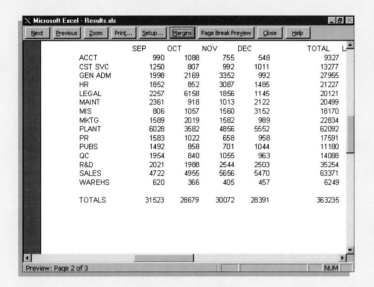

4 If you want a row of data to appear at the top of each printed page, click the Collapse Dialog button at the right end of the Rows to Repeat at Top box. The Page Setup dialog box temporarily disappears from view and is replaced by the collapsed dialog box shown here.

Marquee indicating text to be used as titles

Click here to return to the Page Setup dialog box.

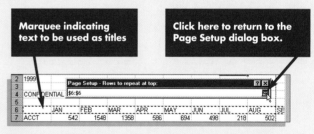

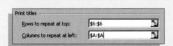

6 If you want a column of data to appear at the left side of each printed page, click the Collapse Dialog button at the right end of the Columns to Repeat at Left box. When the Page Setup dialog box disappears from view, click anywhere within that column in the worksheet. (Feel free to drag to select several rows.) The column is enclosed within a marquee and its column letter appears in the text box. Then click the button at the right end of the text box to return to the Page Setup dialog box.

5 Click anywhere within the desired row in the worksheet itself. (If you want, you can drag to select several rows.) The row is enclosed within a marquee and its row number appears in the text box. Then click the Collapse Dialog button at the right end of the text box to return to the Page Setup dialog box.

TRY IT!

Here is your opportunity to try out the many Excel skills you've picked up in the first five chapters of this book. Follow these steps to build, edit, and print the worksheet pictured here. For many steps, chapter numbers remind you where these topics were covered in detail so you can flip back if necessary to refresh your memory. In upcoming chapters you'll learn about certain techniques that would make this worksheet more pleasing to the eye. For example, you'll learn how to align the column headings over the numbers below them and how to express the numbers using fewer decimal places.

1 With Excel running, click the New toolbar button to display a new worksheet. (You only need to do this to clear an existing worksheet from the screen; if you're starting Excel for the day, it displays a new worksheet automatically.) *Chapter 3*

2

A1	▼ X ✓ =	REVENUE BY CATEGORY, IN THOUSANDS				
A	**B**	**C**	**D**	**E**	**F**	**G**
1 REVENUE BY CATEGORY, IN THOUSANDS						

Press the Caps Lock key to type in all uppercase, and in cell A1 type **REVENUE BY CATEGORY, IN THOUSANDS**.

3

Press the Enter key to enter the text you just typed. *Chapter 2*

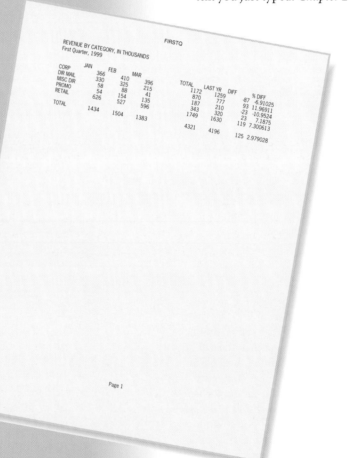

4

	A	B	C	D	E
1	REVENUE BY CATEGORY, IN THOUSANDS				
2	1q, 1999				
3					

Press Caps
Lock to turn off uppercase, type **1q,
1999** (short for First Quarter, 1999), and
press the Enter key. *Chapter 2*

5

	JAN	FEB	MAR	TOTAL	LAST YR	DIFF	%DIFF
4	JAN	FEB	MAR	TOTAL	LAST YR	DIFF	%DIFF
5 CORP							
6 DIR MAIL							
7 MISC DIR							
8 PROMO							
9 RETAIL							
10							
11 TOTAL							

Press Enter
twice to move down to row 5, turn Caps Lock
back on, and enter all the remaining row headings, as shown here and in the printout to the
left. Also enter the column headings JAN and
so forth. See if you can remember a shortcut
for entering those month headings. (Hint: It
involves dragging.)

6

4	JAN	FEB	MAR
5 CORP	366	410	396
6 DIR MAIL	330	325	215
7 MISC DIR	58	88	41
8 PROMO	54	154	135
9 RETAIL	626	527	596

Enter the
January, February, and March data for each
of the five categories, as shown here. (As an
experiment, try selecting B5:D9 before entering your data. When you select a range,
pressing Enter from the last selected cell in a
column moves you to the top selected cell in
the next column to the right, making it easier
to enter several adjacent columns of data.)

7

B11 | =SUM(B5:B9)

	A	B	C	D	E
1	REVENUE BY CATEGORY, IN THOUSANDS				
2	1q, 1999				
3					
4		JAN	FEB	MAR	
5	CORP	366	410	396	
6	DIR MAIL	330	325	215	
7	MISC DIR	58	88	41	
8	PROMO	54	154	135	
9	RETAIL	626	527	596	
10					
11	TOTAL	1434			

In cell B11,
type
=sum(b5:b9)
and click the
Enter button. This function adds together
the five numbers above cell B11. *Chapter 2*

8

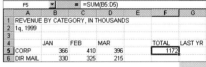

C11 | =SUM(C5:C10)

	A	B	C	D	E
1	REVENUE BY CATEGORY, IN THOUSANDS				
2	1q, 1999				
3					
4		JAN	FEB	MAR	
5	CORP	366	410	396	
6	DIR MAIL	330	325	215	
7	MISC DIR	58	88	41	
8	PROMO	54	154	135	
9	RETAIL	626	527	596	
10					
11	TOTAL	1434	1504	1383	

In cell C11,
enter a func-
tion to sum
the February
data, and in cell D11, enter a function to sum
the March data. (Hint: A handy shortcut for
doing this is to select the range C11:D11 and
click the AutoSum toolbar button.)

9

F5 | =SUM(B5:D5)

	A	B	C	D	E	F	G
1	REVENUE BY CATEGORY, IN THOUSANDS						
2	1q, 1999						
3							
4		JAN	FEB	MAR		TOTAL	LAST YR
5	CORP	366	410	396		1172	
6	DIR MAIL	330	325	215			

In cell F5,
enter
=sum(b5:d5) to add the totals for first-
quarter revenues in row 5. To experiment,
try entering the cell references by dragging
with your mouse. (In other words, enter
=sum(, drag across B5:D5 and then type **)**
and press Enter.) *Chapter 2*

10

F11 | =SUM(B11:E11)

	A	B	C	D	E	F
1	REVENUE BY CATEGORY, IN THOUSANDS					
2	1q, 1999					
3						
4		JAN	FEB	MAR		TOTAL
5	CORP	366	410	396		1172
6	DIR MAIL	330	325	215		870
7	MISC DIR	58	88	41		187
8	PROMO	54	154	135		343
9	RETAIL	626	527	596		1749
10						
11	TOTAL	1434	1504	1383		4321

Fill in the rest
of the TOTAL
column using
the method
that suits you
best. You can enter SUM functions (typing in
coordinates or selecting them with your
mouse), or you can use the AutoSum button.

11

LAST YR
1259
777
210
320
1630
4196

Enter this data into the
LAST YR column. The top
five numbers are plain data,
not formula results. You can
calculate the total at the
bottom with the AutoSum button.

Continue to next page ▶

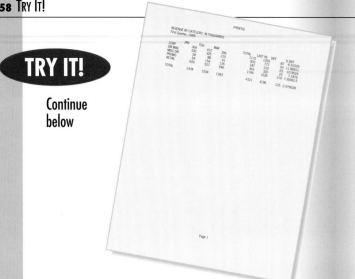

TRY IT!

Continue
below

14

TOTAL	LAST YR	DIFF	%DIFF
1172	1259	-87	=H5/G5
870	777	93	

Double-click
on cell I5 to activate the formula for
editing. Notice that Excel marks the
two cells referred to in the formula by
enclosing them within colored borders.
If the insertion point is not already at
the end of the formula, use the arrow
keys to place it there. *Chapter 4*

12

	H11	▼	=	=F11-G11			
	A	B	C	D	E	F	G	H
1	REVENUE BY CATEGORY, IN THOUSANDS							
2	1q, 1999							
3								
4		JAN	FEB	MAR		TOTAL	LAST YR	DIFF
5	CORP	366	410	396		1172	1259	-87
6	DIR MAIL	330	325	215		870	777	93
7	MISC DIR	58	88	41		187	210	-23
8	PROMO	54	154	135		343	320	23
9	RETAIL	626	527	596		1749	1630	119
10								
11	TOTAL	1434	1504	1383		4321	4196	125
12								

In cell H5,
enter the for-
mula =**f5-g5**
to subtract
last year's first-quarter revenues from this
year's. Then enter similar formulas in cells H6
through H9 and cell H11, adjusting only the
cell references. For example, the formula in cell
H6 should be =F6–G6. (In Chapter 9 you'll
learn a quick way to generate several similar
formulas like this.) *Chapter 2*

15

	I5	▼	=	=H5/G5*100			
	A	B	C	D	E	F	G	H	I
1	REVENUE BY CATEGORY, IN THOUSANDS							
2	1q, 1999							
3								
4		JAN	FEB	MAR		TOTAL	LAST YR	DIFF	%DIFF
5	CORP	366	410	396		1172	1259	-87	-6.91025

Type *100
and press the Enter key or click the
Enter button. Notice that cell I5 now
shows the correct percent figure.
Chapter 4

16

		=	=H11/G11*100				
	C	D	E	F	G	H	I
	GORY, IN THOUSANDS						
	FEB	MAR		TOTAL	LAST YR	DIFF	%DIFF
	410	396		1172	1259	-87	-6.91025
	325	215		870	777	93	11.96911
	88	41		187	210	-23	-10.9524
	154	135		343	320	23	7.1875
	527	596		1749	1630	119	7.300613
	1504	1383		4321	4196	125	2.979028

Enter similar
formulas
(with appro-
priate cell
references) in
cells I6 through I9 and cell I11.

13

		=	=H5/G5				
	C	D	E	F	G	H	I
	GORY, IN THOUSANDS						
	FEB	MAR		TOTAL	LAST YR	DIFF	%DIFF
	410	396		1172	1259	-87	-0.0691
	325	215		870	777	93	

In cell I5,
enter the for-
mula =**h5/g5** and observe the result, –0.0691.
This formula expresses the difference between last year's quarterly revenues in the
Corporate category and this year's as a pro-
portion of last year's quarterly Corporate revenues. You need to multiply this number by
100 to get a percent figure.

17

	A	B	C	D	E
1	REVENUE BY CATEGORY, IN THOUSANDS				
2	First Quarter, 1999				

Click on cell A2, type **First Quarter,
1999** and press the Enter key or click
the Enter button. (You can also modify
instead of overwriting the contents of
this cell if you like.) *Chapter 4*

18

Choose the Save command from the File menu or click the Save toolbar button. *Chapter 3*

19

Type **firstq** in the File Name text box of the Save As dialog box. If necessary, choose a new folder and/or drive for the file. Then click the Save button to save the workbook under the name FIRSTQ. *Chapter 3*

20

If you see a Properties dialog box, click the OK button.

21

Double-click on the Sheet1 worksheet tab. *Chapter 3*

22

Type **Revenue** to give the sheet a new name and then press Enter. Descriptive sheet names make your data more readily accessible. *Chapter 3*

23

Choose the Print command from the File menu or press Ctrl+P. (Remember, you need to resist the temptation to click the Printer toolbar button if you want to make changes to the print settings.) *Chapter 5*

24

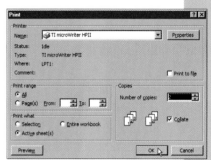

In the Print dialog box, enter 2 in the Number of Copies box, and click the OK button to print two copies of your worksheet. *Chapter 5*

25

Choose Close from the File menu to close the workbook. When asked whether to save the workbook, choose the Yes button. *Chapter 3*

CHAPTER 6

Fixing Mistakes and Getting Help

 Even Excel experts occasionally make errors or stumble into unfamiliar territory. And if you're just starting out in Excel, learning how to get out of trouble is an essential survival skill, because you're bound to get into it. Luckily, Excel provides an assortment of features for bailing yourself out when you take a wrong turn, cleaning up after yourself when you make mistakes, or simply satisfying your curiosity.

Excel's Undo command reverses your most recent action—entering cell contents, deleting data, and so on. Although it can't reverse every action, Undo can often get you out of hot water in a single step.

Excel's new Office Assistant is an animated creature that doles out help. You can search for help information by typing questions and browsing through the responses. In addition, the Assistant spontaneously offers helpful tips related to the actions you take.

Excel also comes with volumes of online help that you can display on your screen and browse through much as you'd flip through a reference book. To get an overview of the help system, you can go to the Contents tab of the Help Topics dialog box; it's much like the table of contents in a book or manual. There's also a help index you can use to quickly track down the information you need.

Finally, Excel lets you fix spelling mistakes using the spelling checker and an invaluable feature called AutoCorrect that literally cleans up after you as you type. Both of these features can hunt down and correct your misspellings, helping to make your worksheets look truly professional in the process.

How to Undo an Action

If it hasn't happened to you yet, it will: You'll edit a formula incorrectly, type something into the wrong cell, or delete too many values and then immediately regret your error. Don't worry. If you notice a mistake quickly enough, you can probably reverse it by issuing Excel's Undo command. Best of all, Excel 97 can undo multiple actions—up to 16 in fact. (In the past, you could reverse only your most recent action.) But keep in mind that Excel cannot undo certain actions, such as opening or saving a workbook.

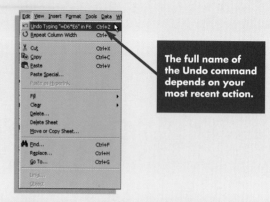

The full name of the Undo command depends on your most recent action.

▶ ❶ If you decide to undo your last action, choose Edit from the menu bar. The first command on the Edit menu reads *Undo* followed by a description of your most recent action.

TIP SHEET

▶ **If you make a slew of changes to a workbook and decide you don't like any of them, it's much easier to close your workbook without saving than to reverse your actions one by one. Just choose Close from the File menu and, when asked whether to save your changes, respond with No. The original copy of the workbook will remain intact on your hard disk and all your changes will be discarded at once.**

▶ **All choices you make in one session with a dialog box constitute a single action, and you can reverse them in one fell swoop with Undo. Better yet, if you haven't closed the dialog box yet, you can nix all your changes simply by clicking the Cancel button or pressing Esc.**

▶ **If you're a real waffler, the Undo and Redo commands are set up just for you: You can use the Redo command to reverse an undo operation. In addition, if you change your mind about the redo, you can choose the Undo command to reverse your redo operation. You can go back and forth between undo and redo as often as you like.**

2 Click on the Undo command to turn back the clock, reversing the effect of your most recent action. You can choose Undo from the Edit menu repeatedly to reverse previous actions one by one.

3 If you're not wild about using the menu system or you have your mouse in hand, you can reverse previous actions by clicking the Undo toolbar button. You can click this button repeatedly to undo several previous actions one at a time.

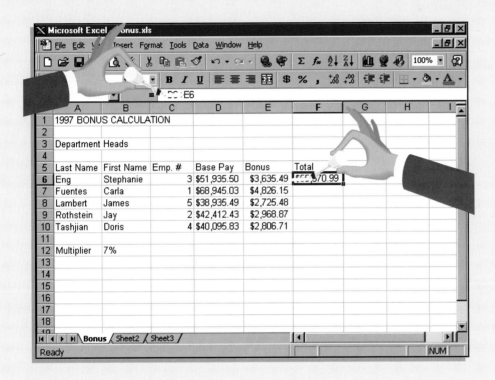

4 To quickly reverse several actions at once, click on the downward-pointing triangle to the right of the Undo button. You'll see a list of the "undoable" actions you've performed, with the most recent at the top. Click on any action to reverse all actions up to that point.

6 Like the Undo button, the Redo button has a drop-down list that lets you redo several actions at a time.

5 If the Undo command doesn't produce the expected result, you can reverse it by clicking the Redo button or choosing Redo from the Edit menu. You can click the Redo button repeatedly if you've undone several actions. But for Redo to work, you must choose it before you do anything else.

How to Use the Office Assistant

Excel 97 is outfitted with a new tool that dishes up help quickly and easily. The Office Assistant is an animated creature—it can take on a number of different forms—that you can keep by your side to deliver help on demand. The Office Assistant has a search feature that lets you look up help on specific topics. It also provides a running commentary of tips about how to streamline your work. As you'll see, the Office Assistant is a friendly and entertaining helper.

TIP SHEET

▶ **To try out a different Office Assistant, right-click the current Assistant and select Choose Assistant. Click the Next and Back buttons to survey the available choices. When you find the one you want, click OK. At this point you might be prompted to insert your Microsoft Office CD-ROM disc or floppy disk or to check that your computer is connected to your network. (Typically, only the default Office Assistant is installed on your hard drive.)**

▶ **You can customize the way the Office Assistant works by right-clicking the Assistant, choosing Options, and making selections from the Office Assistant dialog box that appears. For example, if you find the Office Assistant helpful but noisy (those of you with sound cards will have been hearing noticeable sound effects), you can deselect the Make Sounds option.**

▶ **If your Office Assistant is displayed, Excel doesn't always behave exactly as described in this book. For example, when you exit Excel without saving your changes, you see an Office Assistant "balloon" asking whether you want to save your changes rather than the usual dialog box. It's unlikely that you'll be fazed: Usually the Office Assistant is either displaying the same information in a slightly different manner or providing a bit of extra help.**

▶ **1** If you don't see an Office Assistant on your screen (for an idea of what it looks like, check the figure in the middle of these pages), choose Microsoft Excel Help from the Help menu or click the Office Assistant button (the question mark) on the Standard toolbar.

8 Finally, the Office Assistant is friendly but tends to get underfoot. If you want to move it out of the way, drag its title bar. To conceal it from view altogether, click the Close button (the *x* in its upper-right corner).

7 At times the Office Assistant may hop in unannounced to ask whether you need help with a specific procedure—for example, when you open Excel's ChartWizard, which you'll learn all about in Chapters 12 and 13. As you can guess, click on the top option if you want extra help and the bottom option if you don't.

2 An Office Assistant materializes. It may look like this paper clip, or it might take the form of an animated cat, dog, or robot, to name just a few. (The Tip Sheet describes how to choose a different Assistant.) If you don't see the accompanying "balloon" (dialog box) with a list of options, click on the Office Assistant to bring it into view.

3 To find out how to carry out a particular action, type some descriptive text in the box labeled, "What would you like to do?" For example, to learn how to start a new workbook, type something like **How do I start a new workbook?** (It's best to be quite specific, typing a full sentence or question rather than just a word or two.) Then click on Search or press Enter. You'll see a list of relevant topics.

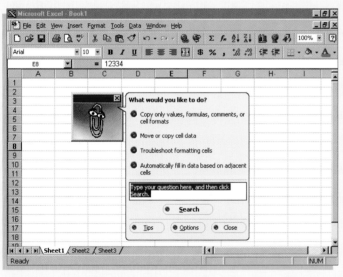

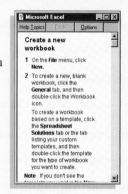

4 Click on the topic you want to read about. You'll arrive at a help screen describing in detail how to do what you want to do. For example, clicking on the topic Create a New Workbook displays this help screen. To remove the help screen from view when you're done reading, click its Close button.

Light bulb indicating that a tip is waiting

5 Besides letting you search for information, the Office Assistant supplies tips about how to accomplish certain tasks more efficiently. For example, if you use the menu system to do something you can pull off by clicking a toolbar button, you may get a tip to that effect. You know a tip is waiting when a light bulb appears. (If the Office Assistant isn't displayed, the Office Assistant toolbar button acquires a light bulb to indicate that there's a tip.)

6 Click on the light bulb to display the tip. If several tips have accumulated, you can move back and forth between them by clicking the Back and Next buttons. To hide the tip, simply click the Close button or press Esc. (To see previous tips when the light bulb is not displayed, either click the Office Assistant icon and click the Tips button or right-click the Office Assistant and choose See Tips.)

How to Look Up Help Topics

If you like a help system that is more businesslike and less boisterous than the Office Assistant, you can explore Excel's Help Topics dialog box. This portion of the help system gives you three ways of hunting for help: You can use the Contents tab to look through help information arranged in a series of topics, you can use the Index tab to go directly to topics that you type in, and you can use the Find tab to search for certain words or phrases that occur within help topics. These tools lead you to much of the same information you can turn up using the Office Assistant—you're just getting there in a different way.

TIP SHEET

▶ **If you're hunting for help on a particular topic, you may be able to find the information you need more quickly by using the Index tab rather than the Contents tab. From within the Index tab, type a few letters of the word or topic you're looking for. When you see a topic that looks promising, click on it and then click the Display button. You'll see either a help screen or a Topics Found dialog box, from which you can click on the desired topic and then click on Display to get to a help screen.**

▶ **Sometimes it's convenient to print a particularly useful help topic as a reference or to share with a friend. It's easy enough to do: Display the help topic, click the Options button, and choose Print Topic; or select a topic in the Contents screen and click the Print button. This lands you in the Print dialog box, which you learned all about in Chapter 5.**

▶ **For more details on the Find tab in the Help Topics dialog box, check your Excel documentation.**

1 Choose Contents and Index from the Help menu.

7 When you're done getting help, click the Close button (the *X*) to exit from Excel's online help system.

Help Topics

6 To return to the main Help Topics: Microsoft Excel dialog box, click the Help Topics button in any help window.

> **worksheet**
> The primary document you use in Microsoft Excel to store and work with data. A worksheet consists of cells organized into columns and rows and is always part of a workbook. Also called a spreadsheet.

5 Clicking on any word or phrase that has dotted underlining displays a pop-up box with a definition of the underlined term. Click anywhere to close the pop-up box when you're done.

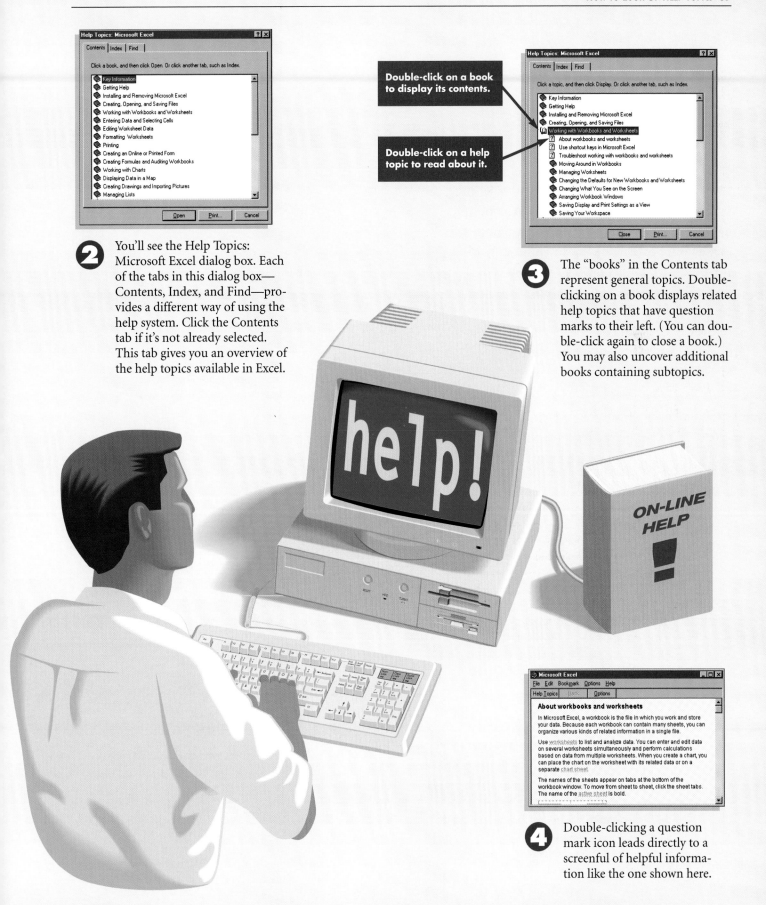

Double-click on a book to display its contents.

Double-click on a help topic to read about it.

2 You'll see the Help Topics: Microsoft Excel dialog box. Each of the tabs in this dialog box—Contents, Index, and Find—provides a different way of using the help system. Click the Contents tab if it's not already selected. This tab gives you an overview of the help topics available in Excel.

3 The "books" in the Contents tab represent general topics. Double-clicking on a book displays related help topics that have question marks to their left. (You can double-click again to close a book.) You may also uncover additional books containing subtopics.

4 Double-clicking a question mark icon leads directly to a screenful of helpful information like the one shown here.

How to Fix Spelling Mistakes

Excel is equipped with a spelling checker you can use to check and remedy your spelling. When Excel encounters a word that's not in its electronic dictionary, it gives you a chance to change the word, much of the time supplying possible corrections from which you can choose. Excel also includes an AutoCorrect feature that can fix your spelling mistakes automatically as you type. This feature is so invaluable that you'll instantly become addicted to it.

 1 To use Excel's spelling checker, choose Spelling from the Tools menu or click the Spelling toolbar button—it has the letters *ABC* on it. (If you have your Office Assistant on, you may get slightly different responses than those described on these pages.)

TIP SHEET

▶ **If you want to spell-check only part of the active worksheet, select that part before you begin. If you don't do this, Excel automatically checks the entire active worksheet.**

▶ **Keep in mind that the spelling checker won't notice a misspelling that forms another legitimate word—for example, if you accidentally type *than* instead of *then*. In other words, spell-checking is no substitute for proofreading your worksheets carefully.**

▶ **The top of the AutoCorrect dialog box includes several check boxes for fixing other kinds of common typing mistakes. All of these options are on by default. You can turn them on and off if you like, but be sure to leave the Replace Text As You Type check box selected, or AutoCorrect won't correct the mistakes listed at the bottom of the dialog box.**

8 You can also use the AutoCorrect feature to lighten your typing load. For instance, repeatedly typing a long name such as **Woody Woodman's Finger Palace** can quickly get pretty tedious. Here's what you can do instead: Enter an abbreviation, such as wwfp, in the Replace text box within the AutoCorrect dialog box, and then enter the full name in the With text box. Now every time you type **wwfp** Excel will automatically convert it into *Woody Woodman's Finger Palace*.

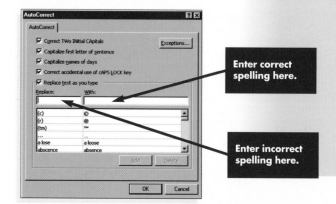

Enter correct spelling here.

Enter incorrect spelling here.

7 You'll see the AutoCorrect dialog box. Scroll through the list at the bottom; the words on the left are misspellings and the words on the right are correct spellings that Excel automatically replaces the misspellings with. To add a new word to the list, enter the misspelling in the Replace text box, enter the correct spelling in the With box, and click the Add button. Click OK to close the AutoCorrect dialog box and return to your worksheet.

This word is spelled correctly but isn't used often.

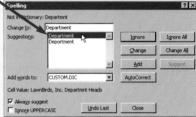

3 If the word is spelled correctly and you plan to use it frequently in other worksheets, click the Add button. This adds the word to the electronic dictionary so Excel won't stop on it in the future.

Double-click on the correct spelling to put it into place.

This word is spelled correctly and is used frequently.

2 If Excel comes upon a word that's not in its dictionary, it presents the Spelling dialog box. If the word is spelled correctly but you don't use it often, click Ignore to skip the word just this once or click Ignore All to skip the word wherever it appears for the rest of this spelling check.

4 If the word is misspelled and you see the correct spelling in the Suggestions list, double-click on that spelling to correct the word and continue the spelling check. If the word is misspelled but the correct spelling doesn't appear under Suggestions, fix the word in the Change To text box and then click the Change button to correct the misspelling and continue the spelling check.

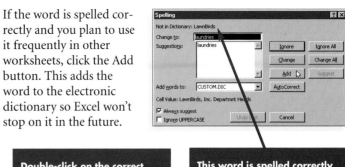

6 If you haven't already noticed Excel fixing some of your spelling mistakes, try typing **teh** and pressing Enter. Excel changes the word to *the* without any intervention on your part; this is AutoCorrect in action. There is a very long list of words that Excel can fix all on its own. In addition, you can add words to this list. The first step is to choose AutoCorrect from the Tools menu.

5 Click OK when Excel tells you it's done with the spelling check.

CHAPTER 7

Changing Worksheet Structure

 As your business evolves, your Excel worksheets should too. What happens to your personnel worksheets when employees come and go? What if accounting tells you that the numbers you budgeted to one category belong under another? Clearly, you need to know how to update your worksheets to keep pace with these and other challenges and surprises.

When making these types of modifications to your worksheets, you can't use the cell editing techniques you learned about in Chapter 4. Instead, you have to learn how to restructure your worksheets—inserting new data, moving and erasing existing data, and more. In the days of paper ledgers, tasks like these were major headaches. With Excel, they're quick and easy.

This chapter covers the most important ways of restructuring your worksheets. You'll learn how to accommodate new data by adding columns and rows to a worksheet. You'll find out how to delete cells and cell contents—including entire columns and rows—to eliminate obsolete data and make way for new data. You'll learn several ways of moving and copying data from one part of a worksheet to another. And you'll see how to adjust column widths so that your worksheet columns display all their data without wasting any space.

How to Insert Columns and Rows

To add new data to a worksheet, you almost always have to make room for it. Suppose you have a personnel worksheet on which the rows are arranged in alphabetical order by last name. When a new employee joins the company, you can't just stick his or her name at the bottom of the list. Instead, you have to insert the name in the proper alphabetical order. To do this, you add a blank row to the appropriate spot in the worksheet and type the new data there.

TIP SHEET

▶ When you insert rows or columns, data below or to the right of the new rows or columns shifts down or to the right. What happens to formulas containing references to the shifted data? Excel updates them automatically. For example, in step 3, Charles Lambert's vacation record, formerly in row 6, moved to row 7. Cell G6 used to contain the formula =SUM(C6:F6). Because Lambert's record shifted down one row, his balance, now in cell G7, is calculated with the formula =SUM(C7:F7).

▶ Proceed with caution when adding data to existing formulas by inserting columns and rows. If you add data within the range of an existing formula, the new results are calculated automatically. For example, if your worksheet contained the function =SUM(D4:D8) and you added a new row of data above row 6, the data in that new row would become part of the calculation, which would now read =SUM(D4:D9). But if you added a row below row 8 and wanted the new data to be part of the SUM function, you'd have to edit the function to read =SUM(D4:D9); Excel wouldn't do this job for you automatically. (You'd also have to edit the function if you added a row above row 4.)

Insert one row above row 6.

If you want to insert a single row, first activate any cell in the row above which you want to insert the new row. To insert multiple rows, select at least one cell in the desired number of adjacent rows. For example, to insert three rows above row 5, select at least one cell in rows 5, 6, and 7.

2 Choose Rows from the Insert menu. Excel inserts one or more blank rows, nudging existing data downward as needed. (If you like, you can instead right-click on a row number and choose Insert from the shortcut menu that appears.)

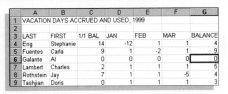

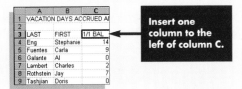

	A	B	C	D	E	F	G
1	VACATION DAYS ACCRUED AND USED, 1999						
2							
3	LAST	FIRST	1/1 BAL	JAN	FEB	MAR	BALANCE
4	Eng	Stephanie	14	-12	1	1	4
5	Fuentes	Carla	9	1	-2	1	9
6	Galante	Al	0	0	0	0	0
7	Lambert	Charles	2	1	1	1	5
8	Rothstein	Jay	7	1	1	-5	4
9	Tashjian	Doris	0	1	1	1	3

3 Now you can add data to the new row or rows in the normal fashion.

VACATION

VACATION DAYS ACCRUED AND USED, 1999								4
LAST	FIRST	EMP #	1/1 BAL	JAN	FEB	MAR	BALANCE	9
Eng	Stephanie	3	14	-12	1	1		5
Fuentes	Carla	1	9	1	-2	1		4
Lambert	Charles	5	2	1	1	1		3
Rothstein	Jay	2	7	1	1	-5		
Tashjian	Doris	4	0	1	1	1		

Please add a new employee
AL GALANTE
employee #6
vacation balance Ø.

	A	B	C
1	VACATION DAYS ACCRUED A		
2			
3	LAST	FIRST	1/1 BAL
4	Eng	Stephanie	14
5	Fuentes	Carla	9
6	Galante	Al	0
7	Lambert	Charles	2
8	Rothstein	Jay	7
9	Tashjian	Doris	0

Insert one column to the left of column C.

4 If you want to insert one column, first activate any cell in the column to the left of which you want to insert the new column. To insert multiple columns, select at least one cell in the desired number of adjacent columns. For example, to insert three columns to the left of column D, select at least one cell in columns D, E, and F.

5 Now choose Columns from the Insert menu. Excel inserts one or more blank columns, shifting any existing data to the right as needed. (You can also right-click on a column letter and choose Insert from the shortcut menu that appears.)

6 You can now add data to the new columns or rows as you normally would.

	A	B	C	D	E
1	VACATION DAYS ACCRUED AND USED, 1999				
2					
3	LAST	FIRST	EMP #	1/1 BAL	JAN
4	Eng	Stephanie	3	14	-12
5	Fuentes	Carla	1	9	1
6	Galante	Al	6	0	0
7	Lambert	Charles	5	2	1
8	Rothstein	Jay	2	7	1
9	Tashjian	Doris	4	0	1

How to Delete or Clear Cells

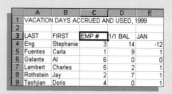

There are two ways to go about erasing data from your worksheets. You can *delete* cells, removing them from the worksheet and closing up the vacated space by relocating the cells below or on the right. Or you can *clear* cells, deleting their contents and leaving them empty, without actually removing them from the worksheet. Often, you delete an entire row or column. For example, in a personnel worksheet, you might delete the row containing the record of a former employee. On the other hand, you may need to clear any number of cells—even nonadjacent ones—when you know that they contain inaccurate data but aren't yet sure what to replace it with.

TIP SHEET

▸ **When you delete cells, any data below or to the right automatically shifts up and/or to the left. But Excel automatically adjusts formulas that refer to the shifted data so that they continue to produce the original result.**

▸ **When you need to replace data, there's often no point in clearing the cell and then entering the new data. You can simply activate the cell and enter the new data, which automatically replaces the old data. One exception is that you might want to clear all the data from a group of cells for which you need to replace the data so you don't unintentionally leave some of the old data in with the new.**

▸ **Here's a confusing quirk in Excel's terminology: The Del key clears cell contents; it doesn't delete cells from the worksheet. In other words, pressing the Del key doesn't accomplish the same thing as issuing the Delete command from the Edit menu.**

 1 To delete a single row or column, activate any cell in the row or column. To delete multiple adjacent rows or columns, select at least one cell in each one. To delete specific cells only, select those cells. (Skip to step 5 if you want to clear cells—removing their contents only—rather than delete them.)

 6 If you want to get fancy when clearing cells, choose Clear from the Edit menu to display this submenu. Choosing All clears the cells' contents, as well as any formatting and special comments. (You'll learn how to apply formatting to your worksheets in Chapter 8.) Choosing Formats clears any formatting (boldfacing and so on) associated with the cells but doesn't clear their contents. Choosing Contents clears the cells' contents but doesn't clear any formatting. (This is the same as pressing the Del key.) Choosing Comments clears any special comments associated with the cells, without clearing anything else.

2 Choose Delete from the Edit menu or right-click on one of the selected cells and choose Delete from the resulting short-cut menu. (*Do not* try pressing the Delete (Del) key as an alternative.)

3 In the Delete dialog box, select the Entire Row option button to delete one or more adjacent rows, or select the Entire Column option button to delete one or more adjacent columns. To delete the selected cells without removing the entire columns or rows that contain them, choose either Shift Cells Left or Shift Cells Up to indicate how you want the empty space filled. Then click OK to delete the selected cells, columns, or rows.

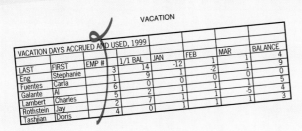

4 To quickly delete entire columns or rows, first select them and then choose Delete from the Edit menu or from the shortcut menu that appears when you right-click the selected cells. This deletes the selected rows or columns automatically, without displaying the Delete dialog box.

5 To clear any number of cells— from a single one to the entire worksheet—simply select them and press the Del key. Note that you can clear both adjacent and nonadjacent cells. (Feel free to flip back to Chapter 4 to refresh your memory about how to select various portions of your worksheet.)

Page 1

How to Move and Copy Data with Drag and Drop

Drag-and-drop editing is a refreshingly intuitive operation. This feature lets you move or copy data by dragging it where you want it with the mouse and then dropping it into place. This technique is especially effective for moving or copying data to areas that are currently visible on the screen.

TIP SHEET

► When you move cells, formulas that refer to these cells individually are updated. But cell ranges in formulas are updated only if you move the entire range of cells. If your worksheet includes any formulas containing cell ranges, double-check them carefully after moving data and update them if necessary.

► You can also move and copy data by right-dragging on the selected cells and choosing the appropriate option from the shortcut menu that appears when you release the mouse button.

► You can easily drag and drop data between worksheets and between workbooks. To move material to a new workbook, make sure both workbooks are visible and simply drag the data from one to the other. Hold down Ctrl while you're at it if you want to copy the material instead. (To display several open workbooks at once, choose Arrange from the Window menu, choose Tiled, Horizontal, or Vertical from the Arrange Windows dialog box and click OK.) To move data to a different worksheet within the same workbook, hold down the Alt key while dragging over the desired worksheet tab. (Hold down both Ctrl and Alt if you want to copy the data.) Once Excel puts you in the new worksheet, continue dragging until you have the data in the right spot, and then release the mouse button.

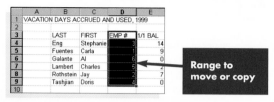

Range to move or copy

▶ ❶ Activate the cell or select the range of cells you want to move or copy.

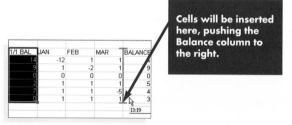

Cells will be inserted here, pushing the Balance column to the right.

❼ To avoid overwriting nonblank cells when moving or copying information, hold down the Shift key before releasing the mouse button. The rectangular outline mentioned in step 3 changes into a vertical or horizontal I-beam, indicating where the cells will be inserted and whether other cells will be pushed to the right (vertical I-beam) or downward (horizontal) to make way for the inserted data.

❻ If you drop cells you're moving into an occupied area of the worksheet, Excel asks whether you want to overwrite the nonblank cells, deleting their previous contents. Click OK if you do or Cancel if you don't. (Be careful: For some reason you aren't warned about overwriting cells when you're copying rather than moving data.)

2 Point to the border of the cell or range so the mouse pointer changes from a cross into an arrow. You can point to any border, but don't point to the fill handle in the range's lower-right corner.

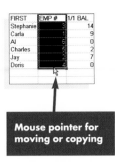

Mouse pointer for moving or copying

Destination

ScreenTip indicating destination range

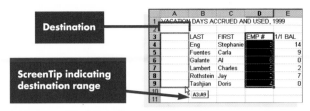

3 Hold down the left mouse button and drag the selected cells to the desired spot. A rectangular outline shows you where the cells you are moving or copying will be inserted if you release the mouse button at that moment. A ScreenTip also tells you what range the cells will be inserted into—A3:A9, in this case.

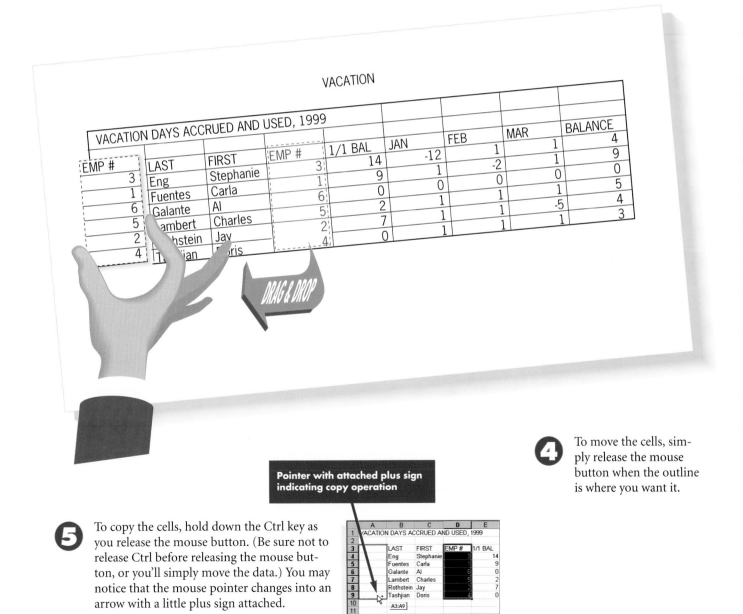

VACATION

DRAG & DROP

4 To move the cells, simply release the mouse button when the outline is where you want it.

Pointer with attached plus sign indicating copy operation

5 To copy the cells, hold down the Ctrl key as you release the mouse button. (Be sure not to release Ctrl before releasing the mouse button, or you'll simply move the data.) You may notice that the mouse pointer changes into an arrow with a little plus sign attached.

How to Move and Copy Data with the Clipboard

Excel's drag-and-drop editing feature is wonderfully handy. However, it does have a few drawbacks. It can be a slippery proposition to drag data over long distances—from cell A1 to Z1111, for instance—or even beyond the visible boundaries of the screen. You may also run into trouble dragging very large blocks of data, since it's hard to maneuver and see what you're doing at the same time. In these situations, you can take advantage of the Windows Clipboard—a temporary storage area where you can stash data. You can "paste" data from the Clipboard back into a different area of the same worksheet, into a new worksheet, into a new workbook, and even into certain other programs.

TIP SHEET

▶ Another convenient shortcut for the Paste command is the Enter key. Just issue the Cut or Copy command using your preferred method. Then decide where you want to place the data, and press Enter to paste in the contents of the Clipboard.

▶ As mentioned, a flashing marquee indicates that there's data on the Clipboard when you issue a Cut or Copy command. The marquee disappears when you paste cut data or when you press Enter to paste the data. But when you use the Copy and Paste commands the marquee remains; in other words, the data is still on the Clipboard and you can paste it in to your worksheet repeatedly. If the flashing marquee gets on your nerves, just press Esc to get rid of it.

▶ Data you paste from the Clipboard into your worksheet overwrites any existing data in its path, with no warning. The moral: Check the area in which you're planning to paste data to make sure it doesn't contain data you want to keep.

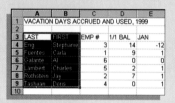

	A	B	C	D	E
1	VACATION DAYS ACCRUED AND USED, 1999				
2					
3	LAST	FIRST	EMP #	1/1 BAL	JAN
4	Eng	Stephanie	3	14	-12
5	Fuentes	Carla	1	9	1
6	Galante	Al	6	0	0
7	Lambert	Charles	5	2	1
8	Rothstein	Jay	2	7	1
9	Tashyuan	Doris	4	0	1
10					

1 Activate the cell or select the range of cells you want to move or copy, as when using the drag-and-drop technique.

6 After choosing where to insert the Clipboard data, you can click the Paste toolbar button to insert the data from the Clipboard into your worksheet.

2 Choose Cut or Copy from the Edit menu. The Cut command places the selected data on the Clipboard and also removes it from your worksheet; the Copy command places the selected data on the Clipboard without removing it from the worksheet. A *marquee*—a flashing border around the selected cells—indicates that there's data on the Clipboard.

3 Select the cell where you want to paste the data. There's no need to select a range the size of the range you cut or copied. You can just select a single cell, which will become the upper-left cell of the block of data being pasted in.

4 Choose Paste from the Edit menu. If you used the Cut command, your data will be moved to its new location; if you used Copy instead, a copy of the data will be inserted in the new location.

5 If you're fond of mouse shortcuts, you'll like the Cut and Copy toolbar buttons, which you can use to cut or copy the selected data to the Clipboard.

The Copy button

The Cut button

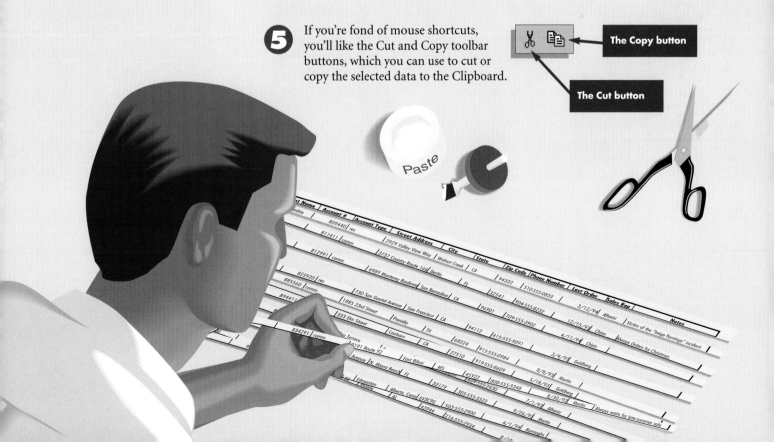

How to Adjust Column Width

Excel's columns often aren't wide enough to accommodate long headings and large numbers. If so, several things can happen. Text entries spill over into cells to the right if those cells are empty; otherwise the display of text is cut off. Numbers with many decimal places may appear to lose some digits to the right of the decimal place. And large numbers are displayed either in scientific notation or as overflow markers (######). To display the complete contents in the cell, you can widen the column. Using the same approach, you can narrow columns so they are no wider than necessary to display their contents.

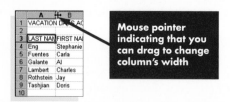

Mouse pointer indicating that you can drag to change column's width

▶ **1** In the column you want to widen or narrow, point to the line at the right of the column heading. Notice the shape of the mouse pointer.

TIP SHEET

▸ Even if an entry is truncated on the screen, Excel "remembers" the complete contents of the cell, displaying it in the formula bar when the cell is active and using it when the cell is referenced in a formula or function.

▸ Double-clicking on the line to the right of a column heading makes the column just wide enough to display its longest entry.

▸ You can adjust row heights much as you adjust column widths. Point to the bottom of the row heading and then drag up or down to change the height of the row. If you like, you can select several rows and adjust their heights all at once by dragging one of their row headings.

▸ Excel sometimes widens columns for you. If you enter a number and then give it a numeric format that increases its size, Excel adjusts the column width accordingly.

5 If you want to simultaneously change the width of several columns—whether adjacent or not—just select them (click on their column letters) and then drag to adjust the width of one of them. This widens or narrows all the selected columns, making them all the same width.

 4 Repeat steps 1 through 3 as needed to further adjust the width of this or other columns. In this case, you would most likely want to adjust the width of the First Name column too.

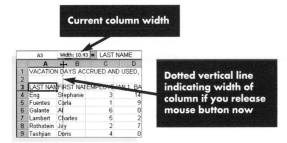

Current column width

Dotted vertical line indicating width of column if you release mouse button now

② Hold down the left mouse button and drag the mouse to the right (to widen the column) or to the left (to narrow it). You'll see a vertical line indicating what the column's width would be if you released the mouse now. A ScreenTip indicating the column's current width also appears as you drag.

③ Release the mouse button and check whether the column has reached a more suitable width. Is your data still truncated? Or is the column too wide now, wasting space? Here the Last Name column looks about right.

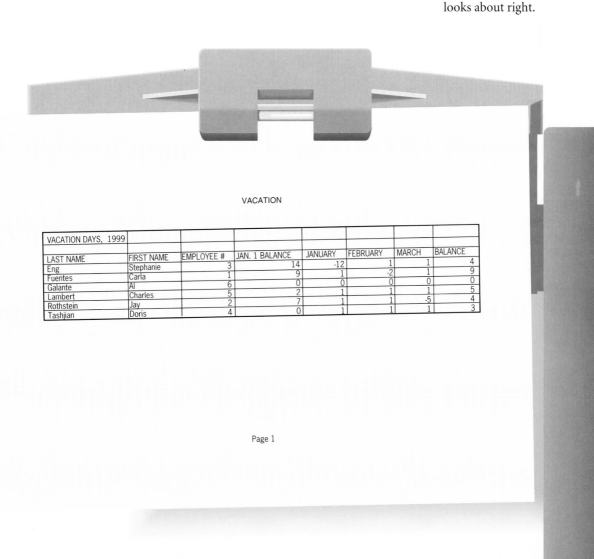

VACATION

VACATION DAYS, 1999							
LAST NAME	FIRST NAME	EMPLOYEE #	JAN. 1 BALANCE	JANUARY	FEBRUARY	MARCH	BALANCE
Eng	Stephanie	3	14	-12	1	1	4
Fuentes	Carla	1	9	1	-2	1	9
Galante	Al	6	0	0	0	0	0
Lambert	Charles	5	2	1	1	1	5
Rothstein	Jay	2	7	1	1	-5	4
Tashjian	Doris	4	0	1	1	1	3

CHAPTER 8

Improving Worksheet Appearance

 It's most important that worksheets be accurate and easy to use. But there's room for aesthetics, too. Boldfacing and italics can draw your eyes toward important information. Rounding off values to a reasonable number of decimal places can make it easier for you and your readers to put data into perspective. And a nice-looking worksheet can both enhance the impact of good news and soften the blow of bad news.

Excel offers a whole range of formatting features that can improve the appearance of your worksheets both on the screen and in print. This chapter describes how to format text and numbers, how to enhance cells by applying shading and borders, and how to change the alignment of cell contents within the cell borders. You'll also discover how to remove formatting when you need to.

Excel makes it refreshingly easy to apply sophisticated formatting to your worksheets. But don't let this tempt you into overdoing it in the formatting department. A worksheet with too much formatting can look cluttered, can be difficult to read, and can take up a lot of your valuable time. Apply formatting with discretion to have it work to your best advantage.

How to Change Font Characteristics

Excel lets you change several standard font characteristics of your data, including the font (typeface), the font style (boldface and italics), and the font size. You can also apply a number of special text effects—everything from the whimsical to the esoteric. When applying this type of formatting, you actually format the cells themselves. Whatever happens to be in a particular cell—whether it's text, numbers, or special characters—takes on the assigned format. If you later edit the data in the formatted cells, any formatting you've applied to the cells still affects the new contents of the cells.

TIP SHEET

▶ **Many of the buttons on the Formatting toolbar are toggles—you punch them once to turn them on and again to turn them off. (They even look pushed in when they're on.) If you see a pushed-in toolbar button when a cell is selected, you can remove the formatting from the cell by clicking the toolbar button to turn it off.**

▶ **To cancel all the selections you've made in the Font tab of the Format Cells dialog box, click on the Normal Font check box.**

▶ **You can format blank cells if you like. When you insert data into the cells, the new contents take on the assigned format. (Remember the formatting is a property of the cell itself, not of any data the cell happens to contain.)**

▶ **Don't confuse underlining with top or bottom borders. Underlining appears under the cell contents, which may not fill the entire width of the cell or may even spill over into adjacent cells. In contrast, top and bottom borders stretch from one end of a cell to the other, regardless of whether there's any data in there. Underlining disappears from view when you delete the cell contents, but borders don't.**

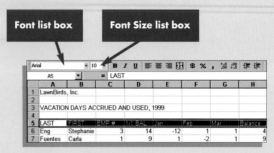

Font list box   Font Size list box

1 Activate the cell you want to format, or select a range of cells to format if you want to apply the same formatting to all of them.

8 When you're ready to put into place all the changes you've selected in the Format Cells dialog box, click OK.

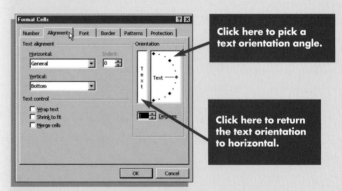

Click here to pick a text orientation angle.

Click here to return the text orientation to horizontal.

7 You can also make some font changes in the Alignment tab of the Format Cells dialog box. In particular, you can change the orientation of your text either by entering an angle in the Degrees text box or by clicking on the mark representing the desired angle in the sample box at the right. (The word *Text* takes on the selected text angle.) To return text to a normal horizontal orientation, click on the sample box at the left.

2 To choose a new font (typeface) for the selected cells, click on the downward-pointing arrow on the Font list box and then click on the desired font in the list of fonts that appears. (The available fonts may vary, depending on your printer and your version of Windows.) The font for the selected cells changes, and the Font list box also displays the new font.

3 To change the font size of the selected cells, click on the downward-pointing arrow on the Font Size list box and then click on the size you want in the list of font sizes that drops down. (The available font sizes may depend on which font you've selected.) The font size for the selected cells changes, and the Font Size list box now displays the new font size.

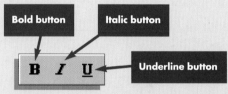

4 To boldface, italicize, or underline the data in the selected cells, click the Bold, Italic, or Underline toolbar button. (These buttons look "pushed in" when they're on; see the Tip Sheet for more details.) You can even use these features in various combinations—you can boldface and italicize text, for instance. (The available font styles may vary depending on which font is selected.)

5 If you need to change several font characteristics for the selected cells or you want to apply some special text effects, start by choosing Cells from the Format menu. (You can also right-click on any of the selected cells and choose Format Cells.)

6 You'll see the Format Cells dialog box. If necessary, click on the Font tab. From here you can change fonts, font sizes, fonts styles—as you can using the toolbar. In addition, you can choose from a variety of underlining styles, pick a text color, and select strikethrough, superscript, or subscript text. (If you have a penchant for colored text, you can change font colors quickly by using the Font Color toolbar button. It's at the far right end of the Formatting toolbar and has the letter *A* on its face.)

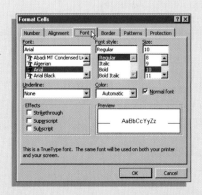

How to Format Numbers

Excel provides a wide assortment of number formats that let you dress up your numbers with dollar signs, commas for thousands separators, percent symbols, and more. Like font characteristics, number formats apply to cells rather than the specific data contained in cells. The complete number, function, or other formula appears in the formula bar when the cell is active, and even when a number is truncated and rounded off for display, the complete number is used in calculations.

TIP SHEET

▸ To remove number formatting, select the cells to be affected, go to the Number portion of the Format Cells dialog box, and choose the General format from the Category list box.

▸ If you type a number that includes commas as thousands separators into a cell that has no number format, Excel automatically assigns that cell the Number format. If you instead type a number that includes a dollar sign or percent symbol, Excel automatically assigns the cell a Currency or Percentage format.

▸ The Percentage format multiplies a number by 100 and adds a percent sign. But if you have applied the Percentage number format to a cell, Excel is bright enough to recognize a variety of data entry formats. For example, if you want to enter 35%, it makes no difference whether you type .35 or 35. Either way, Excel displays 35%.

▸ Applying number formats often lengthens numbers so much that they no longer fit within their cells. If you wind up with a series of pound signs (###) instead of numbers after applying a number format, just widen the appropriate columns (as described in Chapter 7). The numbers will reappear.

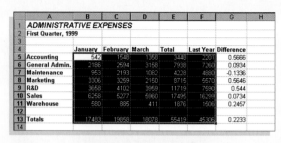

1 Activate the cell for which you want to change the number format, or select a range of cells if you want to assign the same number format to the whole batch of them.

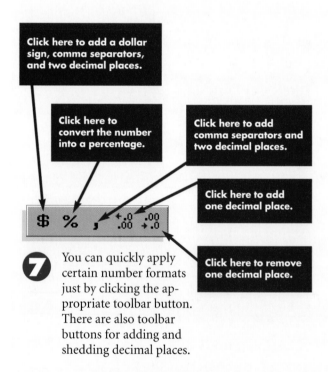

Click here to add a dollar sign, comma separators, and two decimal places.

Click here to convert the number into a percentage.

Click here to add comma separators and two decimal places.

Click here to add one decimal place.

Click here to remove one decimal place.

7 You can quickly apply certain number formats just by clicking the appropriate toolbar button. There are also toolbar buttons for adding and shedding decimal places.

Sample
$542

6 To preview your formatted numbers, look at the number displayed under "Sample." If this sample doesn't look quite right, continue tinkering in the dialog box until you get it the way you want it. Then click the OK button.

2 Choose Cells from the Format menu. Or right-click on one of the selected cells and choose Format Cells from the shortcut menu that appears.

3 At the top of the Format Cells dialog box, click on the Number tab if it's not already active.

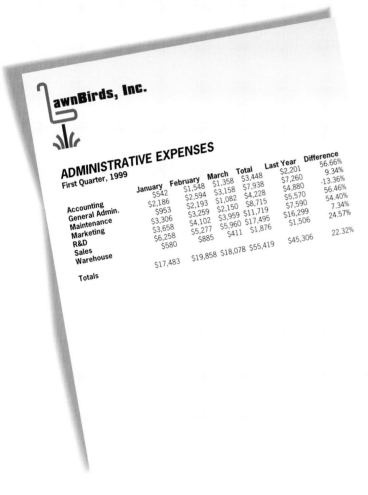

4 In the Category list box, choose the type of number you want to display. For example, click on Currency if you are working with dollar figures. If you're not sure what a particular category is for, click on it and read the description at the bottom of the dialog box.

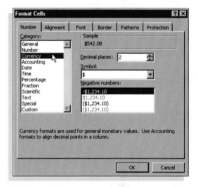

5 Depending on the category you select, you may be able to choose a number of decimal places, a currency symbol, and how you display negative numbers. For example, if you want to display numbers with preceding dollar signs but no decimal places, select Currency under Category, enter **0** in the Decimal Places text box, and leave the Symbol setting at $. By default, negative numbers are shown with a preceding minus sign. You can also display them in red text with no minus sign, in black text within parentheses, and in red text within parentheses.

How to Add Borders and Shading

Borders and shading are great ways to highlight important information and to generally spiff up the appearance of your worksheet, both on the screen and in print. Like all formatting, borders and shading should be applied sparingly so they don't lose their impact. Among other things, you might want to shade column headings or add a thick border to a cell that shows a grand total. When working with ranges of adjacent cells, you have a choice between placing a single border around the outside of the entire range or placing borders along the edges of each selected cell.

TIP SHEET

▶ **To get a better view of your borders and shading, click anywhere in the worksheet to deselect the selected cells.**

▶ **To cancel borders for a selected cell or range, click on None in the Border portion of the Format Cells dialog box. (Or choose the upper-left option from the palette that appears when you click the Borders toolbar button.) To get rid of shading, choose No Color in the Patterns portion of the Format Cells dialog box. (Or choose No Fill from the palette displayed when you click the Fill Color toolbar button.)**

▶ **Unlike cell borders, gridlines (see Chapter 5) don't show up in the worksheet window. They always print on all four sides of every cell, and they print only around existing data. (Actually, gridlines form a big box going from the upper-right to the lower-right worksheet cell containing data.) In contrast, cell borders always print—even if they're in an area of the worksheet that contains no data.**

▶ **1** Activate the cell you want to format, or select a range of cells to format them as a group. Then choose Cells from the Format menu or right-click on one of the selected cells and choose Format Cells from the shortcut menu.

Fill Color button

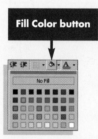

9 You can quickly shade selected cells by clicking on the arrow on the Fill Color toolbar button and choosing from the palette of colors that materializes. (If your choice appears on the button face, click the button itself to apply the currently selected color.)

Borders button

8 You can quickly apply borders by clicking on the arrow on the Borders toolbar button and choosing from the palette of options that appears. (If the choice you want shows up on the button face, just click the button itself to apply the currently selected border style.)

2 In the Format Cells dialog box, click on the Border tab if it's not already active.

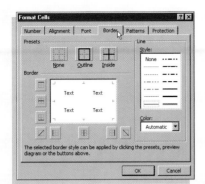

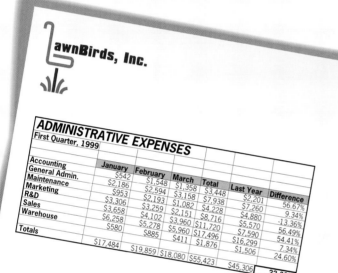

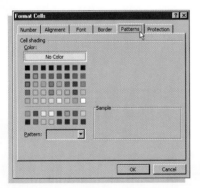

3 To add a border around the active cell or to add a single border around the outside edge of a group of selected cells, click on Outline. If you change your mind, you can click on None to remove the line.

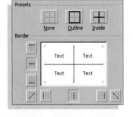

4 To place borders between adjacent cells but not around the outside edge of a group of selected cells, click on Inside. This option is available only if you select two or more cells. As before, you can click on None if you change your mind. (Note that you can select both Outline and Inside; they're not mutually exclusive.)

5 To place borders along specific sides of one or more cells, click the appropriate buttons under Border. There are eight buttons: for applying top, bottom, left, and right borders; horizontal and vertical borders between cells; and two styles of diagonal borders across cells. To remove a border, just click its button again to deselect it; the button will no longer look pushed in.

7 To shade the selected cell or cells, click on the Patterns tab in the Format Cells dialog box. Choose the color or shading you want. If you like, also choose a pattern from the patterns displayed when you click on the arrow in the Pattern list box. Consult the Sample box to check whether your color/pattern combination is palatable. When you're done, click OK to put your borders and shading into place.

6 Pick a border style. You can choose among various dashed, dotted, and double lines, as well as lines of varied thicknesses. In the Style box, the selected line is enclosed within a light dotted rectangle. You can also choose among various border colors by making selections from the color palette that materializes when you click on the Color drop-down list box.

How to Align Cell Contents

By default, Excel right-aligns numbers, including formula results, and left-aligns text; this alignment scheme is called the General option. Sometimes the General alignment is inadequate, especially when you have left-aligned column headings over right-aligned numbers. Luckily, it's easy to realign cell contents within their cell borders. Like font characteristics and number formats, alignment settings apply to the cells themselves rather than to any specific data. Even if you edit your data, the alignment should stay in effect.

TIP SHEET

▸ **To go back to default alignment (right-aligned numbers, left-aligned text), choose General in the Alignment portion of the Format Cells dialog box. Or click the selected alignment toolbar button to deselect it. To reverse the effects of Merge and Center, go to the Alignment tab of the Format Cells dialog box, deselect Merge Cells, and choose the desired alignment under Horizontal.**

▸ **When you use numbers as descriptive labels, Excel right-aligns those numbers by default. To specifically point out when they are labels, type an apostrophe before the number or enter the number and then left-align it with the Align Left toolbar button.**

▸ **You cannot align a column of numbers at the decimal point by following the procedure described here. Instead, simply select any number format that lets you pick a specific number of decimal places. If you want to line up both decimal points and currency symbols, go with the Accounting number format.**

▸ **Don't forget to select the cells across which you want to center your heading. If you don't, the Center Across Columns feature will behave the same as the ordinary center alignment feature.**

1 Activate the cell for which you want to change the alignment, or select a range of cells to specify the same alignment for all of them.

8 Finally, you can use the Fill option under Horizontal to repeat the cell contents until the cell is full—adding decorative touches such as rows packed with dashes or equal signs. When you're done making selections in the Format Cells dialog box, click OK to put your changes into place.

7 If you select the Wrap Text check box, wide text entries break into separate lines within the cell, increasing the row height rather than spilling into any vacant cells to the right. You can then select the Justify option under Horizontal to justify lines within the cell, which adds space between words so your text is both right- and left-aligned between the cell borders.

2 To align the contents of the selected cells with the left cell borders, click the Align Left toolbar button.

3 To center the cell contents between the cell borders, click the Center toolbar button.

4 To align the contents of the selected cells with the right cell borders, click the Align Right toolbar button.

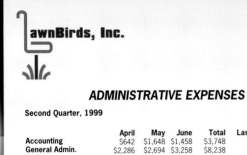

awnBirds, Inc.

ADMINISTRATIVE EXPENSES

Second Quarter, 1999

	April	May	June	Total	Last Year	Difference
Accounting	$642	$1,648	$1,458	$3,748	$2,401	56.10%
General Admin.	$2,286	$2,694	$3,258	$8,238	$7,460	10.43%
Maintenance	$1,053	$2,293	$1,182	$4,528	$4,980	-9.08%
Marketing	$3,406	$3,359	$2,251	$9,016	$7,970	13.12%
R&D	$3,756	$4,202	$4,060	$12,018	$13,886	-13.45%
Sales	$6,358	$5,378	$6,060	$17,796	$16,399	8.52%
Warehouse	$680	$985	$511	$2,176	$1,906	14.17%
Totals	$18,181	$20,559	$18,780	$57,520	$55,002	**4.58%**

Please call Fran at ext. 2077 for more information.

5 To center a heading across several columns, select the heading as well as the columns over which you want to center it. Then click the Merge and Center toolbar button.

6 To make additional alignment selections, choose Format Cells from the Format menu and click on the Alignment tab in the Format Cells dialog box. From here you can shrink text to fit within a cell by selecting the Shrink to Fit check box, you can indent left-aligned text from the left edge of the cell, and you can change the orientation of text, as described earlier in this chapter under "How to Change Font Characteristics."

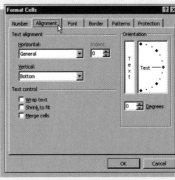

How to Remove Formatting

The prime directive of formatting is not to go overboard. If you add too much formatting, the result will be a cluttered worksheet that's a chore to read. As you fine-tune and tinker with your worksheets, there will inevitably be times when you want to toss out certain formats you've applied. If you're in the midst of the formatting process, it's often easy to reverse course. If you already have a full quota of formatting in place, however, it helps to know a few tricks for eliminating one or more formats quickly and painlessly.

TIP SHEET

▸ **If you've only just put a formatting change into place, you may be able to backtrack with the Undo command; its secrets were unmasked in Chapter 6.**

▸ **If your aim is to obliterate all formatting in the worksheet, select the entire worksheet by pressing Ctrl+A. Then choose the Edit, Clear, Format command.**

▸ **You can use the Clear command to clear a cell's contents without clearing any formatting. (That's what you did in Chapter 7; pressing the Del key is the same as choosing Edit, Clear, Contents.) You can also use Clear to clear a cell's formatting without clearing its contents (as you did here). And if you use the All option, you can use the Clear command to clear both the contents and formatting in a cell.**

▶ **1** To eliminate all formatting, select the cells for which you want to get rid of formatting. You can select anywhere from a single cell to the entire worksheet.

You can tell that boldfacing is still on, because the button looks "pushed in."

Italic is now off; the button doesn't look "pushed in."

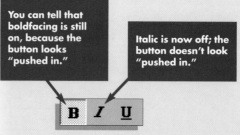

6 If you want to eliminate some but not all formatting, you need to take a more gingerly approach. Often you can get your way by using toolbar buttons judiciously. For example, if you want to remove only the italics from cells that are both bold and italic, you can select the cells and click the Italic toolbar button to turn it off. If you want to get rid of a formatting feature that doesn't have a toolbar button, retrace your steps back to the correct tab in the Format Cells dialog box, where you should be able to find the appropriate "off switch." (Just deselect any options you've selected.)

2 Choose Clear from the Edit menu.

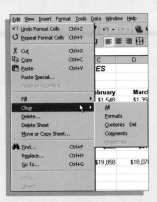

3 Choose Formats from the submenu that appears. This option clears any and all formatting from the selected cells, without throwing out their contents in the process.

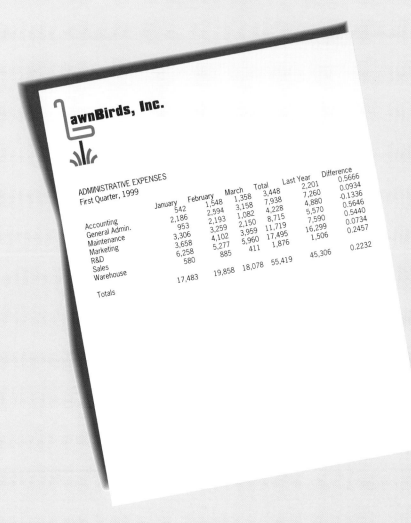

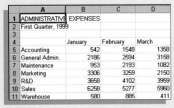

4 If you like, click anywhere in the worksheet to deselect the selected cells. Then scan those cells, noting that they include no formatting whatsoever—no font styles, no number formats, no nothing.

5 If you decide to eliminate both data and formatting from the selected cells, you can use the Edit, Clear, All command instead.

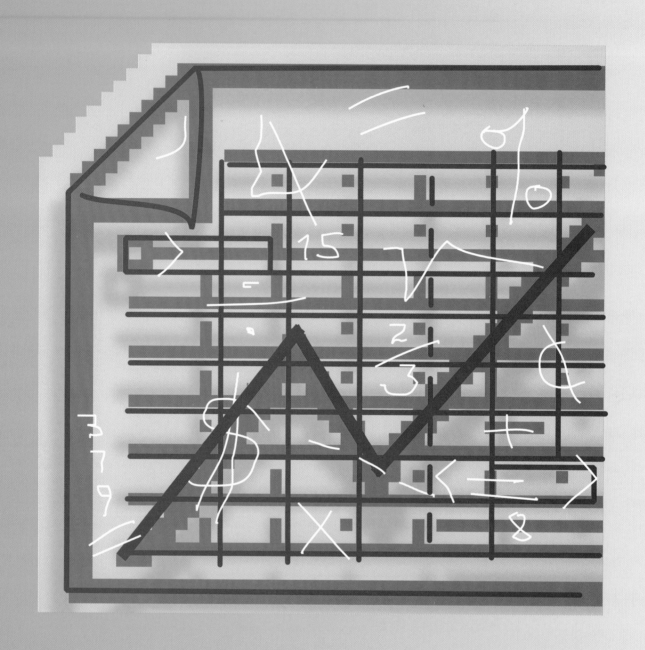

CHAPTER 9

More about Formulas and Functions

Chapter 2 explained how to create formulas that perform calculations based on the data already in your worksheet. You also learned about the SUM function, a tool for adding up numbers—even large groups of numbers—quickly and easily. Remember, a formula is any set of instructions that perform calculations and display their results in the worksheet. A function is a built-in formula that Excel provides for quickly carrying out specific and sometimes complex calculations. This chapter supplies you with more skills for working with formulas and functions.

You'll find out about a few additional Excel functions for carrying out operations that would be inconvenient or impossible to perform with ordinary formulas. You'll learn a great way to build worksheets more quickly by "filling in" repetitive formulas and letting Excel figure out the correct cell references. You'll also discover how to override Excel's automatic adjustment of cell references when necessary. Next you'll find out how to detect and repair some common errors in formulas. Finally, you'll discover how to assign names to cells and ranges. These names can make your formulas easier to type and easier to understand.

Excel lets you build extremely complex formulas and provides literally hundreds of functions for everything from statistical to financial to database calculations. But there's no need to memorize the intricacies of all of Excel's functions, since most of them are tools for specialists. If you gain an understanding of how formulas do their job and a working knowledge of a few functions, you have what it takes to make Excel work for you, and you can learn about additional functions as needed.

How to Use Excel's Functions

These pages present four of Excel's most useful functions: MAX, MIN, AVERAGE, and COUNT. Remember that a function is a built-in formula. For example, the SUM function lets you sum the contents of several cells without building a long formula to add each one. But not all Excel functions are mere conveniences like SUM. Certain Excel functions perform actions that don't duplicate standard formulas. For instance, the MAX function displays the largest (maximum) value in a range you specify. No formula could do that.

TIP SHEET

▶ You can type function names in uppercase, lowercase, or a combination of the two. Excel automatically converts them to uppercase in the interest of tidiness.

▶ To include noncontiguous ranges or individual cells in any function, separate the ranges or cell references with commas, as in =min(b4:d8,f4:g8,i10,j10).

▶ You can also enter functions by using Excel's Paste Function toolbar button (the one with *fx* on its face). This button leads to the Paste Function dialog box, which helps you build complex functions and can save you a lot of typing in the process. Another option is to use the drop-down list of functions that appears on the left end of the formula bar when you type an equal sign. If you're entering short-and-sweet functions, however, it's often just as easy to type them and click or drag across the needed cell references.

▶ A good way to explore Excel's many other functions is to display the Paste Function dialog box and then use the Office Assistant to seek help on specific functions. See Chapter 6 for more details on using the various aspects of Excel's online help system.

	A	B	C	D	E	F	G	H	I
1			VACATION DAYS ACCRUED AND USED, 1999						
2									
3	Last Name	First Name	Emp #	1/1 Balance	January	February	March	Balance	
4	Eng	Stephanie	3	14	-12	1	1	4	
5	Fuentes	Carla	1	9	1	-2	1	9	
6	Lambert	Charles	5	2	1	1	1	5	
7	Rothstein	Jay	2	7	1	1	-5	4	
8	Tashjian	Doris	4	0	1	1	1	3	
9									
10							High:		
11							Low:		
12							Avg:		
13									

▶ **1** Activate the cell in which you want the function result to appear.

The equal sign is missing, so Excel doesn't perform the calculation.

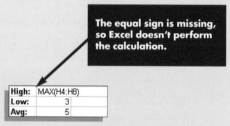

High:	MAX(H4:H8)
Low:	3
Avg:	5

6 Common mistakes in entering functions include misspelling the function name and forgetting the equal sign and/or the opening parenthesis. (If you forget the closing parenthesis, Excel generously adds it for you.) Check for one of these mistakes if Excel tells you that you made an error or displays an obviously incorrect result. Then edit the function as needed, using the techniques you learned in Chapter 4.

March	Balance
1	4
1	9
1	5
-5	4
1	3
High:	=max(H4:H8)
Low:	
Avg:	

2 Enter the function =MAX(*range*) to display the largest number in the designated range. *Range* stands for the function's arguments—that is, the values the function operates on. The argument can be a single cell, a range of cells, or several cells separated by commas. Here the range is H4:H8, the balance values for all employees.

High:	9
Low:	=min(H4:H8)
Avg:	

3 Enter the function =MIN(*range*) to display the smallest number in the designated range.

VACATION DAYS ACCRUED AND USED, 1999

Last Name	First Name	Emp #	1/1 Balance	January	February	March	Balance
Eng	Stephanie	3	14	-12	1	1	4
Fuentes	Carla	1	9	1	-2	1	9
Lambert	Charles	5	2	1	1	1	5
Rothstein	Jay	2	7	1	1	-5	4
Tashjian	Doris	4	0	1	1	1	3

High:	9
Low:	3
Avg:	5

High:	9
Low:	3
Avg:	=average(H4:H8)

4 Enter the function =AVERAGE(*range*) to display the average of the numbers in the designated range. The AVERAGE function sums the numbers in the range and divides the result by the number of values summed.

High:	9
Low:	3
Avg:	5
Count:	=count(H4:H8)

5 If you had a lot of employees and wanted to determine exactly how many employees there were, you could use the COUNT function, as shown here. This function "counts" any column or row that contains numbers since its purpose is to determine how many cells in the designated range contain numbers.

How to Fill in a Formula

Many worksheets contain sequences of very similar formulas. For example, the rightmost column or bottom row in a table often holds a series of SUM functions that total the numbers to their left or above them. Although you could enter all formulas separately, it's much easier to use Excel's fill handle to create a sequence of formulas that are identical except for cell references. When you fill in a row or column, Excel adjusts the cell references accordingly, and usually it guesses right.

TIP SHEET

▶ When you're building a series of SUM functions, the AutoSum button is often just as quick as the fill handle (see Chapter 2). But if you want a series of other functions—such as MIN, MAX, AVERAGE, or COUNT—or if you want to create similar formulas—such as =B8*C8, =B9*C9, and so on—the fill handle is one of the quickest ways to go.

▶ After filling in a row or column, check that Excel adjusted the cell references appropriately. Excel guesses which cell references you want. For example, as you fill cells to the right, every column letter in the formula increases by one; and as you fill cells down, each row number increases by one. Occasionally, you may have to override this automatic cell reference adjustment. The next set of pages explains why and how.

▶ You can also copy formulas. When you do, their cell references automatically adjust themselves. If you're copying formulas down a column or across a column, the fill handle is probably the fastest method. But if you want to copy a formula to a location elsewhere in the worksheet, you can use either the drag-and-drop strategy or the Copy and Paste commands (Chapter 7).

	A	B	C	D	E	F	G	H	I
1				VACATION DAYS ACCRUED AND USED, 1999					
2									
3	Last Name	First Name	Emp #	1/1 Balance	January	February	March	Balance	
4	Eng	Stephanie	3	14	-12	1	1	=sum(d4:g4)	
5	Fuentes	Carla	1	9	1	-2	1		
6	Lambert	Charles	5	2	1	1	1		
7	Rothstein	Jay	2	7	1	1	-5		
8	Tashjian	Doris	4	0	1	1	1		

▶ **1** Enter the topmost or leftmost formula in the sequence. (Feel free to use any of the shortcuts you learned for entering functions, such as the AutoSum button.)

Adjusted cell references

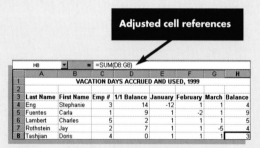

H8		=	=SUM(D8:G8)				
	A	B	C	D	E	F	G	H
1			VACATION DAYS ACCRUED AND USED, 1999					
2								
3	Last Name	First Name	Emp #	1/1 Balance	January	February	March	Balance
4	Eng	Stephanie	3	14	-12	1	1	4
5	Fuentes	Carla	1	9	1	-2	1	9
6	Lambert	Charles	5	2	1	1	1	5
7	Rothstein	Jay	2	7	1	1	-5	4
8	Tashjian	Doris	4	0	1	1	1	3

6 The cells you dragged across now contain the formula results. Activate any of the cells and check the formula bar. Note that Excel has automatically inserted a series of formulas, adjusting the cell references to fit their new location. For example, the original formula =SUM(D4:G4) has been changed to =SUM(D8:G8) in cell H8.

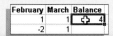

February	March	Balance
1	1	4
-2	1	

2 If necessary, activate the cell containing the formula.

Balance
4

3 Point to the fill handle in the lower-right corner of the cell. Notice that the mouse pointer takes on a new shape—a smaller plus sign.

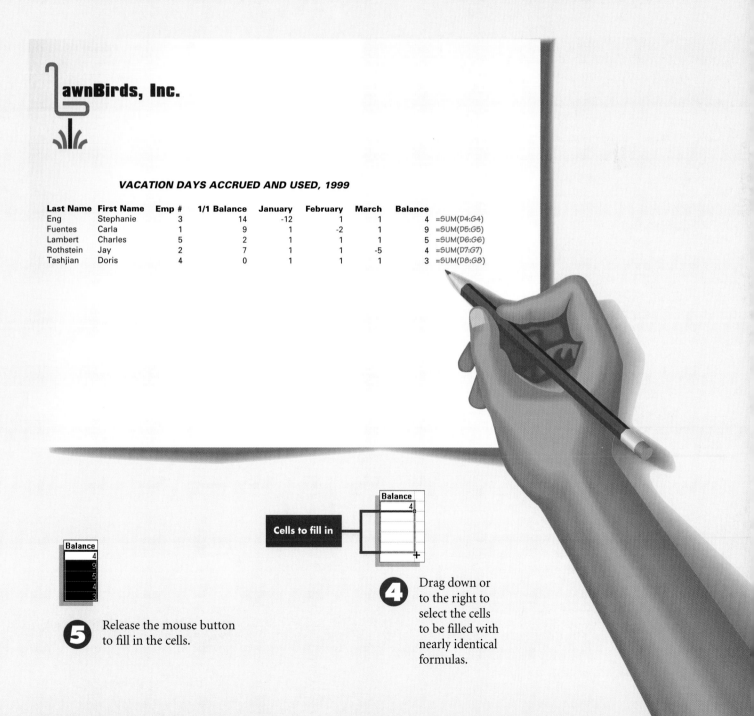

LawnBirds, Inc.

VACATION DAYS ACCRUED AND USED, 1999

Last Name	First Name	Emp #	1/1 Balance	January	February	March	Balance	
Eng	Stephanie	3	14	-12	1	1	4	=SUM(D4:G4)
Fuentes	Carla	1	9	1	-2	1	9	=SUM(D5:G5)
Lambert	Charles	5	2	1	1	1	5	=SUM(D6:G6)
Rothstein	Jay	2	7	1	1	-5	4	=SUM(D7:G7)
Tashjian	Doris	4	0	1	1	1	3	=SUM(D8:G8)

Cells to fill in

Balance
4

4 Drag down or to the right to select the cells to be filled with nearly identical formulas.

Balance
4
9
5
4
3

5 Release the mouse button to fill in the cells.

How to Work with Absolute References

When you used the fill handle to create additional formulas a moment ago, the cell references changed automatically relative to their new location. For this reason, such references are called *relative references*. But sometimes you won't want cell references to change when you copy formulas using the fill handle or another copying strategy. References that don't change when copied are called *absolute references*. In a moment you'll learn how to create absolute references and why they're sometimes necessary.

TIP SHEET

▸ **Don't worry when moving a cell that is referenced absolutely somewhere else in the worksheet. (This would be the case, for example, if you had the formula =C3*D13 and you moved the contents of cell D13 to D15.) The references to the cell adjust automatically to reflect the new location of the cell—and they remain absolute. (The revised formula would be =C3*D15.)**

▸ **Why would you reference the cell containing the multiplier instead of including the multiplier in every bonus calculation? Well, what if you need to decrease the bonuses from 7 percent to 5 percent of base pay? Because you've referenced the cell rather than the actual multiplier in the formula, you can simply enter the new multiplier in the referenced cell. Excel will recalculate all the bonuses instantly.**

▸ **Absolute cell references must have a dollar sign preceding both the column letter and the row number. You can also create mixed cell references, which have a dollar sign preceding the column letter but not the row number, or vice versa.**

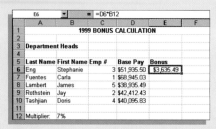

 1 First try entering a standard formula (without any absolute references) and then copying it with the fill handle, as you did earlier. The formula shown here calculates the correct bonus for Stephanie Eng by multiplying her base pay by the percentage listed in cell B12.

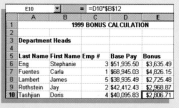

7 If you like, click on one of the cells containing a copied formula to inspect the results. For instance, here the reference to D6 was appropriately changed to D10, but the reference to B12—the cell containing the multiplier—did not change.

 6 Again drag the fill handle to copy the formula in cell E6 down column E. This time you'll get the correct results shown here—to the relief of the rest of the employees.

2 Drag the fill handle to copy this formula down column E.

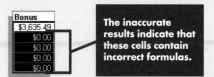

The inaccurate results indicate that these cells contain incorrect formulas.

3 When you release the mouse button, you see these results. What went wrong? How come Stephanie seems to be the only one in line for a bonus?

	A	B	C	D	E
1		*1999 BONUS CALCULATION*			
2					
3	Department Heads				
4					
5	Last Name	First Name	Emp #	Base Pay	Bonus
6	Eng	Stephanie	3	$51,935.50	$3,635.49
7	Fuentes	Carla	1	$68,945.03	$4,826.15
8	Lambert	Charles	5	$38,935.49	$2,725.48
9	Rothstein	Jay	2	$42,412.43	$2,968.87
10	Tashjian	Doris	4	$40,095.83	$2,806.71
11					
12	Multiplier:	7%			

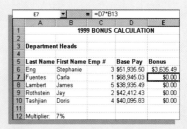

E7   = =D7*B13

	A	B	C	D	E
1		1999 BONUS CALCULATION			
2					
3	Department Heads				
4					
5	Last Name	First Name	Emp #	Base Pay	Bonus
6	Eng	Stephanie	3	$51,935.50	$3,635.49
7	Fuentes	Carla	1	$68,945.03	$0.00
8	Lambert	James	5	$38,935.49	$0.00
9	Rothstein	Jay	2	$42,412.43	$0.00
10	Tashjian	Doris	4	$40,095.83	$0.00
11					
12	Multiplier:	7%			

4 Highlight one of the cells containing a $0.00—and an erroneous formula. For example, here you can see that cell E7 contains the formula =D7*B13. The original reference to D6 was changed to D7, to refer to Carla Fuentes' base pay. That much makes sense. But the reference to the multiplier in cell B12 was also changed to B13, an empty cell! Instead, the reference to cell B12 must remain unchanged—that is, it needs to be an absolute reference.

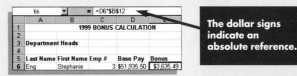

E6   = =D6*B12

	A	B	C	D	E
1		1999 BONUS CALCULATION			
2					
3	Department Heads				
4					
5	Last Name	First Name	Emp #	Base Pay	Bonus
6	Eng	Stephanie	3	$51,935.50	$3,635.49

The dollar signs indicate an absolute reference.

5 Double-click on cell E6. Then type dollar signs ($) in front of the column letter and row number in B12—changing it to B12—and press Enter or click the Enter button. (You can instead make sure the insertion point is within that cell reference and press F4.) The reference to B12 is now absolute (it won't change), but the reference to D6 will adjust itself to its new surroundings when copied.

How to Fix Mistakes in Formulas

Normally, your formulas will work without a hitch. Occasionally, however, something goes wrong. If you forget to include an absolute reference, you might wind up with incorrect results, as you saw on the previous set of pages. In addition, incorrect formulas sometimes yield cryptic results, such as #NAME?, #REF!, and #DIV/0! Here's where you learn what some of these hieroglyphics mean, as well as few other pitfalls to avoid.

TIP SHEET

▶ **If one of your formulas is not coming out as planned and it includes multiple mathematical operators, you might need to use parentheses to fix the problem. Operations aren't automatically performed from left to right. Instead, exponentiation is performed first, then multiplication and division, and finally addition and subtraction. If you need to change this order, you can use parentheses; the operations within parentheses will be performed first. For example, in the formula =2+3*4, 3 is multiplied by 4, and then the result (12) is added to 2. If you instead want to add 2 and 3, and then multiply by four, you can change the formula as follows: =(2+3)*4.**

▶ **You might also see the #NAME? error if you enter an incorrect name for a cell or range. What are cell and range names? Read the next few pages to find out.**

▶ **If a cell fills up with pound signs (####), you've simply generated a number that is too large to fit in the cell at its current width. (In other words, you haven't really done anything wrong.) The solution is simple: Widen the column or columns in question, as described in Chapter 7. Another possible solution is to use a number format with fewer decimal places, as explained in Chapter 8.**

The formula in this cell attempts to divide the value in B1 by B2, which is empty and so is considered to have a value of 0.

This formula attempts to divide the value in A1 by 0.

❶ If you see the message #DIV/0! in a cell, the formula in that cell has attempted to divide a number by 0—a mathematical *faux pas*. (Note that Excel considers blank cells to have a value of 0.) Check that there's a value other than 0 in the cell that is the divisor.

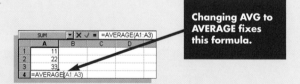

Changing AVG to AVERAGE fixes this formula.

❻ Once you've tracked down your error, you can make corrections by double-clicking on the cell containing the faulty formula and editing it using the techniques you learned in Chapter 4.

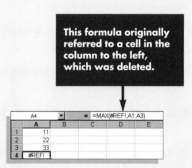

This function name has been misspelled (it should be AVERAGE), so Excel doesn't recognize it.

2 If a cell contains the message #NAME?, the formula contained in that cell includes a name that Excel doesn't recognize. Check whether you typed the wrong cell address or mistyped the function name.

This formula originally referred to a cell in the column to the left, which was deleted.

3 If you see the message #REF!, your formula refers to a cell that is not valid. For example, you may have deleted one of the cells referred to in the formula. You can often avoid receiving this error by using cell ranges instead of individual cell references. Excel knows enough to adjust the range listed in the formula when you delete cells included in the range.

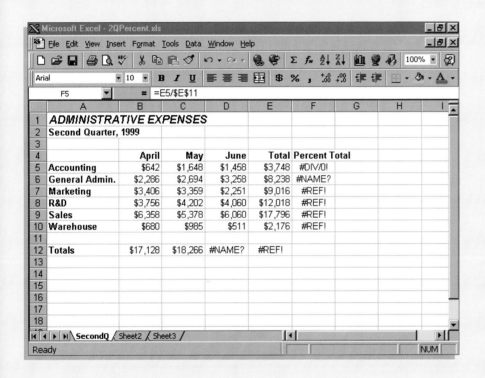

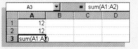

5 If the results you get seem to be off, carefully read through your formulas, even if Excel isn't giving you an error message. You may have included incorrect cell references, among other things. In other words, double-check all your results, even if you don't receive error messages. Excel carries out any mathematical operations that make logical sense, regardless of whether that's what you actually intended.

4 If your formula shows up just as text, stubbornly refusing to carry out any calculations, you probably neglected to precede it with an equal sign, as shown here.

How to Name Cells and Cell Ranges

When referring to ranges of cells, you've so far used notation such as B6:C7 to mean cells B6, B7, C6, and C7. This shorthand notation can be a great convenience, especially when you're referring to large ranges. But you can also assign names to individual cells or to cell ranges. Using names can make your formulas easier to enter and easier to read.

 1 Select the cell or range of cells that you want to name.

Natural language formula

8 Sometimes you can refer to labels without going through the whole naming rigmarole by using what are called *natural language formulas*. For example, in the worksheet shown here, you could enter =**April Sales**+**May Sales** to find the total for those two months, or you could enter =**Marketing**+**Sales** in column E to find the quarterly totals for Marketing and Sales. Natural language formulas are not invariably easier to type than run-of-the-mill formulas, but they are always much easier to read.

TIP SHEET

▶ Be sure not to confuse the Name box, which is on the formula bar, with the Font drop-down list box on the Formatting toolbar.

▶ If you want to delete existing names, simply choose Name from the Insert menu and choose Define to display the Define Name dialog box. From here you can delete names by highlighting them and clicking the Delete button.

▶ If you decide to change a name, choose Name from the Insert menu and then choose Define. Click on the name to be changed. Then click in the Names in Workbook text box, edit the name as desired, and click on Add. Finally, click on the original name (at this point you'll have two names for the same range) and click the Delete button.

The Name box

2 Click on the Name box at the far left end of the formula bar. Type a name for the range and press Enter. The name can be up to 255 characters and must begin with a letter or an underscore. (It's probably best to use fairly short, descriptive names.) These names can include letters, numbers, periods, and underlines but cannot include spaces or any other punctuation or special characters except for the backslash (\) and the question mark.

3 If you want to use existing labels as names, select the range of cells to be named, along with the labels, as shown here.

	April	May	June	Total	Last Year	Difference
					ADMINISTRATIVE EXPENSES	
5	Accounting	$642	$1,648	$1,458	$3,748	$2,401	56.10%
6	General Admin.	$2,286	$2,694	$3,258	$8,238	$7,460	10.43%
7	Maintenance	$1,053	$2,293	$1,182	$4,528	$4,980	-9.08%
8	Marketing	$3,406	$3,359	$2,251	$9,016	$7,970	13.12%
9	R&D	$3,756	$4,202	$4,060	$12,018	$13,886	-13.45%
10	Sales	$6,358	$5,378	$6,060	$17,796	$16,399	8.52%
11	Warehouse	$680	$985	$511	$2,176	$1,906	14.17%
13	Totals	$18,181	$20,559	$18,780	$57,520	$55,002	4.58%

Sum=$55,002

4 Now choose Name from the Insert menu and choose Create from the submenu that appears. (One of the best things about this technique is that you can use it to create several names at once.)

5 In the Create Names dialog box that appears, choose Top Row if the labels to be used as names are above the range(s) to be named. Choose one of the other options if your labels are in a different location. Then click OK.

7 To use a named cell or range in a formula, enter the formula as usual, but instead of typing or pointing out the cells or ranges, choose Name from the Insert menu, choose Paste, and choose the named range from the Paste Name dialog box. You can also type in range names if you like.

6 To select a named range, click the downward-pointing arrow to the right of the Name box and click on the name of the desired range in the drop-down list that appears.

TRY IT!

You've built up quite a set of Excel skills in the last four chapters of this book. Here's your opportunity to put those skills into practice. Follow these steps at your computer to produce the worksheet shown on this page. Most steps include chapter numbers that guide you to more detailed explanations of the required skills. When formatting the worksheet, remember that the available fonts, styles, and point sizes can differ from one computer to the next, so your worksheet may not match the one shown here in every detail.

Start Excel if it's not already running. Unless you already have a blank worksheet on your screen, start a new worksheet by clicking the New button. *Chapter 3*

Enter the basic worksheet exactly as shown here. (Don't worry that it doesn't exactly match the graphic shown below.) All these numbers are plain data, not formula results.

	A	B	C	D	E	F
1	1999 BONUS CALCULATION					
2						
3	Department Heads					
4						
5	Last Name	Emp. #	Base Pay	Bonus	Total	
6	Eng	3	51935.5			
7	Fuentes	1	68945.03			
8	Lambert	5	38935.49			
9	Rothstein	2	42412.43			
10	Tashjian	4	40095.83			
11						
12	Multiplier	7%				

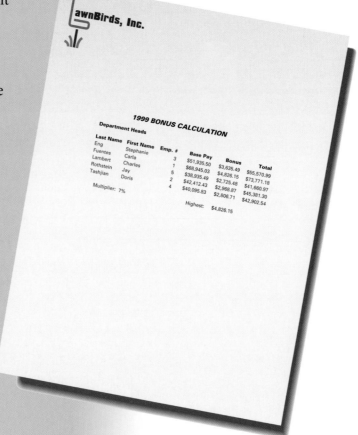

LawnBirds, Inc.

1999 BONUS CALCULATION

Department Heads

Last Name	First Name	Emp. #	Base Pay	Bonus	Total
Eng	Stephanie	3	$51,935.50	$3,635.49	$55,570.99
Fuentes	Carla	1	$68,945.03	$4,826.15	$73,771.18
Lambert	Charles	5	$38,935.49	$2,725.48	$41,660.97
Rothstein	Jay	2	$42,412.43	$2,968.87	$45,381.30
Tashjian	Doris	4	$40,095.83	$2,806.71	$42,902.54

Multiplier: 7%

Highest: $4,826.15

Choose Save
from the File
menu or click
the Save tool-
bar button.
Chapter 3

Choose Cells
from the
Format menu
to display the
Format Cells
dialog box.
Chapter 8

In the File
Name area of
the Save As
dialog box,
type **Bonus** as the workbook name.
Then click the Save button.

Click on the
Number tab
if necessary.
In the
Category list,
click on
Currency.
Under
Symbol,
make sure $ is selected. In the Negative
Numbers list, click on the last currency formatting option. Then click the OK button
to apply this format to the numbers now in
the Base Pay column and to the numbers
that will appear in the Bonus and Total
columns in a moment. *Chapter 8*

If by chance you see a Properties dialog box,
click the OK button. There's no need to fill in
any of the extra details.

Select the
Base Pay numbers and the blank cells beneath
the Bonus and Total headings. *Chapter 4*

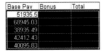

Activate cell
D6, type
=**c6*b12** and press Enter. The dollar
signs in this formula produce an absolute
reference, so when you copy the formula to
other cells, the reference to the multiplier
in cell B12 will not change. *Chapter 9*

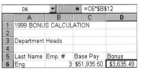

Continue to next page ▶

TRY IT!

Continue below

10

With cell D6 active, point to the fill handle in its lower-right corner and then drag down to fill in the four cells below. Release the mouse button and note that each filled-in cell multiplies the cell to its left by the multiplier in cell B12. *Chapter 9*

11

Base Pay	Bonus	Total
$51,935.50	$3,635.49	$55,570.99
$68,945.03	$4,826.15	$73,771.18
$38,935.49	$2,725.48	$41,660.97
$42,412.43	$2,968.87	$45,381.30
$40,095.83	$2,806.71	$42,902.54

Activate cell E6 and enter the formula =**c6+d6** to calculate Eng's total pay. Then, with cell E6 still active, drag its fill handle to fill in the four cells below it. *Chapter 9*

12   **B**

Select the range A3:E5. Then click the Bold toolbar button to boldface the selected cells. *Chapter 8*

13

Activate any cell in column B. Then choose Columns from the Insert menu. *Chapter 7*

14

First Name
Stephanie
Carla
Charles
Jay
Doris

Enter the data shown here into the newly created column B. Also widen column B just a tad by dragging the right border of its column heading. *Chapter 7*

15

Activate cell C12, point to the cell border so that the mouse pointer becomes an arrow, drag one cell to the left, and release the mouse button to move the cell contents. *Chapter 7*

16

Select the range C5:F5, and click the Align Right toolbar button. *Chapter 8*

17

Using the same technique, right-align cell A12. *Chapter 8*

 21

Select the range A1:F1 and click the Merge and Center toolbar button.

 18

Now left-align cell B12 by clicking on it to activate it and then clicking the Align Left toolbar button.

 22

In cell D12, enter **Highest:** and right-align it using the Align Right toolbar button. *Chapter 8*

 19

Activate cell A1 and click the Bold and Italic toolbar buttons. *Chapter 8*

 23

Base Pay	Bonus	Total
$51,935.50	$3,635.49	$55,570.99
$68,945.03	$4,826.15	$73,771.18
$38,935.49	$2,725.48	$41,660.97
$42,412.43	$2,968.87	$45,381.30
$40,095.83	$2,806.71	$42,902.54
Highest:	=max(e6:e10)	

In cell E12, enter the function =**max(e6:e10)** to display the highest bonus given. *Chapter 9*

 20

With cell A1 still active, choose 14 from the Font Size drop-down list. *Chapter 8*

 **24**

Save the worksheet again, print it if you like, and close it when you're done. *Chapter 3, Chapter 5*

CHAPTER 10

Formatting Shortcuts

 Chapter 8 introduced a whole assortment of tools for formatting your worksheets to make them both more readable and more pleasing to the eye. This chapter presents some shortcuts for simplifying and speeding up your formatting chores.

First you discover how to copy formats. If your worksheet includes a particular formatting combination—maybe bold, italic, and Currency formatting with two decimal places—that you want to use elsewhere, you don't need to reenter the formatting from scratch. Instead, you can copy it from one place to another. Best of all, the process is equally easy whether you're copying a set of two or a set of twelve formats.

You also learn about ready-made spreadsheet designs called Auto-Formats. These designs include anything from lines and shading to special 3D effects. AutoFormats can make your worksheets look truly professional with very little effort on your part.

Next you find out how to work with styles—formatting combinations you can create and save with your workbooks. Styles make it easy to apply formatting combinations in a single step. For example, if you regularly use headings that are 14 point, Times New Roman, and italic, you can create a style called Heading and use it instead of going through several formatting steps each time. And if you alter a style, any cells formatted with that style are updated to reflect those changes. In other words, styles not only speed up your initial formatting tasks, they provide consistency to your spreadsheets.

Finally, you learn a bit about *conditional formatting,* a way of having Excel automatically format cells containing data that meets specified conditions. For instance, you can have your sales figures displayed in blue if they exceed a particular target amount, or in red if they fall short.

How to Copy Formats

If you've already applied a set of formats to one or more areas of your worksheet—maybe you chose a new font, picked a new point size, and changed the alignment—you don't have to enter these formats again from the ground up when you need them elsewhere in the worksheet. Instead you can use a handy tool called the Format Painter to copy them.

TIP SHEET

▶ If you select several cells before choosing the Format Painter toolbar button and then click within the worksheet, Excel formats a range the same size as the originally selected range. It's probably safest to select a single cell containing formatting you want to copy before clicking the Format Painter toolbar button. This way you'll format only the cells you actually click or drag across.

▶ Here's yet another trick for applying formatting from one cell to another cell in your worksheet: Select the cell containing the formatting you want to copy. Then right-drag (drag using the right mouse button) that cell over the cell you want to format. Release the mouse button and choose Copy Here as Formats Only from the shortcut menu that appears. You can copy formatting from a range of cells in the same way. However, this technique permits you to format a group of cells only if they are the same size and shape as the range you selected originally.

▶ When you use Copy and Paste Special, the originally selected cell remains enclosed within a marquee after the paste operation. If you move to another cell and press Enter, you'll copy the entire contents of the original cell, not just its formatting. To get rid of the marquee, just press Esc.

▶ Note that Paste Special works only with the Copy command; it doesn't work with the Cut command.

	January	February	March	Q1		Percent Total
Cat Food	2346	3112	2911	8369		30%
Dog Food	2199	2635	2783	7617		27%
Flea Products	1732	1863	1534	5129		18%
Toys	1184	1321	1429	3934		14%
Treats	972	842	1299	3113		11%
Totals	$ 8,433	$ 9,773	$ 9,956	$ 28,162		

1 If you want to apply the formatting from one cell to one or more other cells in your worksheet, first activate the cell containing the formatting you want to copy.

7 Choose Paste Special from the Edit menu to display the Paste Special dialog box. Click the Formats option button to select it, and then click OK to copy the formatting (but not the contents) of the cell you copied originally. Until you place something else on the Clipboard, you can repeat this step as often as you like to format other sets of cells. (Hint: To hasten the process, choose Repeat from the Edit menu or press the Ctrl+Y keyboard shortcut.)

2 Click the Format Painter toolbar button. The active cell acquires a marquee—remember, that's a moving dashed line—and the Format Painter toolbar button looks pushed in.

was copied to here.

Format from here

	January	February	March	Q1	Percent Total
Cat Food	2346	3112	2911	8369	30%
Dog Food	2199	2635	2783	7617	27%
Flea Products	1732	1863	1534	5129	18%
Toys	1184	1321	1429	3934	14%
Treats	972	842	1299	3113	11%
Totals	$ 8,433	$ 9,773	$ 9,956	$ 28,162	

3 Click or drag across the cells you want to format. When you release your mouse button, the selected cells take on the new format. (Also, the marquee disappears and the Format Painter button no longer looks pushed in.) Instead of applying many different formats in a number of steps, you did it with a couple of mouse moves.

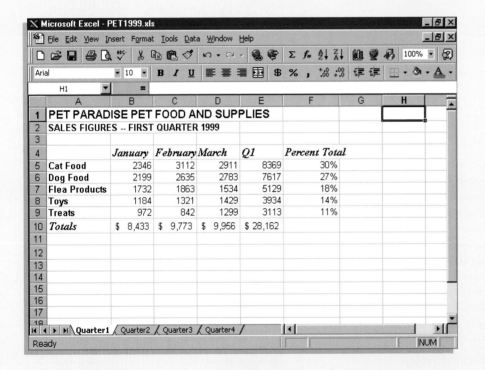

4 If you want to "paint" formatting across several sets of cells, double-click the Format Painter toolbar button. Now you can format as many sets of cells as you want by clicking or dragging across them. When you're done copying formats, press Esc or click the Format Painter toolbar button again.

6 Select the cells you want to format.

5 You can also copy formatting using the Copy command. As before, first activate the cell containing the formatting you want to copy. Then click the Copy toolbar button or choose Copy from the Edit menu. This copies the formatting to the Clipboard.

How to Format Worksheets Automatically

It can take hours of experimentation and hard labor to get your worksheets looking just right. The Format Painter button can speed up the process, but it still leaves you with the job of deciding how best to lay out and format your data. If you use the AutoFormat feature, you can try out some of Excel's ready-made worksheet designs, which both look professional and are easy to apply.

TIP SHEET

▶ You can use the Undo command to get rid of an AutoFormat if you act quickly enough. If not, you can clear the AutoFormat by selecting the range it affects, choosing AutoFormat from the Format menu, and choosing None under Table Format. Note that choosing Undo returns your worksheet to the state it was in before you applied the AutoFormat, while choosing None under Table Format removes all formatting from the selected cells (assuming all check boxes under Formats to Apply are selected).

▶ AutoFormats may override existing formatting. If your worksheet includes formatting you want to keep, click the Options button in the AutoFormat dialog box and deselect the appropriate check boxes. As an example, deselect the Alignment check box if you don't want to change the alignment of any cells in the selected range.

▶ You don't have to select the entire range to be formatted when applying an AutoFormat. If you select a single cell, Excel can often guess which cells it should format. But Excel might not be able to tell which cells you want to format, or it may guess incorrectly. To be safe, select precisely which cells you want to format.

1 Before applying an AutoFormat, it's a good idea to select the portion of the worksheet to be formatted. (If you don't select a range, Excel selects the portion of the worksheet it assumes you want to format, and it doesn't always guess right. Often you'll want to select column and row headings but not spreadsheet titles.)

6 From here, you can deselect check boxes to avoid applying particular formats. For example, if you don't want to change the number formats you've already applied, you can click the Number check box to deselect it. Click OK when you've modified the AutoFormat to your liking.

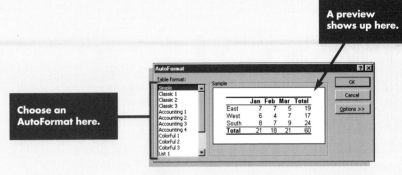

A preview shows up here.

Choose an AutoFormat here.

2 Choose AutoFormat from the Format menu. You'll see the AutoFormat dialog box.

3 Choose a design for your worksheet under Table Format. You'll see an example of the selected format in the Sample box. If you're not familiar with the available AutoFormats, it's a good idea to browse through them by scrolling through the list and clicking on the formats you want to preview.

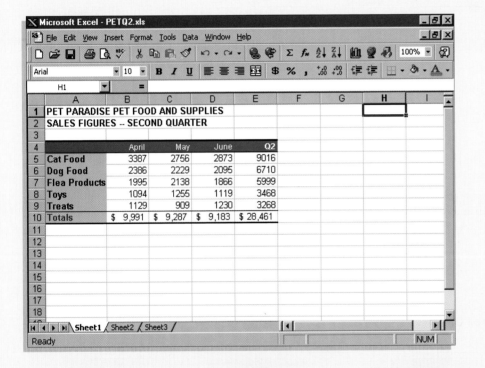

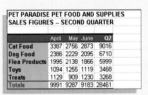

4 When you find an AutoFormat you like, click OK to apply it to the selected range in your worksheet. Then deselect the range so you can get a better picture of the formatting that Excel has applied.

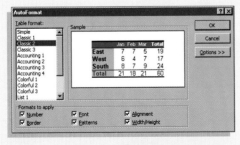

5 At times you may want to use some but not all of the features of a particular AutoFormat design. To do so, get into the AutoFormat dialog box and choose the desired table format, as usual. Then click the Options button. The AutoFormat dialog box expands, acquiring a section called Formats to Apply.

How to Create and Apply Styles

You just learned how to use the Format Painter button to copy existing formats from one cell to other cells. If you repeatedly apply the same formatting combinations, it's more efficient to create a style. A *style* is simply a collection of formats you can define, save with a workbook, and apply at any time to any worksheet within it.

TIP SHEET

▶ You can create styles even if your current worksheet doesn't already contain the desired formatting combination. Choose Style from the Format menu, enter a style name, click the Modify button, choose the desired formats from the Format Cells dialog box, and click OK. In the Style dialog box, choose OK to create the new style and close the Style dialog box; choose Add to create a new style without closing the dialog box.

▶ To copy styles between workbooks, open both workbooks, activate the workbook to copy styles to, choose Style from the Format menu, click the Merge button, choose the name of the workbook to copy styles from, and click OK. (Note that this copies all styles; you can't copy styles selectively.)

▶ The Normal style determines what data looks like before you apply any extra formatting. If you want to strip all formatting from one or more cells, you can apply the Normal style to them. In addition, you can modify the Normal style to change the default look of your workbook. For example, if you want text to appear automatically in a 12-point rather than 10-point font, you can change the Normal style so it provides a 12-point font.

PET PARADISE PET FOOD AND SUPPLIES
SALES FIGURES – THIRD QUARTER

▶ **❶** Select a cell that includes the formatting you want to save as a style.

2 Choose Style from the Format menu.

3 In the Style dialog box that appears, type a name for the style in the Style Name box. Then double-check that the appropriate formatting characteristics show up under Style Includes. If so, click OK. (If not, read the next section, "How to Modify Styles.")

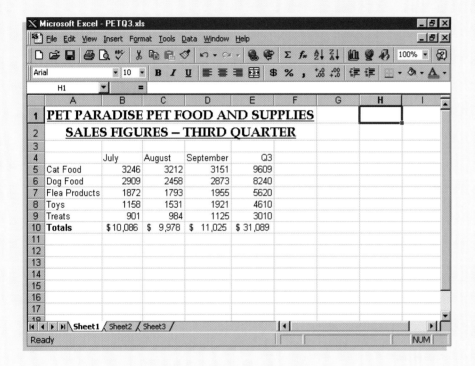

4 To save the style with the current workbook so you can use it in the future, choose Save from the File menu or click the Save toolbar button.

5 Once you've created and saved a style, you can apply it to any worksheet within the workbook you saved it in. Select the cells you want to format and choose Style from the Format menu. In the Style dialog box, choose the Style you want from the Style Name drop-down list box, and then choose OK.

How to Modify Styles

An added benefit of styles is that they're easy to modify—either a little or a lot. As one example, you may decide that the point size in your heading style is too large, or you might conclude that you need an entirely new heading style—with a new font, a new point size, and a new font style. When you modify a style, all cells to which you apply the style in the future have the new formatting characteristics, as you would expect. Even better, all cells to which you already applied that style are also updated automatically to match the revised style.

TIP SHEET

▶ Another way to modify a style is to change an example cell so it contains the desired formats and then activate that cell. Choose Style from the Format menu, type the name of the style to be modified in the Style Name box, and click the Add button. (You have to type the style name; you can't just select the name from the Style Name box.) You are asked whether you want to redefine the style based on the selection. Choose Yes to go ahead with the change.

▶ What if you want to apply some but not all aspects of a style? It's simple: Choose the cells to be formatted, choose Style from the Format menu, and choose the style you want to apply, as usual. But before you go forward with the command, deselect any relevant check boxes under Style Includes. For example, if you want to apply the fonts associated with a particular style but not the alignment or number formatting, choose the style but deselect the Number and Alignment check boxes.

▶ It's also very easy to delete styles. Simply open the Style dialog box, choose the style in question from the Style Name list, and click the Delete button. (Note, however, that you can't delete the Normal style.) Keep in mind that if you delete a style, all cells formatted with that style will be stripped of their formatting.

 To modify an existing style, choose Style from the Format menu to display the Style dialog box.

7 Choose Save from the File menu or click the Save toolbar button to save your new style with the current workbook so you can use it in the future.

6 Choose OK to revise the style and close the dialog box. Notice that any cells to which the format had been applied are updated automatically to reflect the changes.

2 Choose the name of the style you want to change in the Style Name list box.

3 Click the Modify button. You'll land in the Format Cells dialog box, which you saw and explored a bit in Chapter 8.

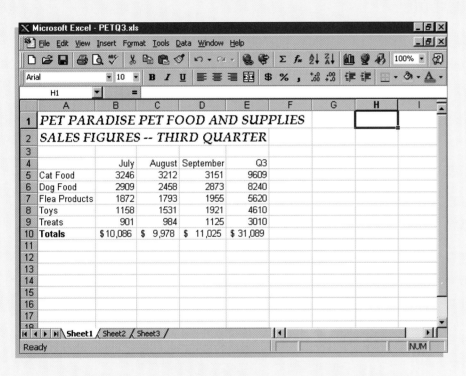

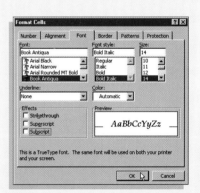

4 Make any changes you want in any of the tabs in this dialog box. For instance, you could choose a new point size and font style from the Font tab and a new alignment from the Alignment tab.

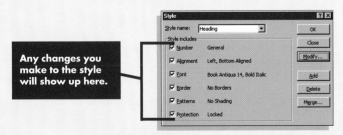

Any changes you make to the style will show up here.

5 When you've made all your selections in the Format Cells dialog box, click OK to both confirm your selections and return to the Style dialog box. You can check your changes under Style Includes.

How to Use Conditional Formatting

Excel lets you apply conditional formatting—formatting that appears only when the data in the formatted cells meets certain conditions you specify. You could tell Excel to show values of over a million dollars underlined and in green, for example. Conditional formatting can make specific values stand out from the crowd, and that makes it much easier for you to hone in on them.

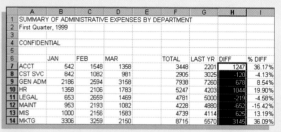

1 Select the cells to which you want to apply conditional formatting.

TIP SHEET

- ▶ You can copy conditional formatting from one cell to another with the Format Painter toolbar button you learned about a little bit earlier in the chapter.

- ▶ You can apply multiple conditions. To do so, set up the initial condition as described on these pages. Then click the Add button in the Conditional Formatting dialog box to specify a second and, if you like, even a third condition. (You can't have more than three at once.) For example, you could tell Excel to display negative values in one way and values of over 50,000 in another. (Values over 0 and under 50,000 wouldn't receive any special treatment.)

- ▶ To delete conditions, click the Delete button in the Conditional Formatting dialog box, choose which condition(s) to delete in the Delete Conditional Format dialog box, and click OK.

- ▶ Like other types of formatting, conditional formatting doesn't "go away" if you delete the contents of the formatted cells. It's also still associated with the designated cells even if their data doesn't meet the specified conditions. To get rid of it, choose Edit, Clear, Formats.

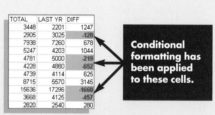

Conditional formatting has been applied to these cells.

7 Click OK to apply the newly created conditional format to the selected cells.

6 Click OK in the Format Cells dialog box to return to the Conditional Formatting dialog box. Here the Preview box indicates which formatting you've chosen.

2 Choose Conditional Formatting from the Format menu.

3 You'll see the Conditional Formatting dialog box shown here. (Your Office Assistant may chime in to ask if you want help. Click on "Yes, please provide help" if you do. The Office Assistant was covered in Chapter 6, in case you need to jog your memory.)

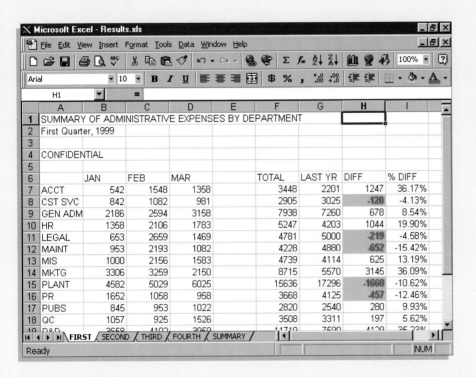

4 In the leftmost drop-down list box, select Cell Value Is to use the cell values to determine which cells are formatted. In the next drop-down list box, choose an operator with which to evaluate the cell values. In the rightmost text box, enter values or formulas indicating the condition you want to format. (You can also click the Collapse Dialog button at the right end of this text box to select a value or formula from within the worksheet.)For example, you can choose the operator Less Than and then enter **0** in the list box to format all values that are less than zero. (Most operators provide only one list box. If you choose Between or Not Between, however, two list boxes appear so you can enter top and bottom values for the range.)

5 Click the Format button. In the Format Cells dialog box that appears, choose which formatting—font styles, font colors, underlining, shading, and borders—to apply to the cells that meet your conditions. (Note that not all cell formatting choices are available. For instance, you can change the font color but not the font or size.) You can always click the Clear button if you decide to revert to the standard formatting.

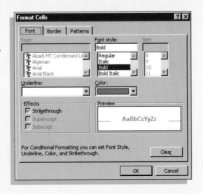

CHAPTER 11

Modifying the Display

Often you'll want to change what you see on screen, without necessarily affecting your printed worksheets. For example, you might want to get a close-up view of a particular portion of your worksheet, or you may decide to hide certain rows or columns temporarily from view. This chapter introduces a variety of strategies for modifying the display to suit your purposes.

First, you discover how to shrink or magnify the display. You can "zoom in" to get a detailed view of a small portion of your worksheet; or you can "zoom out" to get an overview, seeing more information in less detail.

You also learn how to "freeze" columns and rows so they stay in view at all times. You'll often want to freeze column and/or row headings in larger worksheets so you can identify your data no matter where you scroll.

Next you learn how to hide columns or rows from view—either to conceal confidential information or to sift out detailed information you may not need at the moment.

Last of all, you find out how to split the screen so you can view several parts of a single worksheet at the same time. You might do this, for example, to see both the top and the bottom of a large worksheet at once.

How to Magnify and Shrink the Display

Sometimes you may have trouble reading what's on your screen, or you may want to see more information on the screen at once. One possible solution is to enlarge or reduce the font size, but that affects your printed document, which may not be what you want. To see less or more on screen without affecting your printouts, you can use Excel's Zoom feature.

TIP SHEET

▶ Zooming affects what you see on screen but doesn't affect your printed documents. If you want to print larger or smaller, you can change the font size, as explained in Chapter 8, or you can adjust the print scaling, as described in Chapter 5.

▶ Although you can zoom in and out in the print preview screen (Chapter 5), you can't do any editing there. When you zoom in the regular worksheet window, in contrast, you can still edit as usual. (This holds true whether or not you're in page break preview.) The only limitation is that it might be difficult to gauge what you're doing if the display is very small.

▶ Another way of squeezing a bit more data onto the screen is to choose Full Screen from the View menu. This maximizes the Excel window and removes from view the toolbars, the formula bar, and the status bar. (The menu bar remains in view, however.) To return the screen to its previous state, click the Close Full Screen button (it shows up in the middle of the screen when you choose Full Screen) or choose Full Screen from the View menu a second time.

▶ You can also eliminate screen clutter by hiding just the toolbars. Choose Toolbars from the View menu and deselect the check boxes for the toolbars you want to hide. If you somehow lose a toolbar, or you decide to reinstate a hidden toolbar, choose Toolbars again from the View menu and select the check box representing the toolbar you want to display.

▶ **①** To magnify or shrink the display, click on the downward-pointing triangle to the right of the Zoom Control box on the Standard toolbar.

⑦ Anytime you want to return the display to its original size, choose a zoom percentage of 100%, either from the Zoom Control box or from the Zoom dialog box.

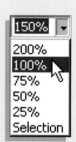

	A	B	C	D	E	F
1	VACATION DAYS ACCRUED AND USED, 1999					
2						
3	LAST	FIRST	EMP #	1/1 BAL	JAN	FEB
4	Eng	Stephanie	3	14	-12	1
5	Fuentes	Carla	1	9	1	-2
6	Lambert	Charles	5	2	1	1
7	Rothstein	Jay	2	7	1	1
8	Tashjian	Doris	4	0	1	1
9						

⑥ Another option is to enlarge or shrink the display just enough to fill the screen with data you've selected. To do this, select the data and then either choose Selection from the Zoom Control box or choose Fit Selection from the Zoom dialog box. The selected range of data enlarges or reduces itself to fit the screen, as shown here.

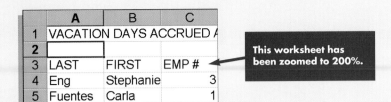

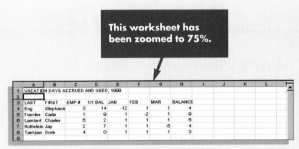

This worksheet has been zoomed to 200%.

This worksheet has been zoomed to 75%.

2 Choosing a setting of greater than 100% (the default) zooms in on (enlarges) your worksheet, so you see less of it but in greater detail. This is handy if you have impaired vision, or even if your eyes are simply blurring over from too many hours in front of the computer.

3 If instead you want to see more of your worksheet in less detail, choose a setting of less that 100% from the Zoom Control box. Zooming out like this is a good way to get an overview of larger worksheets.

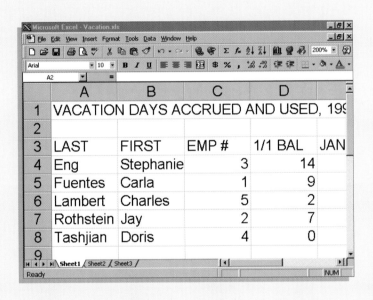

4 You can also zoom in or out using the menu system if you prefer. Start by choosing Zoom from the View menu.

5 In the Zoom dialog box, just click on a setting and click OK to shrink or enlarge the display. You aren't limited to the default magnification settings; you can click on Custom and enter any percentage between 10 and 400. (You can also type any percentage between 10 and 400 in the Zoom Control box on the toolbar.)

How to Keep Columns and Rows in View

When there's a lot of data in your work-sheets, column and row headings have an inconvenient tendency to disappear from view when you scroll through your data. This makes it hard to identify the information at the far reaches of your worksheet. A simple solution is to "freeze" columns or rows so that they remain in view, even when you scroll.

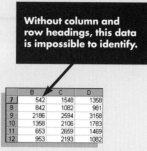

Without column and row headings, this data is impossible to identify.

1 Normally, scrolling down and/or to the right in a large worksheet removes column and row headings from view, making your data very difficult to identify.

TIP SHEET

▶ **Frozen panes don't affect your printed output.** In other words, even if you freeze column and row headings, those headings won't necessarily appear on each page of your printed spreadsheet. If you want them to, consult the section "How to Print Column and Row Titles" in Chapter 5.

▶ **You can freeze columns but not rows, and vice versa.** To freeze rows only, activate a cell in column A of the row just below any rows you want to freeze. To freeze columns only, activate a cell in row 1 of the column immediately to the right of any columns you want to freeze. For example, if you want to freeze rows 1 and 2 only, activate cell A3 before issuing the Freeze Panes command.

▶ **When you freeze columns and rows,** it doesn't mean that the data they contain will always stay within view. Instead, what it means is that column headings will remain in view to identify the data beneath them even if you scroll down, and row headings will stay visible to identify the data to their right even if you scroll to the right.

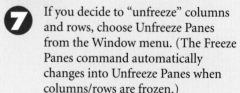

7 If you decide to "unfreeze" columns and rows, choose Unfreeze Panes from the Window menu. (The Freeze Panes command automatically changes into Unfreeze Panes when columns/rows are frozen.)

	A	B	C	D
1	SUMMARY OF ADMINISTRATIVE EXPENS			
2	First Quarter, 1999			
3				
4	CONFIDENTIAL			
5				
6		JAN	FEB	MAR
7	ACCT	542	1548	1358
8	CST SVC	842	1082	981
9	GEN ADM	2186	2594	3158
10	HR	1358	2106	1783

2 To freeze columns or rows, first activate the cell below any rows you want to freeze, and/or to the right of any columns you want to freeze. (You have to activate just a single cell, not an entire row or column.) For example, if you activate cell B7, you'll freeze rows 1 through 6 and column A.

3 Choose Freeze Panes from the Window menu.

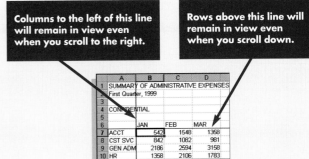

Columns to the left of this line will remain in view even when you scroll to the right.

Rows above this line will remain in view even when you scroll down.

	A	B	C	D
1	SUMMARY OF ADMINISTRATIVE EXPENSES			
2	First Quarter, 1999			
3				
4	CONFIDENTIAL			
5				
6		JAN	FEB	MAR
7	ACCT	542	1548	1358
8	CST SVC	842	1082	981
9	GEN ADM	2186	2594	3158
10	HR	1358	2106	1783

4 Excel inserts a horizontal line indicating which rows are frozen and a vertical line indicating which columns are frozen. (All the rows above the horizontal line are frozen and all columns to the left of the vertical line are frozen.)

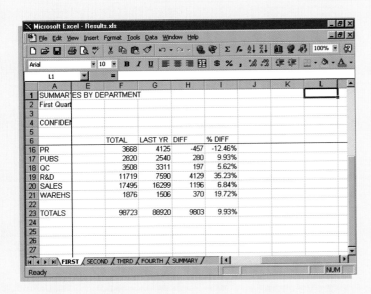

Microsoft Excel - Results.xls

File Edit View Insert Format Tools Data Window Help

Arial   10   B I U

L1   =

	A	E	F	G	H	I	J	K	L
1	SUMMARIES BY DEPARTMENT								
2	First Quart								
3									
4	CONFIDEN								
5									
6			TOTAL	LAST YR	DIFF	% DIFF			
16	PR		3668	4125	-457	-12.46%			
17	PUBS		2820	2540	280	9.93%			
18	QC		3508	3311	197	5.62%			
19	R&D		11719	7590	4129	35.23%			
20	SALES		17495	16299	1196	6.84%			
21	WAREHS		1876	1506	370	19.72%			
22									
23	TOTALS		98723	88920	9803	9.93%			
24									
25									
26									
27									

FIRST / SECOND / THIRD / FOURTH / SUMMARY /

Ready   NUM

	A	F	G	H
1	SUMMAR	PARTMENT		
2	First Quart			
3				
4	CONFIDEN			
5				
6		TOTAL	LAST YR	DIFF
7	ACCT	3448	2201	1247
8	CST SVC	2905	3025	-120
9	GEN ADM	7938	7260	678
10	HR	5247	4203	1044

6 If you scroll to the right in your worksheet, the frozen columns stay in view instead of scrolling to the left and out of view.

	A	B	C	D
1	SUMMARY OF ADMINISTRATIVE EXPENSES			
2	First Quarter, 1999			
3				
4	CONFIDENTIAL			
5				
6		JAN	FEB	MAR
19	R&D	3658	4102	3959
20	SALES	6258	5277	5960
21	WAREHS	580	885	411
22				
23	TOTALS	29472	35826	33425

5 Now if you scroll down in the worksheet, the frozen rows remain in view instead of scrolling up and out of view as they normally would. This way you can always see the headings that identify your data.

How to Hide Columns or Rows

Sometimes you'll want columns and/or rows to remain in view when you scroll through the worksheet. But at other times you'll want to hide data temporarily from view. For example, you may want to conceal the salary column in a personnel worksheet or hide the monthly details in a sales worksheet and show just the quarterly information. You can do this easily with the Hide command. This command doesn't get rid of anything, but instead temporarily conceals columns and rows from view, until you decide to call them back with the Unhide command.

TIP SHEET

▶ Hidden columns and rows don't show up on the screen or in your printouts. If you want to print hidden columns or rows, you need to unhide them first.

▶ Another way to hide and unhide columns or rows is to select them (or the range containing them), right-click on them, and choose Hide or Unhide from the Shortcut menu that appears.

▶ You can use the mouse to hide rows and columns. To hide a column, drag from the right to the left edge of its column border; to hide a row, drag from the bottom to the top edge of its row border. (To hide multiple columns or rows, first select them, and then drag any one of their borders.) To unhide columns or rows with the mouse, point to the column or row border where rows or columns are hidden. When the mouse pointer turns into a double bar with a double-headed arrow attached, drag to the right to reveal hidden columns, or drag down to reveal hidden rows.

▶ Unfortunately, you can't unhide columns and rows at the same time. You need to do this in two separate operations.

 1 To hide one or more rows, select the rows to be hidden. (Click on or drag across their row numbers.) Then choose Row from the Format menu and choose Hide from the submenu that appears.

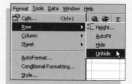

 6 If you decide to reveal hidden rows, select a range containing those rows, choose Row from the Format menu, and choose Unhide.

You can tell that rows are hidden because some row numbers are missing.

	A	B	C	D
1	*ADMINISTRATIVE EXPENSES*			
2	Second Quarter, 1999			
3				
4		April	May	June
8	**Marketing**	$3,406	$3,359	$2,251
9	**R&D**	$3,756	$4,202	$4,060
10	**Sales**	$6,358	$5,378	$6,060
11	**Warehouse**	$680	$985	$511

2 The selected rows disappear from view. Your only clue that they're still in your worksheet is that some row numbers are missing from the left edge of the worksheet window.

3 To hide columns, select the columns to be hidden. (Click on or drag across their column letters.) Then choose Column from the Format menu and choose Hide from the submenu that appears.

X Microsoft Excel - SecondQ.xls

File Edit View Insert Format Tools Data Window Help

Arial 10 B I U

J1 =

	A	E	F	G	H	I	J	K
1	*ADMINISTRATIVE EXPENSES*							
2	Second Quarter, 1999							
3								
4		Total	Last Year	Difference				
5	**Accounting**	$3,748	$2,401	56.10%				
6	**General Admin.**	$8,238	$7,460	10.43%				
7	**Maintenance**	$4,528	$4,980	-9.08%				
8	**Marketing**	$9,016	$7,970	13.12%				
9	**R&D**	$12,018	$13,886	-13.45%				
10	**Sales**	$17,796	$16,399	8.52%				
11	**Warehouse**	$2,176	$1,906	14.17%				
12								
13	**Totals**	$57,520	$55,002	4.58%				
14								
15								
16								
17								
18								

SecondQ / Sheet2 / Sheet3 /

Ready NUM

You can tell that columns are hidden because some column letters are missing.

	A	E	F	G
1	*ADMINISTRATIVE EXPENSES*			
2	Second Quarter, 1999			
3				
4		Total	Last Year	Difference
5	**Accounting**	$3,748	$2,401	56.10%
6	**General Admin.**	$8,238	$7,460	10.43%
7	**Maintenance**	$4,528	$4,980	-9.08%
8	**Marketing**	$9,016	$7,970	13.12%

4 The selected columns disappear from view. You can tell that they're still in the worksheet, however, because some column letters are missing from the worksheet window.

5 If you decide to reveal hidden columns, first select a range containing the hidden columns. (If you want to unhide all columns, you can select the entire worksheet by clicking the Select All button.) Then choose Column from the Format menu, and choose Unhide from the submenu that appears.

How to Split the Screen

You can split the screen into two or four panes, the better to view data from different areas in a single worksheet. For example, you might want to look at the top and bottom of a long worksheet at the same time. You can split the screen vertically, horizontally, or both—whichever works best for you. (Splitting the screen allows you to view several different portions of the *same* worksheet. Don't confuse this with displaying several different workbooks at once, which you can do with the Window, Arrange command.)

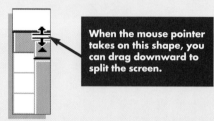

When the mouse pointer takes on this shape, you can drag downward to split the screen.

1 If you want to split the screen horizontally, first place your mouse pointer over the split box immediately above the vertical scroll bar. The mouse pointer changes into a horizontal double bar with vertical arrows attached, as shown here.

TIP SHEET

▶ **A shortcut for splitting the screen is to double-click on one of the split boxes. This splits the screen vertically to the left of the active cell or horizontally immediately above the active cell.**

▶ **You can also split the screen by choosing Split from the Window menu. This command splits the screen above and to the left of the active cell. So if you want to split the screen vertically but not horizontally using this method, first be sure to activate a cell in row 1; if you want to split the screen horizontally but not vertically, activate a cell in column A of your worksheet.**

8 A quick way to remove horizontal and vertical splits at the same time is to choose Remove Split from the Window menu.

7 If you want to remove a split from the screen, you can drag the split bar to the edge of the screen. Or you can double-click on the split bar.

6 If you want to adjust the position of a split, you can simply drag the split bar.

This line indicates where the split will occur.

2 Drag downward. As you drag, a gray horizontal line indicates where the split will occur if you release the mouse button. Let go of the mouse button where you want the screen to split.

When the mouse pointer takes on this shape, you can drag to the left to split the screen.

3 If you want to split the screen vertically, first place your mouse pointer over the split box immediately to the right of the horizontal scroll bar. The mouse pointer changes into a vertical double bar with horizontal arrows attached.

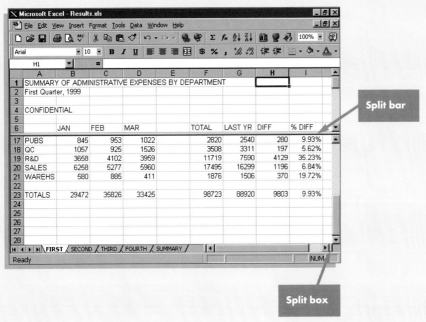

Split bar

Split box

4 Drag to the left. As you drag, a gray vertical line indicates where the split will occur if you let go of the mouse button. Release the mouse button where you want the screen to split.

5 Once you've split the screen, you can scroll independently in either pane. (When you split the screen horizontally, each pane has its own vertical scroll bar; when you split the screen vertically, each pane acquires its own horizontal scroll bar.)

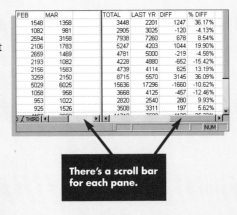

There's a scroll bar for each pane.

CHAPTER 12

Charts

 You probably have a pretty good sense of the data you work with. But hand a printout of an Excel worksheet to a colleague or show a worksheet to a client in a presentation, and you may get a puzzled reaction. Columns and rows of numbers are not always the best way to give someone information at a glance.

That's where charts (often called graphs) come into play. Charts are specialized diagrams that usually represent numbers as circles, lines, or bars. By displaying numbers as pictures, well-conceived charts can convey information much more quickly and forcefully than a large quantity of numbers in a grid. Because they emphasize trends and comparative factors, charts can tell a story more concisely than a mass of raw numbers can.

Excel makes it easy to present all or part of your data in one of several chart types. Even better, as you edit the data on which the chart is based, the chart is updated instantly to reflect the revised data. This chapter explains how to create, improve, and print charts based on your Excel worksheet data. The next chapter describes a number of additional ways of fine-tuning existing graphs.

How to Use the ChartWizard

Excel's ChartWizard guides you step by step through the charting process, asking you which data to chart, which type of chart to create, and which special features—such as legends and chart titles—to add to your chart. As you'll see, the ChartWizard offers a lot of options but also makes life very easy for you.

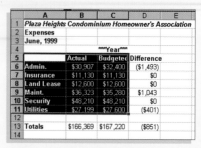

▶ **1** Select the data you want to chart. Be sure to include any column and row headings you want to use within the graph. (If you accidentally forget this step, you can always select the data later from within the ChartWizard.) Be sure *not* to include totals or you'll skew the chart.

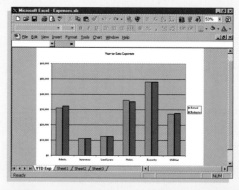

8 If you instead chose As New Sheet, Excel places your chart in a chart sheet that it adds to your workbook. Notice that the chart practically fills this sheet.

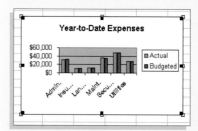

7 If you elected to place your chart in a worksheet, Excel places the chart within the specified sheet. (If that sheet already contains data, the chart may obscure some of it. Flip to the next chapter for the news on how to change a chart's placement and size.) Excel may also display the chart toolbar at this point.

TIP SHEET

▶ **Starting with the second Chart-Wizard dialog box, you can click the Back button to backtrack and alter your selections. To change a chart you've finished creating, see the upcoming pages of this chapter, as well as Chapter 13. To bail out of the chart creation process at any stage, click the Cancel button or press the Esc key.**

▶ **You can rename chart sheets the same way you rename worksheets: Double-click on the sheet tab, type a new sheet name, and press Enter.**

▶ **You don't need to go through any special procedure to save a chart. Instead, you just save the workbook it's in. This saves all charts in the workbook, whether they're on chart sheets of their own or on worksheets that contain data.**

2 Choose Chart from the Insert menu or click the Chart-Wizard toolbar button. The Office Assistant (see Chapter 6) may ask whether you need help with this feature.

3 In this first ChartWizard dialog box, click on the chart type and subtype you want. (If these dozens of chart types aren't enough, check out what's available on the Custom Types tab of this dialog box.) To see a sample of the selected chart, use the Press and Hold to View Sample button. When you're ready to move on, click the Next button.

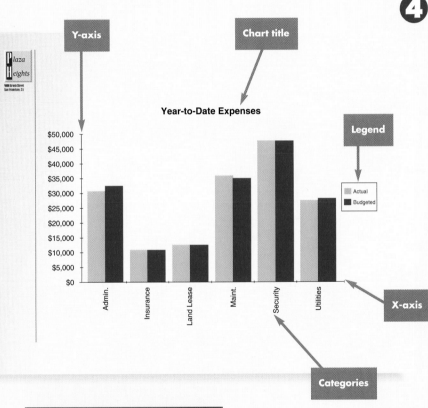

Y-axis

Chart title

Legend

Year-to-Date Expenses

Actual
Budgeted

X-axis

Categories

4 This second Chart-Wizard dialog box is where you choose or confirm which data to graph. If the sample chart looks okay, simply click the Next button. If not, you may have to click the Rows option button to tell Excel to take the data series from rows in your worksheet rather than columns. You can also type a different data range or click the Collapse Dialog button and select a new data range by dragging across it. In the Series tab of this dialog box, you can add, remove, or alter data series, as well as choose which cells to use as X-axis labels. When you're done, click the Next button.

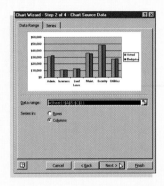

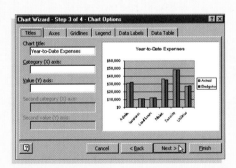

6 In the final ChartWizard dialog box, you can choose to place your chart in an existing worksheet, creating what is sometimes called an *embedded chart*: Select the As Object In option button and choose a worksheet from the drop-down list. Or you can place your chart in a separate chart sheet: Select the As New Sheet option button and, if you like, type a sheet name in the text box that's provided. (A *chart sheet* is a special worksheet that contains only a chart, not the data it's based upon.) When you've made your selection, click the Finish button.

5 The third ChartWizard dialog box lets you choose from a huge assortment of chart features. Among other things, you can enter a chart title and axis titles, turn gridlines on and off, and specify whether to include a legend and where to place it. It's good to do a little exploring here to find out just which features are available. (To a certain extent this will vary depending on the selected chart type.) When you're done, click the Next button.

How to Change the Chart Type

Excel offers an almost dizzying array of chart types. Don't worry if you have trouble settling on just the right type of chart or if you're not even sure what some of the chart types are. It's easy enough to experiment with the different chart types to see which one conveys your point most effectively.

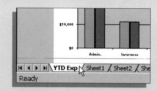

▶ **1** To modify a chart on a chart sheet, activate the sheet containing the chart you want to change.

TIP SHEET

▶ **To hide the Chart toolbar, you can choose View, Toolbars, Chart again. Better yet, you can simply click on the toolbar's close box (the x in its upper-right corner).**

▶ **Excel provides a number of "three-dimensional" chart subtypes. (Their descriptions say "3-D.") These charts can look impressive, but they aren't suitable for every purpose. In particular, black-and-white printouts of three-dimensional charts are sometimes hard to interpret. Also, a three-dimensional chart may make some data harder to see and harder to compare. Use your judgment: If you pick a three-dimensional chart type and the results are anywhere from borderline to impossible to decipher, change back to a non-3D chart type and see if that fixes the problem.**

▶ **If you're having trouble reading the labels and titles on a chart, you can zoom in on it using the techniques discussed in Chapter 11.**

▶ **If you double-click on an embedded chart instead of single-clicking when you're attempting to select the chart, you'll probably see some sort of Format dialog box. Don't worry about it; just cancel out of the dialog box and single-click on the chart to select it, if it isn't already selected as a result of your double-click.**

7 When the Chart toolbar is displayed, you can quickly change the chart type of embedded charts or charts on chart sheets. (If you're working with an embedded chart, make sure it's selected first.) Click on the downward-pointing arrow on the Chart Type button and then click on a chart type in the list that appears.

② Choose Chart Type from the Chart menu.

③ You'll see a Chart Type dialog box that's almost identical to the first ChartWizard dialog box you saw on the previous set of pages. Choose the chart type and subtype you want and then click the OK button.

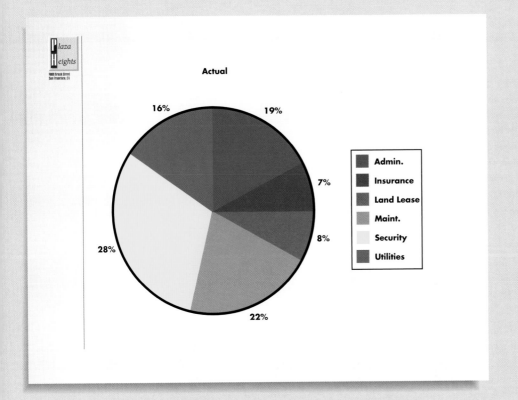

Handles indicating that the chart is selected

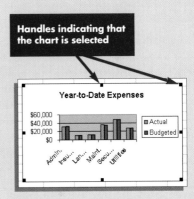

④ To change the chart type of a chart that's embedded within a worksheet, first click on the chart. It acquires a set of square handles, indicating that it's selected. Also note that the menu bar gains a new option: Chart.

⑤ As before, choose Chart Type from the Chart menu and choose a new chart type and subtype from the Chart Type dialog box that appears.

⑥ You can also change the chart type—as well as other chart attributes—with the Chart toolbar. To display this toolbar if it's not already displayed, choose View, Toolbars, Chart.

How to Work with Chart and Axis Titles

You can specify a chart title, an X-axis title, and a Y-axis title while using the Chart-Wizard to create your chart, as you learned earlier in this chapter. But it's also easy to add, change, and delete these titles later, as described here.

TIP SHEET

▶ Obviously, you can change many more options than the chart and axis titles from within the Chart Options dialog box. To give you just a few examples, you can add and remove gridlines, change the position of the legend, and add data labels that show the value or percentage for a particular data point or series. In a pie chart, for instance, you could add labels showing what percentage each slice made up of the whole.

▶ Axis titles make sense only for chart types that are based on axes. Pie charts, for example, have no axes, and Excel wisely prevents you from wasting time specifying axis titles for these kinds of charts.

▶ When you're done working with a chart or axis title, it's a good idea to get rid of the selection handles. To do so, simply press the Esc key. If you don't remove the handles, you might inadvertently change or delete a title. If this happens and you notice it fairly soon after, it's easy enough to retrieve the title by choosing Undo from the Edit menu or clicking the Undo toolbar button.

▶ You can delete a legend the same way you delete a chart or axis title: Click on the legend (it will acquire selection handles) and then press the Del key, or right-click the legend and choose Clear from the menu that materializes. If you have the Chart toolbar displayed, clicking the Legend button displays a legend if one is not displayed and removes the legend if it is displayed.

▶ **1** If you're altering a chart on a chart sheet, activate the sheet containing the chart for which you want to change the titles. If you're working with an embedded chart, make sure it's selected. (Remember, that means it is enclosed within a set of square selection handles.)

6 To delete a chart or axis title, click on it (you'll see selection handles) and then press the Del key. You can also right-click on the title and choose Clear from the resulting menu.

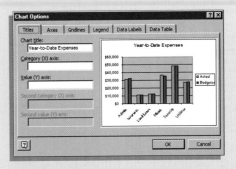

2 Choose Chart Options from the Chart menu.

3 You'll see a Chart Options dialog box that's almost identical to the third ChartWizard dialog box you saw at the beginning of this chapter. Make sure the Titles tab of this dialog box is active. (Click on it if necessary to activate it.) It displays any existing titles for the chart.

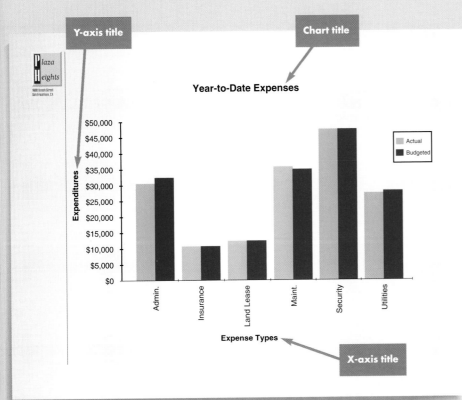

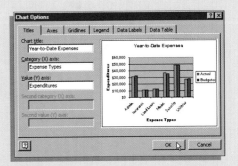

4 Enter or modify any of the titles listed here. (Note that the available titles may depend on the chart type.) Then click the OK button to put your changes into place.

5 You can also modify existing titles directly on the chart. Just click on the title to select it, click again to position your insertion point, and then modify the title as you would modify text in any word processing program: Move the insertion point with the arrow keys, add text as needed, and delete characters with the Del and Backspace keys.

How to Print a Chart

Printing a chart is not much different from printing anything else in Excel. But there are a few tricks to the trade. In particular, with embedded charts you have the option of printing the chart by itself or of printing the chart along with the worksheet data.

▶ **1** To print a chart that's on a chart sheet, simply activate that sheet and click the Print toolbar button. (You can instead use the Print command on the File menu if you want to change any print settings.)

TIP SHEET

▶ **For the lowdown on printing, flip back to Chapter 5. You can use many of the standard printing features when printing charts. For example, you might want to change the print scaling, alter the page orientation, modify the margins, and more.**

▶ **You may have noticed that Excel doesn't print headers and footers by default. If you want to add headers and footers to help identify your charts, use the techniques described under "How to Print Headers and Footers" in Chapter 5.**

▶ **If you're using a black-and-white printer and the various data series and/or data points on your chart are hard to distinguish, here's what you can do: With the chart selected, choose Chart, Chart Type, click on the Custom Types tab in the Chart Types dialog box, and then choose one of the black-and-white (B&W) chart types from the Chart Type list. If you still aren't pleased with your results, another option is to change the colors or fill patterns of data points and/or series individually, as described in the next chapter under "How to Change the Colors in a Chart." This process is quite a bit more laborious but also gives you a great deal more control over your results.**

▶ **When a chart is on a chart sheet, you can't print it on the same page as the data it's based on.**

6 Click the Print toolbar button. This time Excel prints your chart along with your data, as shown above right.

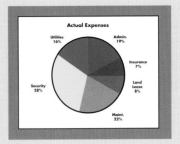

2 To print an embedded chart by itself, first click on the chart to select it.

3 Click the Print toolbar button. Excel prints the chart alone, without the worksheet data.

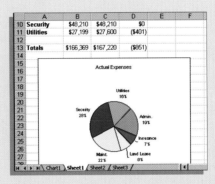

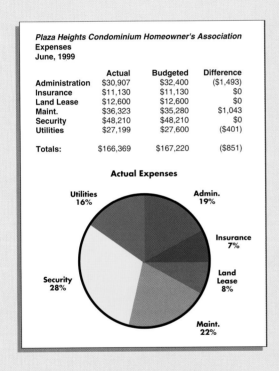

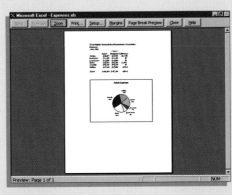

4 To print a chart along with the worksheet data, make sure the chart isn't selected. (If you need to, press Esc or click anywhere outside the chart to deselect it.) Also make sure it's positioned where you want it with respect to the worksheet data. (If you don't know or haven't guessed how to do this, you'll learn how to move and resize charts first thing in the next chapter.)

5 To be safe, do a print preview to see what the results will look like. This tells you right away if your chart is selected. (You'll see that only the chart is going to print.) It also gives you a good idea of whether the chart and data are laid out satisfactorily on the page.

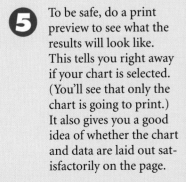

CHAPTER 13

Enhancing Charts

 In the previous chapter, you learned a few basics about creating charts in order to convey information visually. You also discovered some simple ways of altering charts—changing the chart type and adding or modifying titles—so they fill your needs.

This chapter makes it even clearer that once you've put together a chart with the help of the ChartWizard, you are in no way stuck with it. Quite the contrary: You can modify and enhance a chart to your heart's content. This chapter explores some of the many ways you can do this.

First, you learn how to move charts, as well as how to change their size—skills that are particularly handy when you're working with charts embedded in a worksheet. You find out how to explode pie slices to draw attention to them. You also learn how to add data to a chart, in case you didn't initially add all the needed data. (You can remove data even more easily.) You discover how to change the colors in a chart, how to format chart text, and how to add extra text (outside of the standard titles, axis labels, and so on). Finally, you find out how to draw shapes on a chart. With the skills outlined in this chapter under your belt, you'll have no trouble creating charts that both meet your specifications and look great.

How to Move and Resize Charts

When you create an embedded chart, Excel gives it a predetermined size and places it in a predetermined position on the worksheet. But there's a good chance you want the chart to be a different size. There's an even better chance you want the chart in a different location; if you place it on the same sheet as your data, it's probably obscuring at least some of that data from view. But it's child's play to move and resize charts after the fact, as you'll learn here.

TIP SHEET

▸ **You can also change the size of a printed chart by changing the print scaling, as described in Chapter 5. Of course, if you're scaling an embedded chart, this changes the size not only of the chart, but of the worksheet too.**

▸ **These pages describe how to move charts within the current sheet. If you instead want to move a chart from one worksheet to another, or between a worksheet and a chart sheet, do this: Select the chart or activate the chart sheet and choose Chart, Location. In the Chart Location dialog box, choose the worksheet or chart sheet you want to move the chart to. (Keep in mind that this moves the chart rather than just making a copy of it on the specified sheet.)**

▸ **You can move and resize charts on a chart sheet if you like. To do this, choose Page Setup from the File menu, click on the Chart tab, choose the Custom option button, and click OK. This places a dashed border around the chart. Click on the chart area (the area within the border) to introduce selection handles and a heavier border. At this point you can drag these handles to resize the chart or drag on the chart area to move the chart. To return the chart to its original size, repeat the previous steps but choose the Use Full Page option button from the Chart tab of the Page Setup dialog box.**

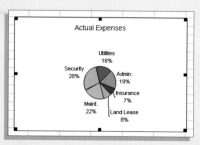

▶ **1** If necessary, activate the worksheet containing your chart. Select the chart if it's not already selected. (Just in case you're confused, note that an embedded chart can be placed anywhere within a worksheet but may not be "embedded" within a batch of data.)

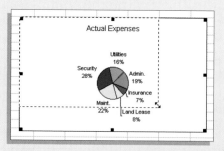

7 To change the chart's size in two directions at once, place the mouse pointer over one of the corner selection handles. The pointer changes into a diagonal double-headed arrow. Dragging now changes both the height and width of the chart. As before, a dashed rectangle indicates the chart's modified size.

2 To move the chart, place the mouse pointer anywhere over the chart. The pointer changes into an arrow. Notice that a ScreenTip also tells you which portion of the chart you're pointing to. Ideally, you should point to the chart area (the blank part of the chart) so you don't accidentally move some portion of the chart rather than the whole thing.

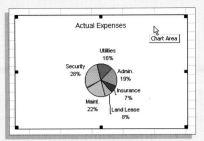

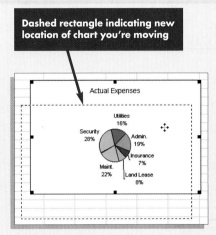

Dashed rectangle indicating new location of chart you're moving

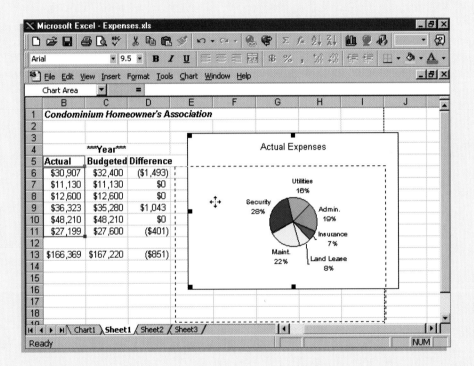

3 Drag the chart to a new location. As you drag, the mouse pointer changes into a four-headed arrow, and a dashed rectangle indicates where the chart will be placed if you release the mouse button. Release the mouse button when you're satisfied with the chart's new location.

4 To resize a chart, again first make sure it's selected.

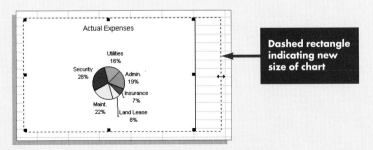

Dashed rectangle indicating new size of chart

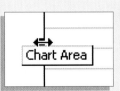

5 To change the chart's size in a single direction, place the mouse pointer over one of the side selection handles (the handles at the top, bottom, right side, or left side). The pointer changes into a double-headed arrow, as shown here.

6 Drag to shrink or enlarge the chart. As you drag, a dashed rectangle shows the new size of the chart. Release the mouse button when the chart looks as though it's the right size.

How to Explode a Pie Slice

Exploding pie slices is not as dramatic or as risky as it sounds. What it means is simply pulling one or more slices away from the chart to make them stand out from the crowd. You can choose to explode pie slices when selecting a pie chart format with the ChartWizard. In addition, you can explode pie slices after the fact, as you'll see here.

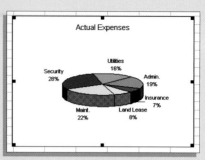

▶ **1** If your chart is on a chart sheet, first activate the chart sheet. If you're exploding a slice of an embedded pie chart, you can select the chart by clicking on it.

TIP SHEET

▶ **You can explode several pie slices. However, the more exploded slices there are, the less impact they have. For this reason, it's probably most effective just to explode one pie slice, or perhaps two on special occasions.**

▶ **Warning: If you drag on a single pie slice when the entire chart (as opposed to one slice) is selected, you'll explode all slices of the pie at once. If this wasn't what you intended, quickly choose the Undo command. Or select the entire chart (there should be one selection handle per pie slice) and drag the slices back together.**

▶ **You can have Excel explode pie slices for you by choosing the exploded pie chart formats from the ChartWizard or from the Chart Type dialog box. However, this explodes all slices at once. In other words, it's probably better to explode slices yourself, as described on these pages, so you can explode selected slices.**

7 If you decide you don't want to keep the pie slice exploded, you can just select it and drag it back inward to reattach it to the rest of the pie.

6 Follow the same procedure if you want to explode additional pie slices.

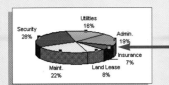

When there's one selection handle per slice, the entire chart is selected.

2 Click on the chart itself. It should acquire a set of handles, one per pie slice, as shown here.

When there are six handles on a single slice, only the individual slice is selected.

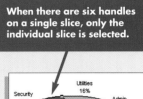

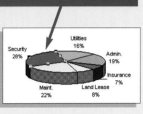

3 Now click on the slice that you want to pull away from the rest of the pie. It should take on a set of six handles of its own. (Warning: You can't double-click on a slice to get here more speedily. You have to single-click on the chart and then single-click on the slice you want to select.)

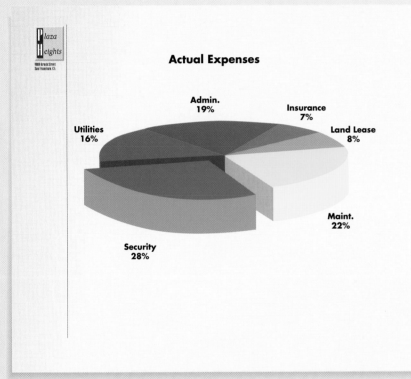

Actual Expenses

Admin.
19%

Insurance
7%

Land Lease
8%

Utilities
16%

Maint.
22%

Security
28%

This outline shows how far away from the pie the exploded slice will be.

4 Drag the selected slice away from the chart. You'll see an outline indicating how far the slice is from the pie.

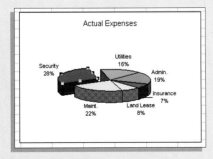

5 Release the mouse button to explode the selected slice. Notice that the label moved automatically with the selected pie slice.

How to Change the Data Being Graphed

What happens if you create a chart and realize that you didn't include all the necessary data? Or what if you included too much data and need to toss out some of it? Do you need to re-create the chart from scratch? Fortunately, the answer is no. If you're in the middle of creating a chart with the ChartWizard, you can just retrace your steps with the Back button and choose a new range of cells from the second ChartWizard dialog box. What's more likely is that you finish creating the chart and only then discover that you have too much or too little data. These pages describe what to do when you find yourself in this particular boat.

TIP SHEET

▶ You might hear the terms *data series* and *data point* used to refer to chart data. A data series is just a set of related values that you're charting. A data point is a single value in a data series. For example, the actual expenses for the year so far is one data series, and the budgeted expenses is another. The budgeted utilities expenses are a data point. Data series typically are laid out as columns or rows of data in the worksheet. All charts are made up of one or more data series.

▶ You can also add data to an embedded chart by selecting the data to add to the chart (be sure to include text to be used as chart labels) and dragging the selected data over the chart (drag the selection by its border). When the mouse pointer turns into an arrow with an attached plus sign, release the mouse button to "drop" the new data onto the chart.

▶ You can add data to a chart sheet by selecting the data to be added, copying it to the Clipboard, activating the appropriate chart sheet, and pasting in the data from the Clipboard. Excel automatically integrates the new data into the chart.

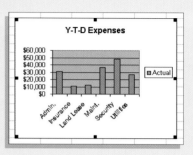

▶ **1** To add data to a chart, first activate the chart sheet containing the chart you want to modify or select the embedded chart to be changed.

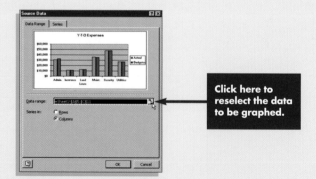

Click here to reselect the data to be graphed.

7 To either add or remove data, or to choose completely new data, you can choose Source Data from the Chart menu. In the Source Data dialog box that appears, make sure the Data Range tab is selected, click the Collapse Dialog button to the right of the Data Range text box, drag across the new data to be graphed, press Enter or click the Collapse Dialog button a second time, and then click OK.

2 Choose Add Data from the Chart menu.

3 You'll see the Add Data dialog box shown here.

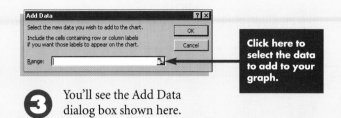

Click here to select the data to add to your graph.

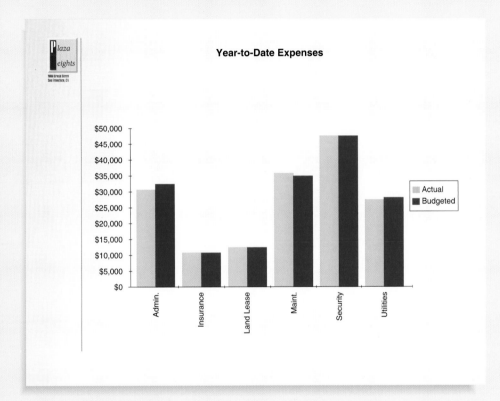

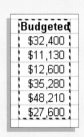

4 Click the Collapse Dialog button to the right of the Range text box. Then simply drag across the range to be added to your graph, being sure to include any labels you want Excel to use as chart text.

6 If you instead want to remove data from your chart, first click on any component of the data series. You could click on any one of the columns representing the Budgeted series, for instance. (Every element in the series will acquire square selection handles. For example, here each column in the Budgeted series is selected.) Then press the Del key. (See the Tip Sheet for more about data series.)

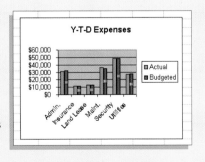

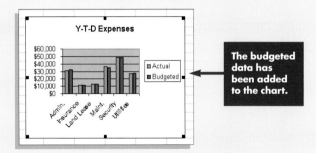

The budgeted data has been added to the chart.

5 Either press Enter or click the Collapse Dialog button again (it's on the far right end of the collapsed dialog box) to return to the Add Data dialog box. Then click OK to return to your worksheet or chart sheet and inspect the revised chart.

How to Change the Colors in a Chart

When you build a chart with the Chart-Wizard, Excel colors the chart automatically, carefully using various shades to distinguish different data series (groups of related data) and data points (single values in a data series). But you also have a lot of leeway to change the colors Excel uses, as well as to color some chart components—such as grid lines or text—that are normally displayed in functional, if unexciting, black. You can change the colors in a chart to emphasize particular data or just to make the chart look more appealing.

TIP SHEET

▸ **When you hold your mouse pointer over a chart, Excel displays a ScreenTip indicating which portion of the chart you're pointing to. This way you know which Format dialog box will materialize if you double-click on that spot.**

▸ **Besides choosing colors, you can choose patterns such as horizontal and diagonal lines. (If you're printing in black and white, using patterns rather than colors makes the various data points and/or data series in your chart much easier to distinguish.) To do so, click the Fill Effects button in the Format dialog box and click on the Pattern tab in the Fill Effects dialog box. Then choose a pattern from the palette that appears. You can also choose colors for the selected pattern. And be sure you explore the Gradient and Texture tabs in the Fill Effects dialog box to find out about some spectacular new fills offered in Excel 97.**

▸ **If you alter some chart colors and have a change of heart, you may be able to backtrack by using the Undo command. In addition, you can revert to the original colors by redisplaying the Patterns portion of the Format dialog box, clicking on Automatic in the relevant area of the dialog box, and clicking OK.**

▶ **1** If your chart is embedded within a worksheet, check that it's selected. If it's on a chart sheet, simply activate the chart sheet.

8 A quick way to change text colors in your chart is to click once on the item you want to change, click on the downward-pointing arrow on the Font Color toolbar button, and click on the desired color.

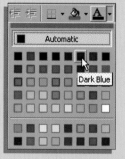

2 Double-click on the part of the chart containing the color you want to change. (You can instead right-click and choose the Format command.) Excel brings up a Format dialog box for the item you clicked on. For example, if you click on a column in a column chart, you'll see a Format Data Series dialog box similar to this one.

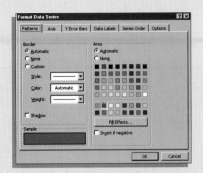

3 If necessary, click on the Patterns tab to activate that portion of the Format dialog box.

4 Under Area, click on the color you want to use and check the Sample in the lower-left corner of the dialog box. (If you like, you can also change the border color of the selected item by choosing a color from the Color drop-down list box in the Border portion of the dialog box.)

Year-to-Date Expenses

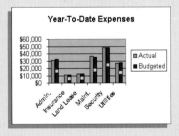

5 Click OK to place the new color in your chart. Note that this changes the color of the selected item or items only—in this case, the selected data series—not the entire chart.

7 A speedy way to change colors in your chart is to click once on the item you want to change, click on the downward-pointing arrow on the Fill Color toolbar button, and click on the color you want to use.

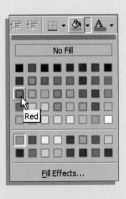

6 Repeat steps 2 through 5 to change the colors of other parts of your chart.

How to Format Chart Text

You learned how to format worksheet text in Chapter 8. You can change the font, font size, font style (bold and italic), and more. It's a simple job to make many of the same changes to the text in your charts, as you'll discover here. When changing chart text, be sure to do frequent print previews because what you see on the screen may not be a very close approximation of the final printout.

TIP SHEET

▸ **You can also make simple font changes to chart text by selecting the text to be changed and choosing a new font, font size, font style, or font color from the Formatting toolbar. The Format dialog box is primarily convenient when you're making a batch of changes at once and/or when you want to preview changes before putting them into effect.**

▸ **In some cases, you can also change the orientation and alignment of your text in the Format dialog box. To do so, choose the Alignment tab in the Format dialog box, and choose the options you want under Orientation and Text Alignment.**

▸ **You can't change the orientation of text in a chart's legend, but you can change its placement. For example, you can choose to position it at the bottom of the chart or to the left of the chart.**

▸ **In certain cases, if chart text is already selected, double-clicking on it doesn't bring up a Format dialog box, but instead highlights some of the text or introduces an insertion point. If this happens, just click away from the text to deselect it, and then double-click on it again. You should get a Format dialog box this time around.**

▸ **1** If your chart is embedded, make sure it's selected. If it's on a chart sheet, activate the chart sheet.

8 Check the Preview box to make your selections look workable. Then click OK to put the font changes into place.

7 You can also choose an underlining style from the Underline drop-down list box, a text color from the Color drop-down list box, and any special text effects, such as strikethrough or superscript. Finally, you can choose whether the background behind chart text is transparent or opaque. (If you select Automatic, Excel chooses for you.)

2 Double-click on the text you want to modify. (You can also right-click on the text and choose the Format command.) Excel displays a Format dialog box for the text you clicked on. For instance, if you double-click on your chart's title, you'll see this Format Chart Title dialog box.

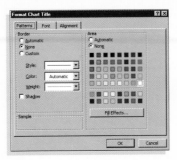

3 If necessary, click on the Font tab of the Format dialog box.

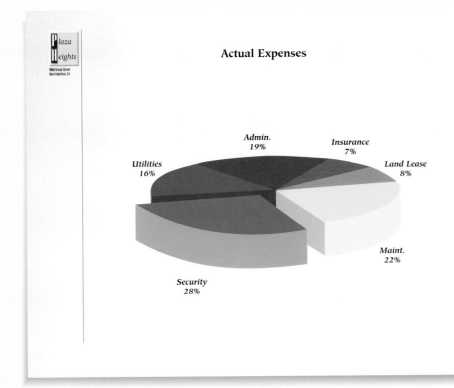

Actual Expenses

Admin.
19%

Insurance
7%

Utilities
16%

Land Lease
8%

Maint.
22%

Security
28%

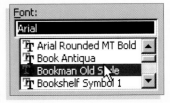

4 If you like, choose a new font from the Font list box.

6 If appropriate, choose a font size from the Size list box.

5 You can also choose a font style—such as bold or italic—from the Font Style list box.

How to Add Extra Text to a Chart

When you create charts, you can have the ChartWizard include text such as legends and axis labels. And you can add certain text elements—chart titles and axis titles, for example—to your chart after the fact, as you learned in the previous chapter. In addition, you can add extra text anywhere you want on your chart. For instance, you may want to include a label pointing out numbers of special significance. To do this, you have to add independent text in text boxes, as you'll learn here.

TIP SHEET

▶ **If you need to change the size of text in a text box, first select the text box. (Click the Select Objects toolbar button and then click on the text box.) Then choose fonts, font sizes, or font styles from the Formatting toolbar, as described in Chapter 8. To change the size of the text box itself, select it and then drag its selection handles, the same way you drag a chart's selection handles to resize it, as described earlier in this chapter.**

▶ **You can use the techniques described on these pages to add text to your worksheets as well as to charts.**

▶ **1** Select the desired chart or activate the chart sheet for the chart you're changing. Click the Drawing toolbar button.

Highest values!

Selected text box

8 If you need to get rid of a text box, click the Select Object button on the Drawing toolbar, click on the text box to select it, and then press Del.

2 You'll see the Drawing toolbar. (If it turns up in the middle of the screen and you need to move it out of the way, drag its title bar.) This toolbar includes a whole batch of tools for drawing shapes, some of which you'll learn about in the next set of pages.

3 Click the Text Box tool in the Drawing toolbar.

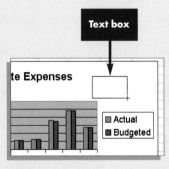

Text box

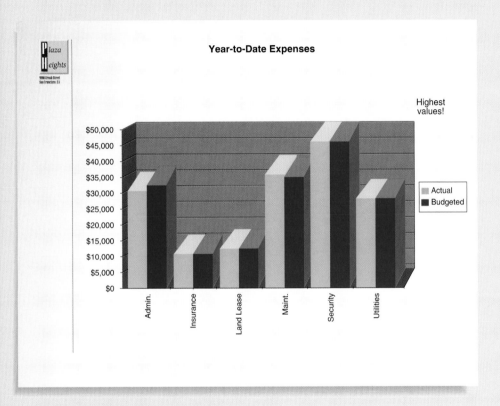

Year-to-Date Expenses

Highest values!

$50,000
$45,000
$40,000
$35,000
$30,000
$25,000
$20,000
$15,000
$10,000
$5,000
$0

Admin. Insurance Land Lease Maint. Security Utilities

☐ Actual
■ Budgeted

4 Drag across your chart to create a box into which you can type text.

Highest values!

Text wrapped within a text box

5 Type the text. If you type enough text, it "wraps" to fit within its text box. (Don't type too much! If your text doesn't fit within the text box, some of it just won't show up. Check the Tip Sheet for details on how to change the size of text boxes.)

Highest values!

7 To remove the Drawing toolbar from view, you can just click the Drawing toolbar button again. (If you're in the mood to use the menus, choose View, Toolbars, Drawing.)

6 When you're done, click outside the text box. (Note that the border doesn't print; it just shows you the bounds of the text box.) Especially if you're working in a chart sheet, you may want to zoom the display to get a better view of the text.

How to Draw Shapes on a Chart

S ometimes adding text is enough, but often you'll want to add shapes too: You might need arrows pointing from labels to items on the chart, boxes enclosing added text, or other shapes to clarify or embellish your charts. You can use the tools on the Drawing toolbar to add a wide variety of shapes both to charts and to the worksheet itself.

▶ **1** Either activate the appropriate chart sheet or select the chart you want to change.

TIP SHEET

▸ **The AutoShapes option on the Drawing toolbar supplies an almost mind-boggling array of shapes you can use. Here's how it works: Click on AutoShapes, highlight the desired option in the menu that appears, and click on the desired shape in the resulting palette. Then simply drag on your chart to draw. (If your mouse pointer persistently continues to draw even when you're finished, double-click to stop drawing; this happens with several of the tools on the Lines palette.)**

▸ **You can introduce text box borders by drawing rectangles around them. Or you can select the text box, choose Text Box from the Format menu, choose the Colors and Lines tab if necessary, choose a color from the Color drop-down list box under Line, and then choose a line style and weight.**

8 If you need to delete a shape you've drawn, click the Select Objects toolbar button, click on the object to select it, and then press Del.

2 If the Drawing toolbar is not already visible, display it by clicking the Drawing toolbar button.

3 To draw a rectangle, first click the Rectangle button on the Drawing toolbar.

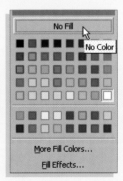

4 Drag over the chart to create a rectangle of the size you want in the spot you want. Release the mouse button to insert the rectangle into your chart.

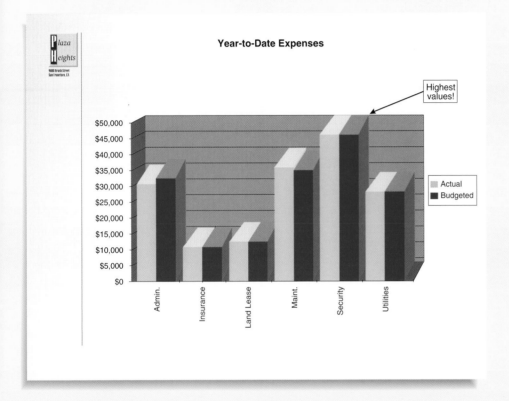

5 If the rectangle obscures your text, you have a couple of options: You can choose No Fill from the Fill Color palette. (Click the drop-down arrow on the Fill Color toolbar button.) Or you can choose Draw from the Drawing toolbar, choose Order, and choose Send to Back to bring the text to the front and put the rectangle behind it.

7 To draw other shapes, repeat the previous steps: Select the appropriate tool and drag across the chart to produce the shape you want.

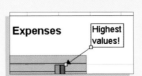

6 To draw an arrow, click the Arrow tool on the Drawing toolbar. Then drag on the chart to produce an arrow. Note that the arrowhead appears where you stop dragging, not where you start dragging.

TRY IT!

In the last four chapters, you acquired a whole new set of useful worksheet tools. Perhaps the most exciting skills you learned were how to create and modify graphs. Here's your chance to test these newfound abilities. Follow the instructions spelled out here to experiment with Excel's graphing features. As usual, chapter numbers indicate where topics came up initially so you can turn back if you need to jog your memory.

By the way, don't be too concerned if your results don't match the ones shown here exactly. You may have slightly different defaults, things may look different on your monitor, or you might simply choose to use different colors, fonts, or graph types.

Start Excel if you haven't already. If you don't have a blank worksheet on your screen, create a new workbook by clicking the New toolbar button. *Chapter 3*

Enter the worksheet shown here. Note that all these numbers are plain data, not formula results. *Chapter 2*

	A	B	C	D
1	PET PARADISE PET FOOD AND SUPPLIES			
2	SALES FIGURES -- FIRST QUARTER 1999			
3				
4		January	February	March
5	Cat Food	2346	3112	2911
6	Dog Food	2199	2635	2783
7	Flea Products	1732	1863	1534
8	Toys	1184	1321	1429
9	Treats	972	842	1299
10				

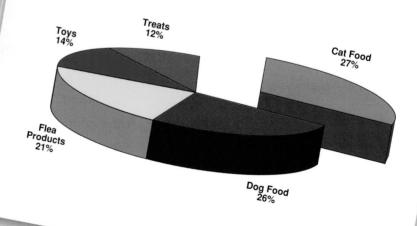

January Sales

3

Select the row headings and the January data, as shown here. *Chapter 4*

4

Click the ChartWizard toolbar button. *Chapter 12*

5

In the first ChartWizard dialog box, choose a chart type of Pie and leave the subtype of Pie se-lected. Then click the Next button to move on to the next ChartWizard dialog box. *Chapter 12*

6

In the second ChartWizard dialog box, check that the selected data range looks correct by re-viewing the sample chart, as well as the selected range listed in the Data Range text box. (Remember, if you need to change the data range, simply click the Data Range Collapse Dialog button, select the desired range, and press Enter.) Click on Next to continue. *Chapter 12*

7

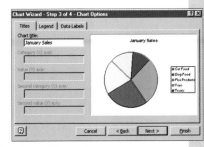

Make sure the Titles tab is selected in the third ChartWizard dialog box. Then change the chart title to *January Sales. Chapter 12*

8

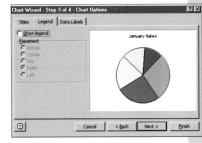

Select the Legend tab of the third ChartWizard dialog box. Then deselect the Show Legend check box. *Chapter 12*

9

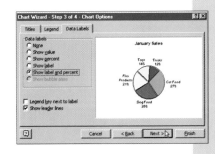

Select the Data Labels tab and click the Show Label and Percent op-tion button to select it. These labels work better than a legend to tell you which pie slice represents which bit of data. When you're ready, click the Next button to go to the final ChartWizard dialog box. *Chapter 12*

10

Leave the As Object In op-tion button selected and leave Sheet1 selected in the drop-down list box to its right. Then click the Finish button. *Chapter 12*

Continue to next page ▶

TRY IT!

Continue below

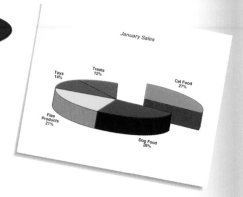

Excel places your newly created chart in Sheet1 of
the workbook, obscuring much of your data. Drag the chart to move it away from your data. (Remember, it's best to drag on the portion of the chart called the chart area—a ScreenTip indicates when your mouse pointer is over this area—so you don't unintentionally move just part of the chart.) *Chapter 13*

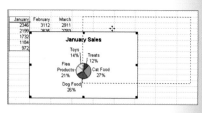

Drag the chart's lower-right handle to enlarge the chart. (If you wanted to
enlarge the chart in a single direction only, you would drag one of the side, top, or bottom handles instead.) *Chapter 13*

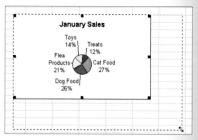

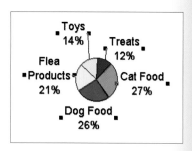

Click on the chart's data labels to select them. *Chapter 13*

Choose a font size of 10 from the Font Size drop-down list box on the Formatting toolbar. *Chapter 13*

Choose Chart Type from the Chart menu. *Chapter 12*

In the Chart Type dialog box that appears, click on the 3D Pie chart under Chart Subtype; it's the
middle option on the top. Then click OK.

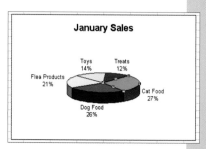

Click once on your three-dimensional pie chart, and then click once on the slice labeled
Cat Food. It should acquire a set of six selection handles. *Chapter 13*

18

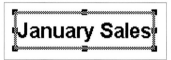

Drag on the
selected slice
to pull it
away from
the pie, creating an exploded pie slice.
The cat food sales were highest, so you
want them to stand out. *Chapter 13*

19

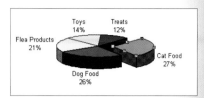

Click on the
chart title
January Sales to select it. *Chapter 13*

20

Notice that
the chart title is boldfaced (the Bold
toolbar button looks pressed in), and
click the Italic toolbar button to italicize
it as well. *Chapter 13*

21

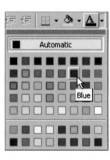

With the
chart title
still selected,
click on the
arrow to the
right of the
Font Color
toolbar button to display the Font
Color palette. *Chapter 13*

22

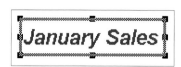

Click on the
desired font
color to change your chart title to that color.

23

Click the
Save toolbar button or choose Save
from the File menu to save the chart
and the worksheet. *Chapter 3*

24

In the Save
As dialog
box, enter a
name for the
file you just created and click the Save
button. If you see a Properties dialog
box, just press Enter to go ahead with
the save operation. *Chapter 3*

25

To see how
your chart looks on the printed page,
check that the chart is selected and click
the Print toolbar button. (If you have a
black-and-white printer and the various elements of the chart are difficult to
distinguish, select the chart to be
changed, choose Chart Type from the
Chart menu, choose the Custom Types
tab, choose a black-and-white (B&W)
chart type, and click OK.)

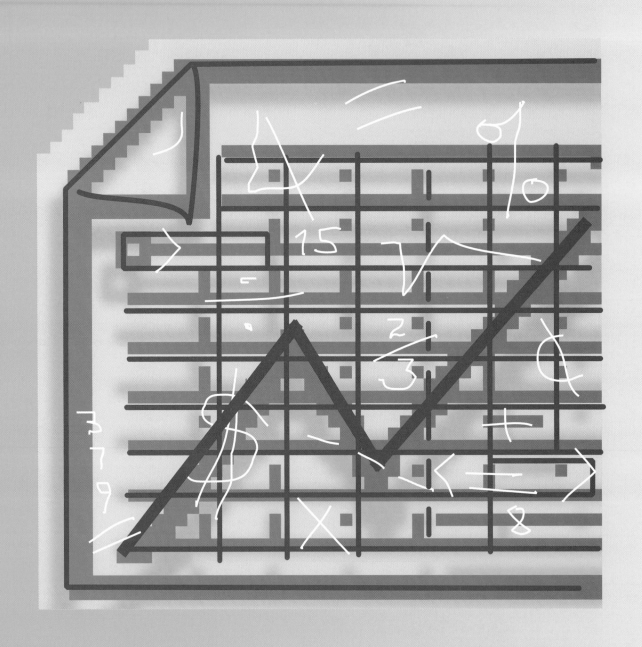

CHAPTER 14

Working with Lists of Data

The data in an Excel worksheet is often referred to as a list. A *list* is simply a series of rows that contain similar data sets and that are topped by a row of identifying labels. (Much of the data you've worked with so far has been in the form of lists.) The advantage of lists is that you can manipulate them to suit your needs. You can search for data that meets specific conditions, filtering out other data that you don't need to see at the moment. In a personnel list, you could hunt for someone named Lambert or for employees who earn over $50,000 a year. You can also sort the list in a variety of ways—arranging it in alphabetical order by last name, for example.

There's some unavoidable jargon associated with lists. (Lists are often referred to as *databases*.) A *record* is all the data about one subject—all the personnel data about an employee named Rothstein, for instance. A *field* is a data category. For example, the fields in a personnel database might include name, social security number, and pay rate. Typically, each record is one row of data and each field is one column of data. The column headings are often called *field names*.

It's best not to have more than one list per worksheet. You should also leave at least one blank column and row between the list and any other data in your worksheet so Excel can identify the list automatically.

How to Perform a Simple Search

Often you'll want to see all the data in your worksheet. But sometimes you'll want to see only selected portions of your data—and the bigger your worksheets grow, the more important this becomes. Excel lets you temporarily "filter" your data, searching for and displaying only those records that meet certain conditions. This section introduces some of the simplest ways of weeding out excess data from your worksheet so you can concentrate on just the data you need. Once you filter your database, you can view, edit, copy, or print the remaining records, just as you can with any data in Excel.

TIP SHEET

▶ **AutoFilter does *not* delete data from your worksheet. It just hides records temporarily.**

▶ **Remember, to undo the effects of a filter on a specific field, you choose All from that field's drop-down list box. To undo the effects of several filters, choose Filter from the Data menu and then choose Show All. To turn off the AutoFilter altogether—that is, display all records and turn off the drop-down arrows—choose Filter from the Data menu and then choose AutoFilter.**

▶ **When your list is filtered, Excel changes the color of the row numbers to remind you that you aren't viewing the entire list; you'll also notice that row numbers aren't consecutive where there's missing data. The drop-down arrow on any fields you've filtered also changes color to indicate that records are hidden.**

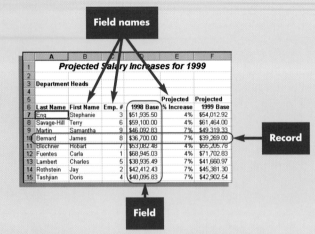

1 If your list is separated from any other data in the worksheet by at least one column and row, select any cell in your list. Otherwise, select the entire list.

9 When you've made the selections you want, click OK to see the filtered version of your list. Notice that rows 10 and 13–15 are hidden here since these employees aren't among the top five money earners.

8 Select the desired number of values from the middle spin box. For example, to view the top five salaries, you would choose 5. You can also view the set of values at the bottom of your list by choosing Bottom (rather than Top) from the leftmost drop-down list, and you can view a top or bottom percentage by choosing Percent (rather than Items) from the rightmost drop-down list.

2 Choose Filter from the Data menu, and then choose AutoFilter from the submenu that appears.

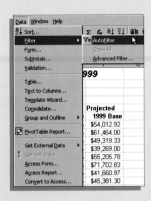

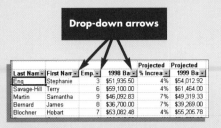

Drop-down arrows

3 Each field name now has a drop-down arrow associated with it. These arrows let you filter the list by values in particular fields (columns). For example, in this worksheet you could choose to view only the records of employees who are up for a 7 percent raise. (There's a value of 7% in the Projected % Increase field for their record.)

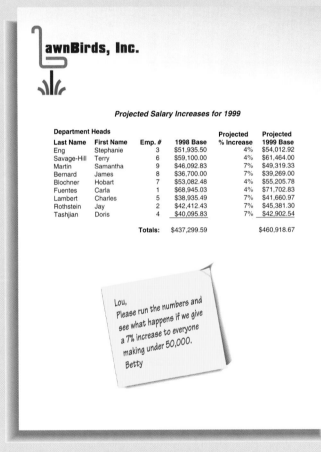

4 Click on any drop-down arrow. The drop-down list that appears shows the contents of each cell in the column, plus some special entries, such as (All) and (Custom).

5 If you choose a particular item from the list, Excel "filters out" all records that don't match the selected value. For instance, if you choose 7% from the Projected % Increase drop-down list, you'll see only the records for all employees who are due for a 7 percent pay increase, as shown here. (Note that there's nothing to prevent you from setting up several such filters.)

6 If you decide to view all records once again, you can choose All from the drop-down list you used to filter your data.

7 To display the top ten values in a particular field—or the top eight, the top three, and so on—choose the Top 10 item from the appropriate drop-down list. You might do this, for example, to see the five employees with the highest salaries. You'll see the Top 10 AutoFilter dialog box shown here. ("Top 10" is a misnomer; you can choose to view anywhere between 1 and 500 items.)

How to Perform Searches Using Operators

You just learned how to filter your data in some simple ways—finding records that match a specified value or hunting down the highest (or lowest) set of records in a specified field. But sometimes you'll need to find a range of values—such as all employees with salaries less than $50,000 or everyone whose last name falls in the second half of the alphabet. In these cases you can't just pick options directly from the AutoFilter drop-down lists. Instead, you need to choose the Custom option and use special comparison operators to tell Excel which range of values you want to track down.

TIP SHEET

▶ It's just as easy to filter fields that contain text rather than numbers. In this case, the letter *a* is considered to be less than the letter *b*, and so on. For instance, you could enter the name *Smith* and choose the "is greater than" operator to find names that fall later in the alphabet than Smith.

▶ After filtering your database once, you can narrow down the data further by applying another criterion. Simply repeat the steps outlined here. For example, after filtering a list to show only employees in the Marketing department, you could filter the list of marketing employees to show only those earning over $50,000 a year.

▶ You can also filter a single field based on more than one criterion. For example, you can hunt for all employees who earn less than $50,000 but more than $40,000. You'll learn how to do this in a moment, under "How to Perform More Complicated Searches."

Last Name	First Name	Emp.	1998 Ba	Projected % Increa	Projected 1999 Ba
Eng	Stephanie	3	$51,935.50	4%	$54,012.92
Savage-Hill	Terry	6	$59,100.00	4%	$61,464.00
Martin	Samantha	9	$46,092.83	7%	$49,319.33
Bernard	James	8	$36,700.00	7%	$39,269.00
Blochner	Hobart	7	$53,082.48	4%	$55,205.78
Fuentes	Carla	1	$68,945.03	4%	$71,702.83
Lambert	Charles	5	$38,935.49	7%	$41,660.97
Rothstein	Jay	2	$42,412.43	7%	$45,381.30
Tashjian	Doris	4	$40,095.83	7%	$42,902.54

▶ **1** If you don't see the AutoFilter drop-down arrows, display them by selecting any cell in the list, choosing Filter from the Data menu, and then choosing AutoFilter. (Also turn off any previous AutoFilters if you want to search through the entire list. Flip back to the previous set of pages if you can't remember how to do this.)

6 As before, you can choose Filter from the Data menu and then choose Show All to bring all your records back into view. The other alternative is to choose All from the drop-down list you used to filter your data.

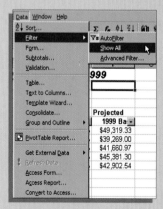

2 Click on the arrow for the field you want to filter. For example, if you want to filter out records based on a certain salary level, click on the arrow for the salary field.

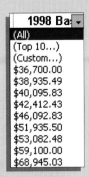

1998 Ba▼
(All)
(Top 10...)
(Custom...)
$36,700.00
$38,935.49
$40,095.83
$42,412.43
$46,092.83
$51,935.50
$53,082.48
$59,100.00
$68,945.03

Name of field being used to filter data

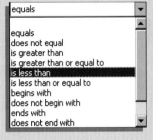

3 Choose Custom to display the Custom AutoFilter dialog box. In the upper-right text box, type the number or text that will be used to filter the list. For example, if you're going to hunt for salaries under $50,000, start by entering **50000**.

LawnBirds, Inc.

Projected Salary Increases for 1999

Department Heads

Last Name	First Name	Emp. #	1998 Base	Projected % Increase	Projected 1999 Base
Eng	Stephanie	3	$51,935.50	4%	$54,012.92
Savage-Hill	Terry	6	$59,100.00	4%	$61,464.00
Martin	Samantha	9	$46,092.83	7%	$49,319.33
Bernard	James	8	$36,700.00	7%	$39,269.00
Blochner	Hobart	7	$53,082.48	4%	$55,205.78
Fuentes	Carla	1	$68,945.03	4%	$71,702.83
Lambert	Charles	5	$38,935.49	7%	$41,660.97
Rothstein	Jay	2	$42,412.43	7%	$45,381.30
Tashjian	Doris	4	$40,095.83	7%	$42,902.54
		Totals:	$437,299.59		$460,918.67

Records for which 1998 base is less than $50,000

equals ▼
equals
does not equal
is greater than
is greater than or equal to
is less than
is less than or equal to
begins with
does not begin with
ends with
does not end with

4 In the upper-left list box, choose an operator to specify how records should be tested against this number or text. You can choose from a whole range of comparison operators: "equals," "does not equal," "is greater than," "is greater than or equal to," "is less than," "is less than or equal to," and so on. To find salaries under $50,000, choose the "is less than" operator.

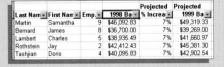

Last Name ▼	First Nam ▼	Emp. ▼	1998 Ba ▼	Projected % Increa ▼	Projected 1999 Ba ▼
Martin	Samantha	9	$46,092.83	7%	$49,319.33
Bernard	James	8	$36,700.00	7%	$39,269.00
Lambert	Charles	5	$38,935.49	7%	$41,660.97
Rothstein	Jay	2	$42,412.43	7%	$45,381.30
Tashjian	Doris	4	$40,095.83	7%	$42,902.54

5 Click OK to filter the list, temporarily screening out any records that don't meet the specified criteria—in this case, any records for which the salary is not under $50,000.

How to Search Using Wildcards

Sometimes you'll have a very precise idea of the data you need—maybe you want a list of all customers named Smith or all employees who earn over $50,000. But at other times you won't be so sure. As one example, you might need to browse through a list of customers whose last names begin with the letter *b* if you're searching for someone whose name you can't remember in full. Here you find out how to carry out searches using *wildcards*, special characters that can stand in for one or more other characters.

TIP SHEET

▶ **When using wildcards, as before, you can filter on more than a single field. For instance, you could look for all employees whose last names started with *b* and then hunt for those whose first names started with the letter *s*.**

▶ **As you may have noticed, it worked just fine to enter b* in the Custom AutoFilter dialog box, even though the last names in this list all begin with capital letters. Excel is not case sensitive when searching for records. That's just a fancy way of saying that Excel doesn't care whether you enter the letters in uppercase, lowercase, or a combination of the two.**

▶ **If you're looking for a value that contains a specific letter or digit that may not fall at the beginning of the word or number, just enter *, the character in question, and another *. For example, if you know that someone's last name contains an *x* somewhere, but perhaps not as the first letter, you can enter *x* in the Custom AutoFilter dialog box to search for that name.**

 1 If the AutoFilter drop-down arrows aren't already displayed, select any cell in the list, choose Filter from the Data menu, and then choose AutoFilter. (Also reverse the effects of any previous AutoFilters if you want to search the entire list.)

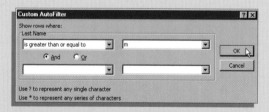

7 You can also use wildcards with operators other than "equals." For example, if you wanted to find all employees whose last names fell in the second half of the alphabet, you could enter **m** in the Custom AutoFilter dialog box, choose the "is greater than or equal to operator," and click OK.

2 Click on the arrow for the field you want to use as a filter. If you decide to find records in which the last name begins with the letter *b*, for example, click on the arrow for the Last Name field.

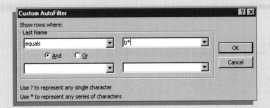

3 Choose Custom to display the Custom AutoFilter dialog box. Then type the value you want to use to filter the list. Since you don't know the exact value in this case, you can type **b*** to indicate any names that begin with the letter *b* and are followed by any other characters. (The asterisk is a wildcard that stands in for any number of characters.)

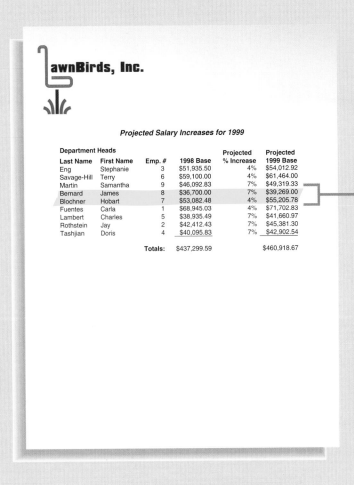

LawnBirds, Inc.

Projected Salary Increases for 1999

Department Heads

Last Name	First Name	Emp. #	1998 Base	Projected % Increase	Projected 1999 Base
Eng	Stephanie	3	$51,935.50	4%	$54,012.92
Savage-Hill	Terry	6	$59,100.00	4%	$61,464.00
Martin	Samantha	9	$46,092.83	7%	$49,319.33
Bernard	James	8	$36,700.00	7%	$39,269.00
Blochner	Hobart	7	$53,082.48	4%	$55,205.78
Fuentes	Carla	1	$68,945.03	4%	$71,702.83
Lambert	Charles	5	$38,935.49	7%	$41,660.97
Rothstein	Jay	2	$42,412.43	7%	$45,381.30
Tashjian	Doris	4	$40,095.83	7%	$42,902.54
	Totals:		$437,299.59		$460,918.67

Records for which last name begins with b

Last Name	First Name	Emp.	1998 Base	Projected % Increase	Projected 1999 Base
Bernard	James	8	$36,700.00	7%	$39,269.00
Blochner	Hobart	7	$53,082.48	4%	$55,205.78

4 In this case you don't need to choose an operator, since the "equals" operator is selected by default. Go ahead and click OK to carry out the Auto-Filter command. You'll wind up with a list of records in which the last name begins with the letter *b*.

Last Name	First Name	Emp.	1998 Base	Projected % Increase	Projected 1999 Base
Rothstein	Jay	2	$42,412.43	7%	$45,381.30

5 As usual, choose All from the drop-down list if you want to redisplay all records.

6 You can use the question mark (?) wildcard character to represent a single character. For example, in the First Name field, you could choose Custom and enter **j??** (leave the "equals" operator selected) to look for three-letter names beginning with the letter *j*. Excel will find *Jay* but not *James*. If you had typed **j*** instead, the filtered list would have included both *Jay* and *James*.

How to Perform More Complicated Searches

You can use the second set of drop-down list boxes at the bottom of the Custom Auto-Filter dialog box to perform more complex searches—ferreting out records that meet two criteria instead of one or finding records that meet at least one of two criteria. As an example, you could hunt for employees who earn between $40,000 and $50,000 a year. Or you could track down people who are in either the Marketing or the Sales department.

TIP SHEET

▶ When you enter two criteria in the Custom AutoFilter dialog box, it doesn't matter what order you list them in. For example, you could enter "is greater than 40000" as the first criterion and "is less than 50000" as the second one, or vice versa. The results will be the same, whether you're using the Or or the And option button.

▶ A quick way to use existing values as criteria in the Custom AutoFilter dialog box is to choose them from the drop-down lists. For example, if you're looking for all employees in Sales and Marketing, you should be able to choose the appropriate department names or codes from the drop-down lists.

1 If you need to display the AutoFilter drop-down arrows, select any cell in the list and then choose Data, Filter, AutoFilter. (If you want to search the entire list, first undo any previous AutoFilters by choosing Data, Filter, Show All.)

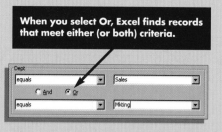

When you select Or, Excel finds records that meet either (or both) criteria.

7 To find records that meet either of two criteria, choose the Or option button. For example, if your list specified departments, you could find all employees in either Marketing or Sales by entering Sales as one criterion, Mkting as another, and choosing the Or option button. (It wouldn't make sense to use the And operator here, since nobody will be in both the Sales and Marketing departments.)

2 Display the drop-down list for the field to be used as a filter. For instance, to find records in which the salary is between $40,000 and $50,000, click on the arrow for the salary field (1998 Base).

3 Choose Custom to display the Custom AutoFilter dialog box. Then, in the top two list boxes, enter the first criterion by which to filter the list. To find all employees earning over $40,000, for example, enter **40000** and choose the "is greater than" comparison operator.

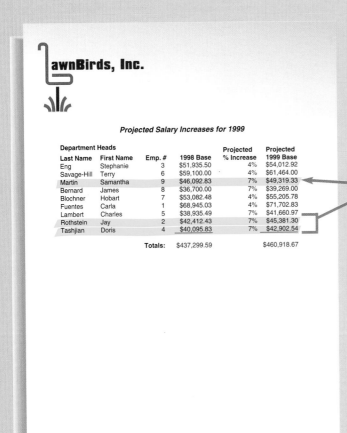

LawnBirds, Inc.

Projected Salary Increases for 1999

Department Heads

Last Name	First Name	Emp. #	1998 Base	Projected % Increase	Projected 1999 Base
Eng	Stephanie	3	$51,935.50	4%	$54,012.92
Savage-Hill	Terry	6	$59,100.00	4%	$61,464.00
Martin	Samantha	9	$46,092.83	7%	$49,319.33
Bernard	James	8	$36,700.00	7%	$39,269.00
Blochner	Hobart	7	$53,082.48	4%	$55,205.78
Fuentes	Carla	1	$68,945.03	4%	$71,702.83
Lambert	Charles	5	$38,935.49	7%	$41,660.97
Rothstein	Jay	2	$42,412.43	7%	$45,381.30
Tashjian	Doris	4	$40,095.83	7%	$42,902.54
		Totals:	$437,299.59		$460,918.67

Records for which 1998 base is between $40,000 and $50,000

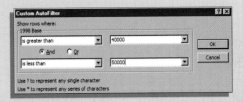

4 Now enter the second criterion in the list boxes at the bottom of the dialog box. For example, enter **50000** and choose the "is less than" operator to find all employees who earn under $50,000 a year.

Records for which 1998 base is between $40,000 and $50,000

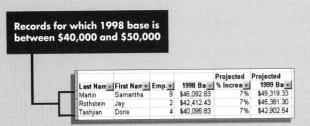

Last Name	First Name	Emp.	1998 Base	Projected % Increase	Projected 1999 Base
Martin	Samantha	9	$46,092.83	7%	$49,319.33
Rothstein	Jay	2	$42,412.43	7%	$45,381.30
Tashjian	Doris	4	$40,095.83	7%	$42,902.54

6 Click OK to filter your list. This filtered view of the list displays only the records for employees who earn more than $40,000 and less than $50,000 a year.

When you select And, Excel finds records that meet both criteria.

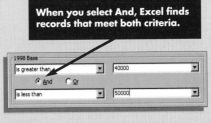

5 Notice that the And option button is selected. This means that Excel will track down records that meet *both* criteria. (It's not enough for the records to meet just one of the criteria.)

How to Find Specific Records

So far in this chapter you've used Excel's AutoFilter command to display subsets of your data on the worksheet. If you want to single out records instead of displaying sets of records, you can use the Form command. The Form command tracks down the records you want, displaying one record at a time in a special onscreen form. The Form command lets you view your data in a different way and lets you edit records, delete records, and enter new records while you're at it.

TIP SHEET

▶ Besides using the Form dialog box to view specified records, you can use it to add new records: Just click the New command button, type data in the empty text boxes that appear, and then press Enter. You can also use it to delete existing records: Simply find the record to be deleted and then click the Delete button. Finally, you can use it to edit records: Display the desired record, make any changes you need, and press Enter.

▶ You can use the vertical scroll bar in the Form dialog box to scroll through the records that meet the designated criteria or, if you haven't specified any criteria, to scroll through all records in the list.

▶ There are some limits to the changes you can make through the Form dialog box. You can't add new records to a list if there's existing data below it that might get overwritten. In addition, you can change only values that are displayed in (white) text boxes. You can't change values that aren't displayed in text boxes (such as 1999 Base), because they contain formulas.

1 Activate any cell in the list and choose Form from the Data menu.

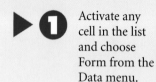

8 When you're done looking over records, you can remove the form from view by clicking its Close button or the Close box (the *x*) in its upper-right corner.

7 You can also find a range of records by using the comparison operators (=, <, >, <=, >=, and <>). For example, you could click the Criteria button, enter >=50000 in the 1998 Base field, and use the Find Next and Find Prev buttons to find all records with a salary greater than or equal to $50,000.

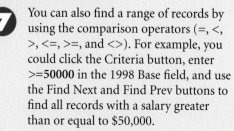

2 You'll see the dialog box shown in the middle of the page. (The name in the title bar is the name of the current worksheet.) Notice that the left side of the dialog box displays all the field names from your list, and to their right is the data for the first record in the list.

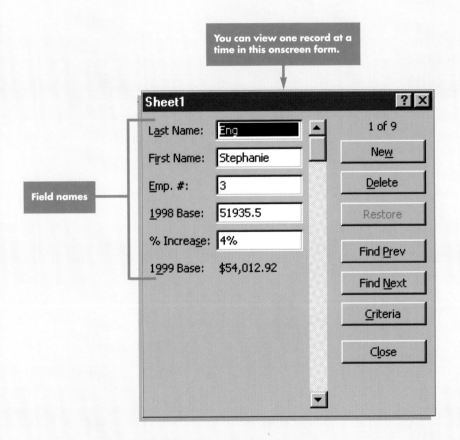

You can view one record at a time in this onscreen form.

Field names

Criteria

3 To find records meeting certain criteria, first click the Criteria button.

4 Click in the text box in which you want to specify a criterion. Then type in values if you want to match them. For example, to find all employees with the last name Fuentes, type **Fuentes** in the Last Name field. (You could also find all records in which the last name begins with *f* by entering **f*** in the Last Name text box.)

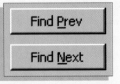

Clear

Form

6 To view all records again, click the Criteria button, click Clear to remove any criteria, and then click the Form button. Once you do this, you can use Find Prev and Find Next to browse through all records in the list.

Find Prev

Find Next

5 Click the Find Next button to search forward through the records that meet the specified criteria. Click the Find Prev button to search backward. You can click either button repeatedly to find additional records that meet the criteria.

How to Sort Data

So far you've learned a whole batch of techniques for narrowing down your lists, viewing selected subsets of your data. Another way to change the way you view your data is to sort it, rearranging the records in your list based on the contents of one or more fields. As an example, you could sort the list in alphabetical order by last name. Or you could sort by departmental budget, starting with the highest budget and ending with the lowest. Perhaps the best thing about sorting in Excel is that you're not stuck with any one arrangement of your data. If you sort a list in one way and then decide to view it from another perspective, you can simply issue another sort command to rearrange the records again.

TIP SHEET

▶ **To be safe, you'll want to save your worksheet immediately before performing a sort. This way, if the sort doesn't work out as planned and you don't perform an Undo fairly soon afterward, you can simply close the worksheet without saving it and then reopen it in its presorted state (see Chapter 3).**

▶ **If you haven't laid out your list correctly—separating the list from other data in the worksheet—Excel may not be able to figure out which data to sort. It's a good idea to check that Excel selects the correct records when you choose the Sort command. (It highlights what it considers to be the list.) Another alternative is to select the data to be sorted before issuing the Sort command, but be sure to select entire records, or your data will be scrambled.**

▶ **Sorting the result of an AutoFilter—and then perhaps printing or charting it—is a great way to pull out snippets of data for presentation. For example, from a personnel worksheet, you could filter a list of employees with more than five years of service and then sort the resulting list in descending order by years of service.**

▶ **1** Activate any cell in your list and choose Sort from the Data menu; this brings up the Sort dialog box.

8 To quickly sort a list into descending order, activate any cell in the column on which you want to sort, and then click the Sort Descending toolbar button.

7 To quickly sort a list into ascending order, select a cell in the column to sort by and then click the Sort Ascending toolbar button. Excel sorts the list in ascending order based on the contents of the selected column. (You can sort on only a single column this way.)

2 Under Sort By, click on the drop-down arrow to display a list of fields (columns) on which you can sort, and then select the field on which to sort your list. In this case, if you want to sort according to budget, you would choose the 1999 Budget field.

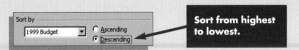

Sort from highest to lowest.

3 By default, Excel sorts in ascending order (A to Z, lowest to highest numbers, and earliest to latest dates and times). If you want to sort in descending order instead (Z to A, highest to lowest numbers, and latest to earliest dates and times), select the Descending option button in the Sort By area.

awnBirds, Inc.

Department Summary
(Ranked by budget size)

Department	Headquarters	Dept. Head	1999 Budget	# Employees
Manufacturing	Emeryville	Tashjian	$5,465,900	26
R&D	San Francisco	Lambert	$4,958,300	20
Marketing	San Francisco	Eng	$4,109,373	12
Sales	Chapel Hill	Savage-Hill	$3,100,000	16
Shipping	Emeryville	Rothstein	$3,100,000	14
Cust. Service	San Francisco	Martin	$1,894,380	7
Maintenance	Emeryville	Blochner	$1,258,445	10
Genl. Admin.	San Francisco	Fuentes	$1,009,894	8
Accounting	San Francisco	Bernard	$902,435	7

Departments with the same budget are sorted in alphabetical order.

4 You may want to sort on one or two additional fields to break ties—that is, records with matching values in the field being sorted on. If so, repeat steps 2 and 3 to specify a sort field and sort order (ascending or descending) in the first and, if necessary, the second Then By area. You could do this, for example, to sort by Department where the budget figures match. You can also sort by last name and then by first name.

Department Summary
(Ranked by budget size)

Department	Headquarters	Dept. Head	1999 Budget	# Employees
Manufacturing	Emeryville	Tashjian	$5,465,900	26
R&D	San Francisco	Lambert	$4,958,300	20
Marketing	San Francisco	Eng	$4,109,373	12
Sales	Chapel Hill	Savage-Hill	$3,100,000	16
Shipping	Emeryville	Rothstein	$3,100,000	14
Cust. Service	San Francisco	Martin	$1,894,380	7
Maintenance	Emeryville	Blochner	$1,258,445	10
Genl. Admin.	San Francisco	Fuentes	$1,009,894	8
Accounting	San Francisco	Bernard	$902,435	7

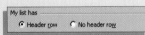

5 By default, the Header Row option button is selected under My List Has. This way Excel won't sort the row containing column headings. If your list doesn't include column headings and you want the topmost row sorted along with the rest, select the option button No Header Row.

6 When you're done making selections from the Sort dialog box, click OK to perform the sort.

How to Calculate Subtotals

You've learned quite a bit about searching for specific records and sorting a list into a variety of orders. Another way to manipulate a list is to summarize the data it contains. As just one example, you can calculate subtotals and grand totals based upon a specified field, as you'll discover here.

TIP SHEET

▶ The steps on these pages illustrate how to sum a series of values, producing subtotals in various categories. But you can use functions other than SUM with the Subtotals command. For instance, you can use the **AVERAGE** function to determine the average value in a particular set of records. (You could find out the average salary in each department.) You can also use the **MIN** and **MAX** functions to see the minimum and maximum values in a particular category, and the **COUNT** function to count the number of items in a designated category.

▶ Once you set up subtotals, you can display different levels of detail in your list. If you click on the number 1 in the upper-left corner of the worksheet, Excel displays the grand total only. If you click on the number 2, Excel shows the grand total and the subtotals, but not the individual records. If you click on the number 3, Excel displays the grand total, subtotals, and all the individual records.

▶ To get rid of subtotals, activate any cell in the list and choose Subtotals from the Data menu. Then choose the Remove All button in the Subtotal dialog box. Note, however, that you can't undo this action.

▶ **1** If you want to determine subtotals based upon a particular column, you first need to sort the column. For example, you could sort this Salaries list by department by selecting any cell in the department column and clicking the Sort Ascending toolbar button.

 If necessary, scroll to the bottom of your list, where you'll see the grand total. Here you can see the total salaries from all departments.

2 Choose Subtotals from the Data menu. Excel displays the Subtotal dialog box.

3 If necessary, select the field you sorted by in the top drop-down list box. Excel calculates subtotals each time the value in this field changes. As an example, if you choose Dept, you can have Excel tally up salary totals for a department each time the department name changes.

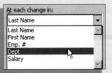

4 If necessary, choose a function from the Use Function drop-down list box. For example, if SUM is selected, Excel adds together all the salaries in each department.

5 Now choose the field in which you want to display subtotals. In this case, since you want to see subtotals in the Salary field, leave Salary selected. Also, click to deselect any other fields that are selected. (Note, however, that there's nothing to prevent you from displaying subtotals for multiple fields if you like.)

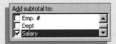

1998 Salaries
(By Department)

Last Name	First Name	Emp. #	Dept	Salary
Bernard	James	8	Accounting	$36,700.00
Stele	Emilie	13	Accounting	$47,872.50
			Accounting Total	$84,572.50
Martin	Samantha	9	Cust. Service	$46,092.83
Yee	Joanne	16	Cust. Service	$42,330.99
			Cust. Service Total	$88,423.82
Fuentes	Carla	1	Genl. Admin.	$68,945.03
Schumofsky	Mara	17	Genl. Admin.	$83,922.00
			Genl. Admin. Total	$152,867.03
Blochner	Hobart	7	Maintenance	$53,082.48
			Maintenance Total	$53,082.48
Gonzalez	Rosa	15	Manufacturing	$38,971.20
Tashjian	Doris	4	Manufacturing	$40,095.53
			Manufacturing Total	$79,067.03
Eng	Stephanie	3	Marketing	$51,935.50
Biow	Lynn	10	Marketing	$69,472.00
Washington	Peter	18	Marketing	$31,457.00
			Marketing Total	$152,864.50
Light	Julie	11	R&D	$73,250.00
Lambert	Charles	5	R&D	$38,935.49
			R&D Total	$112,185.49
Savage-Hill	Terry	6	Sales	$59,100.00
Kenber	Fred	12	Sales	$38,845.00
Gaboury	Thomasine	19	Sales	$72,900.00
Whitman	Frank	20	Sales	$81,115.00
			Sales Total	$251,960.00
Zadeh	Leopold	14	Shipping	$32,419.75
Rothstein	Jay	2	Shipping	$42,412.43
			Shipping Total	$74,832.16
			Grand Total	$1,049,855.03

6 When you're done making selections, click OK. Excel automatically adds the total salaries per department to your list. (You may need to widen columns to see labels in full; see Chapter 7 for details.)

Subtotal labels (Excel inserts these automatically.)

Departmental subtotals

CHAPTER 15

Working with Multiple Worksheets

 Chapter 3 explained a little bit about working with more than one worksheet. (Remember, workbook files are like binders; they contain multiple worksheets you can use to organize your data.) There you discovered how to switch between worksheets, how to name worksheets, and how to add and delete worksheets. There's a great deal more to learn about worksheets, and here's where you get your feet wet on the subject.

You'll learn how to enter data or apply formatting in more than one worksheet at once. For example, you could enter column or row headings into several worksheets at the same time and then enter different data into each worksheet. You'll also discover how to move and copy data between worksheets. This is a simple process that's even easier if you read up on moving and copying data in Chapter 7.

You'll find out how to build formulas that refer to data in other worksheets. This feature is great for creating summary worksheets since it permits you to use data in calculations without having to enter that data into the current worksheet. And as you'd expect, if the data being referred to changes, the formula results change right along with it. You can also link data in different worksheets. When data is linked and you change the data in the original worksheet, the linked data in the other worksheet changes automatically to match.

Finally, you'll acquire some worksheet management skills—such as how to move and copy worksheets—that are essential for keeping your workbooks up to date.

How to Affect Several Worksheets at Once

When your workbook contains multiple worksheets, you'll frequently want to enter data and apply formatting to individual worksheets. But sometimes it can be convenient to affect several worksheets at once—entering the same set of data (column headings or worksheet titles), applying the same formatting (boldfacing or italicizing those titles), and so on. Here's where you learn how to do this. The first step is to group all the worksheets together by selecting them all.

TIP SHEET

▸ **If you want to remove individual worksheets from a group instead of ungrouping them all, hold down the Ctrl key while clicking on the tab of the worksheet you want to remove from the group.**

▸ **To select nonadjacent worksheets, click on the tab of the first worksheet to include in the group, and then hold down the Ctrl key while clicking on additional tabs to add more worksheets to the group.**

▸ **A whole host of other changes will affect all worksheets in a group. To name just a few, you can insert and delete columns and rows in the whole group, clear and delete data in all worksheets in a group, and spell-check all worksheets in the group.**

▸ **You can quickly select all worksheets in a workbook by right-clicking on any worksheet tab and choosing Select All Sheets from the shortcut menu that appears.**

1 Open or create the workbook containing multiple worksheets that you want to operate on as a group. If you need help with any of the details, refer back to Chapter 3. If you plan on entering data in several worksheets at once, make sure the relevant cells of all the worksheets are blank so you don't overwrite existing data.

7 To work on individual worksheets again, right-click on any of the selected tabs and choose Ungroup Sheets from the shortcut menu that appears. You can also click on any tab outside the group to deselect all worksheets in the group. (If your group includes all worksheets in the workbook, clicking on any single tab deselects the group.)

Calculating the totals on any one worksheet in the group calculates them automatically on all other worksheets.

	October	November	December	Q4
Cat Food	2136	4001	3211	9348
Dog Food	2953	2375	2803	8131
Flea Products	1852	1939	1634	5425
Toys	1289	1431	1592	4312
Treats	867	1182	1187	3236
Totals	9097	10928	10427	30452

6 You can even calculate totals on all worksheets in a group, provided that the worksheets are laid out in an identical fashion. Here, for example, you could calculate totals for all sheets in the group by selecting cells B10:E10 on any sheet and then clicking the AutoSum toolbar button.

2 To select a group of adjacent worksheets, click on the tab for the first worksheet, hold down the Shift key, and then click on the tab for the last worksheet. The selected tabs will turn white and you'll see the word *Group* in the title bar, indicating that you can act on all these worksheets as a group.

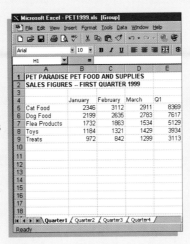

This text was entered into the Quarter1 worksheet, but it also shows up in Quarter2, Quarter3, and Quarter4 because the worksheets are grouped together.

3 When you've selected a group of worksheets, you can enter data into every sheet in the group simultaneously by typing it into any single sheet. For example, if you entered **Totals** in cell A10 of the first sheet shown here, it would show up in cell A10 in all four grouped sheets. (Keep in mind that it doesn't matter which sheet you enter the data in, as long as all the sheets are grouped.)

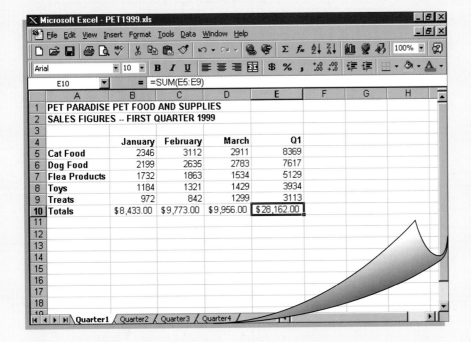

4 You can also apply formatting to all the worksheets in a group. For example, if you wanted to boldface a series of column and row headings that appeared in row 4 and column A on each worksheet, you could select the relevant cells in any one of the sheets and apply boldfacing to them. The headings on all grouped sheets would be boldfaced.

5 You can apply a whole range of other formatting effects to multiple worksheets. For example, here the column headings of all worksheets have been right-aligned. (To do this, just select the headings in any one of the selected sheets and click the Align Right toolbar button.)

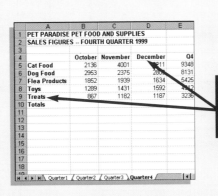

Even though boldfacing was applied in the Quarter1 worksheet, it affects all worksheets in the group.

How to Copy and Move Data between Worksheets

Chapter 7 explained a couple of ways of copying and moving data within a single worksheet. You discovered both how to drag and drop data and how to move and copy data via the Cut, Copy, and Paste commands. Here you'll learn how easy it is to move or copy data to another worksheet. As you'll find out, you can even copy formulas and have them calculate new results based on their new location.

TIP SHEET

▶ You can also drag and drop data between worksheets. To move data in this way, point to the border of the selected cells and hold down the Alt key while dragging over the desired worksheet tab. Once Excel activates that worksheet, continue dragging until you have the data in the right spot and then release the mouse button. To copy data, hold down both Ctrl and Alt while dragging.

▶ It's easy to copy and move data between workbooks, too. Just cut or copy the data as usual using the Cut or Copy command or toolbar button. Then activate the workbook to receive the data—either choose it from the Window menu or click on it if it's already visible. Finally, select the destination cell and click the Paste toolbar button or choose Paste from the Edit menu.

▶ To move data between workbooks by dragging, display both workbooks at once. (Open both workbooks; choose Arrange from the Window menu; choose Tiled, Vertical, or Horizontal; and then click OK.) Then drag the data from one workbook to the other. To copy the data, hold down the Ctrl key while you drag.

	January	February	March	Q1	Percent Total
5 Cat Food	2346	3112	2911	8369	30%
6 Dog Food	2199	2635	2783	7617	27%
7 Flea Products	1732	1863	1534	5129	18%
8 Toys	1184	1321	1429	3934	14%
9 Treats	972	842	1299	3113	11%
10 Totals	$8,433.00	$9,773.00	$9,956.00	$28,162.00	

Quarter1 / Quarter2 / Quarter3 / Quarter4

1 Select the data you want to move or copy to another worksheet.

	October	November	December	Q4	Percent Total
5 Cat Food	2136	4001	3211	9348	31%
6 Dog Food	2953	2375	2803	8131	27%
7 Flea Products	1852	1939	1634	5425	18%
8 Toys	1289	1431	1592	4312	14%
9 Treats	867	1182	1187	3236	11%
10 Totals	$9,097.00	$10,928.00	$10,427.00	$30,452.00	

Quarter1 / Quarter2 / Quarter3 / Quarter4

7 If you use the Copy and Paste toolbar buttons (or the Copy and Paste commands on the Edit menu), you can paste the same set of data repeatedly by going through steps 4 and 5 as often as you want. When you are finished, press Esc to remove the marquee from the source data. If you use the Cut command and/or you paste data with the Enter key, you only have one opportunity to paste in the data from the Clipboard.

6 If necessary, make any adjustments to the worksheet. For example, here you'll have to adjust column width because column widths aren't copied automatically.

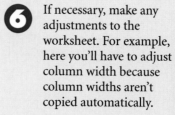
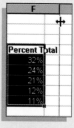

F
Percent Total
32%
24%
21%
12%
11%

2 If you want to move the data, click the Cut toolbar button. To instead copy the data, click the Copy toolbar button. (You can use the Cut and Copy commands on the Edit menu—or their Ctrl+X and Ctrl+C keyboard shortcuts—if that suits you better.)

3 A marquee will enclose the selected data, indicating that you can paste it elsewhere. (As an additional hint, the status bar reads "Select destination and press ENTER or choose Paste.")

Select destination and press ENTER or choose Paste

4 Click on the tab of the worksheet you want to move or copy data to.

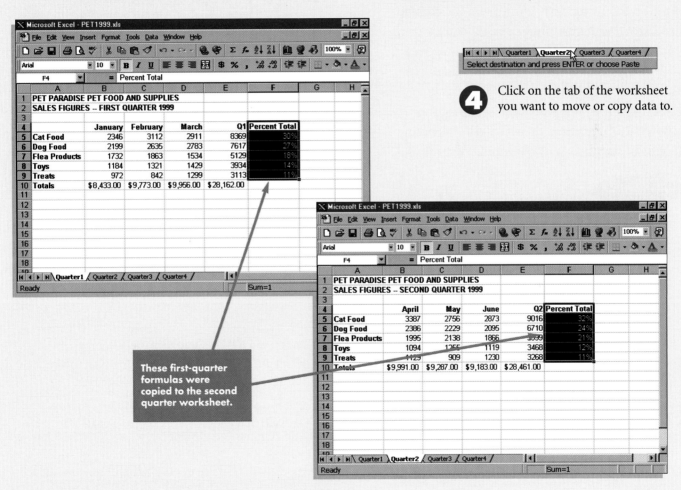

These first-quarter formulas were copied to the second quarter worksheet.

5 Click in the cell that you want to be the upper-left corner of the range of data you're inserting. Then press the Enter key to paste the cut or copied data into the new worksheet. In this case, a column of formulas was copied, so the formula results are updated to reflect the data in the Quarter2 worksheet.

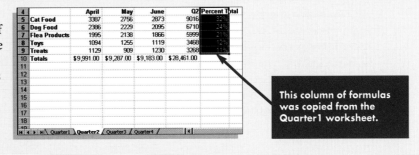

This column of formulas was copied from the Quarter1 worksheet.

How to Build Formulas That Refer to Other Worksheets

So far all the formulas you've created have referred only to cells or ranges in the current worksheet. But it's certainly possible (easy, in fact) to build formulas that refer to cells or ranges in other worksheets in the current workbook. You might want to do this, for example, to create a summary worksheet that adds up the figures from several other worksheets without repeating all of these numbers in the summary worksheet.

TIP SHEET

▶ Although the formula shown in steps 5 and 6 just refers to single cells on various worksheets, you can also use cell ranges from one or more worksheets in your formulas.

▶ You can create 3-D references, which refer to a cell or range in multiple worksheets within a single workbook. 3-D references consist of the first sheet name, a colon, the last sheet name, an exclamation point, and the cell or range reference. For example, the 3-D reference Sheet1:Sheet4!A1:C5 refers to the range A1:C5 on worksheets Sheet1 through Sheet4. A 3-D reference could simplify the example formula shown in steps 5 and 6 to =SUM(Quarter1: Quarter4!E5) and would save you from having to select each cell reference individually. To enter this formula, you would type =SUM, select the worksheets Quarter1 through Quarter4, click on cell E5, and press Enter.

▶ Excel even lets you create formulas that refer to data in other workbooks. (These are called linked formulas.) Basically, the procedure is much like building formulas that draw data from multiple worksheets, but instead you select cells or ranges from one or more other workbooks. For additional details, check your Excel documentation.

1 Activate the worksheet and the cell to contain the formula. Depending on the circumstances, you may also need to add descriptive data, such as worksheet titles and column and row headings. (If you need to add a new worksheet, check "How to Manage Worksheets" later in this chapter. To refresh your memory on how to activate worksheets for which tabs don't currently show up at the bottom of the screen, turn back to "How to Work with Worksheets" in Chapter 3.)

6 When you're done building the formula, press the Enter key or click the Enter button. Excel returns you to the worksheet in which you started the formula, displaying the formula results in the selected cell and the formula itself in the formula bar (when the cell containing it is selected), as shown here.

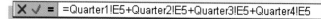

5 Repeat steps 3 and 4 as often as necessary to add more data—from the current worksheet or other worksheets—to your formula. As one example, the formula shown here adds together the values in E5 from the worksheets Quarter1, Quarter2, Quarter3, and Quarter4.

4 Type an operator. For example, to add the value in the current cell to the value in some other cell, type a plus sign (+).

Cat Food	=
Dog Food	
Flea Products	
Toys	
Treats	
Totals	

② Type an equal sign (=) to indicate to Excel that you intend to enter a formula.

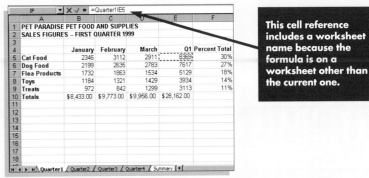

This cell reference includes a worksheet name because the formula is on a worksheet other than the current one.

③ Activate the worksheet that contains data to be used in the formula. Then click on the cell you want to include in the formula. The cell will acquire a marquee, and the formula in the formula bar will include the worksheet name followed by an exclamation point and the cell name. (If the worksheet name includes spaces, it will be enclosed within single quotes.)

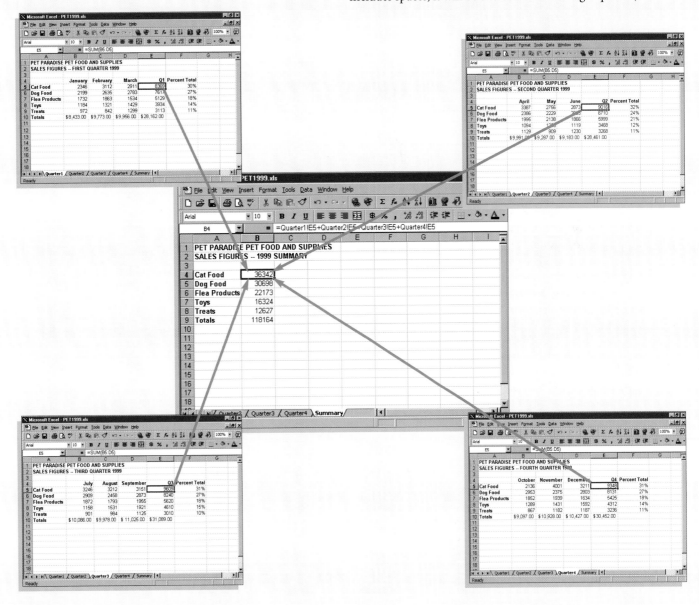

How to Link Data in Different Worksheets

W hen you build formulas that rely on data in other worksheets, you're creating a link between various worksheets. If the data referred to in the formula changes, the formula results change, even though they're on a different worksheet in the workbook. Excel also lets you use the Paste Special command to link data between worksheets. When you do this, the data in one worksheet is always updated to match the data in the original worksheet. This feature comes in particularly handy when you have values—such as fixed expenses—that you want to remain the same across several worksheets.

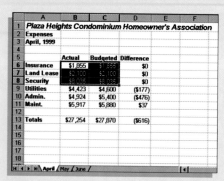

> **1** Select the cell or cells that include data you want to link to data in another worksheet. For example, here the actual and budgeted Insurance, Land Lease, and Security values should stay the same in all worksheets.

TIP SHEET

▶ **Issuing a Paste Special command and choosing the Paste Link button links the data you're pasting to the original worksheet. But the link doesn't work the other way around—that is, you can't modify the linked data and have those changes show up in the original worksheet.**

▶ **You can link data within the same worksheet, too. For example, in any of the worksheets shown here, you could link the actual and budgeted values for the fixed expenses, such as Insurance and Security. That way, each time the insurance went up, for example, the budgeted amount would increase correspondingly.**

7 If you want to link additional data, just follow the procedure outlined in steps 1 through 4. For example, in this case you'd want to link the data from the April worksheet to the June worksheet as well. If you hadn't done anything since the last Paste Special command, you could just move to the desired cell in the June worksheet and issue another Paste Special command.

6 If you want to verify that the data is linked, return to the original worksheet and change one of the linked values. Here, for example, if you changed the Actual Insurance value to $1,900 in the April worksheet, the Actual Insurance value in the May worksheet would change to match

2 Click the Copy toolbar button or choose Copy from the Edit menu. (It doesn't work to use the Cut command or toolbar button in this case.)

3 Click on the tab for the worksheet you want to link data to and then select the cell in which to place the data you copied. (Select the upper-left cell of the range if you're pasting in more than a single cell.)

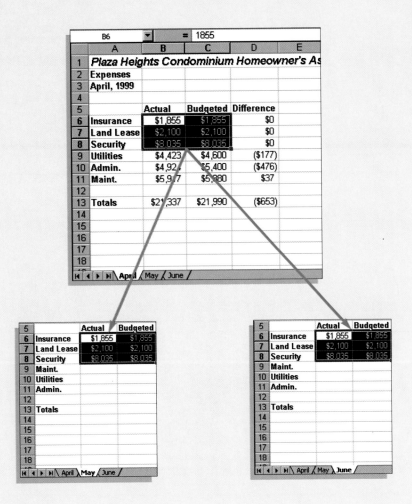

4 Choose Paste Special from the Edit menu. You'll see the Paste Special dialog box. Click the Paste Link button to paste data into the worksheet. The pasted-in data is linked to the data in the worksheet it was copied from. If the data in that original worksheet changes, the data in this worksheet will change correspondingly.

5 Activate one of the cells with linked data. Notice that the formula bar includes a formula containing both the worksheet and the cell to which data is linked.

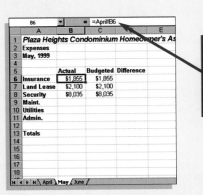

This formula tells you which worksheet (April) and cell (B6) this data is linked to

How to Manage Worksheets

What if you decide to rearrange your existing worksheets more logically to give them some semblance of order? Or what if you want to make a copy of a worksheet to use as the basis for a new worksheet? These and other tasks are easy once you master a few simple worksheet management skills, several of which are described on these pages.

TIP SHEET

▶ **You can use the dragging technique to move and copy worksheets within the current workbook, as described on these pages. In addition, you can move or copy worksheets within the current workbook or to another existing workbook by choosing the Move or Copy Sheet option from the Edit menu. In the Move or Copy dialog box, choose a workbook from the To Book drop-down list. (It displays a list of all open workbooks.) Then choose a sheet you want to place the worksheet in front of, click on the Create a Copy check box if you want to copy rather than move the worksheet, and, finally, click OK.**

▶ **By default, Excel creates workbooks that include three worksheets. If you regularly create workbooks that consist of more than that many worksheets, you can have Excel automatically create larger workbooks (with more worksheets). Choose Options from the Tools menu, click on the General tab, and enter a higher value in the Sheets in New Workbook box. (You can choose any number between 1 and 255 here.) Then click OK.**

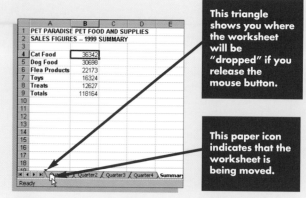

This triangle shows you where the worksheet will be "dropped" if you release the mouse button.

This paper icon indicates that the worksheet is being moved.

▶ **❶** To move a worksheet, activate it by clicking on its worksheet tab, and then drag the tab left or right to move the worksheet to the desired location. As you drag, the mouse pointer acquires an icon (it looks like a sheet of paper) indicating that the worksheet is being moved, and a triangle indicates where the worksheet will move to.

❼ Remember, you add new worksheets by choosing Worksheet from the Insert menu. You can also add several sheets at once by selecting the desired number of sheets before issuing the Worksheet command. (Don't choose Insert from the shortcut menu, or you'll be greeted with a dialog box offering a baffling range of choices. Here's where you choose templates—essentially prefab workbook designs—which you'll learn about in a few chapters.)

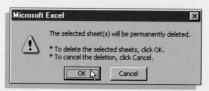

❻ When you delete one or more sheets, you'll see this warning message. Be absolutely certain you want to delete the worksheets since there's no way of retrieving them afterwards. Click OK to go ahead with the deletion.

2 When you release the mouse button, the sheet is "dropped" in its new spot. You can move several worksheets at once using this technique; just group them first, as described at the beginning of this chapter.

This paper icon with a plus sign indicates that the worksheet is being copied.

3 If you instead want to copy a worksheet, hold down the Ctrl key while dragging on its worksheet tab. As you drag, the mouse pointer acquires an icon (it looks like a sheet of paper with a plus sign in it) indicating that the worksheet is being copied, and as before, a triangle indicates where a copy of the worksheet will be deposited.

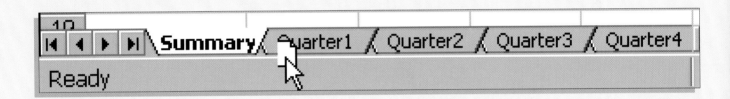

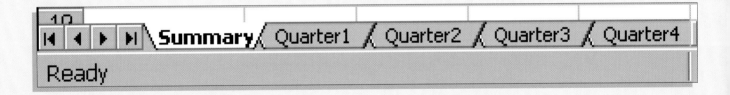

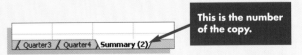

This is the number of the copy.

4 When you release the mouse button, a copy of the worksheet is dropped in the designated location. This copy has the name of the original worksheet, followed by the number of the copy within parentheses. If you like, you can copy several worksheets simply by grouping them before you Ctrl-drag.

5 You learned how to delete a worksheet in Chapter 3. (Remember, you just right-click on the sheet and choose Delete from the shortcut menu.) You can also delete several sheets at once by grouping the sheets before you issue the Delete command.

CHAPTER 16

More Advanced Functions

Both Chapters 2 and 9 explored the topics of functions. There are literally hundreds of other things you can do with functions in Excel, and this chapter touches on just a few of them. You'll learn how to round and truncate numbers with the ROUND and INT functions. You'll use the SUMIF function to sum numbers only if they meet specified conditions. You'll discover how to use the PMT function to calculate regular loan payments. You'll also find out how to use the IF function to make decisions—calculating one percentage raise for employees earning over $50,000 and another percentage for all other employees, for example. You'll see how to use the LOOKUP functions to look up values in a table of data. You could, for instance, look in an inventory price list for the price of an item for which you have the part number. Finally, you'll learn how to perform arithmetic with dates. For example, you find out how to subtract one date from another to determine the number of days between them.

What you learn in this chapter is clearly just the very tip of the proverbial iceberg. Don't feel obligated to memorize this information, and certainly don't feel you need to learn all of Excel's functions just because they're there. But if you're curious about functions, or there's some task you need to accomplish, investigate the functions described in your documentation or the help system. You might just discover a function that can lighten your workload.

How to Round and Truncate Numbers

Frequently when you perform calculations, the result is a batch of numbers with multiple digits after the decimal point. If necessary, you can widen columns so the numbers show up in full, or you can drop the display of one or more decimal places by fiddling with the number format. These strategies alter the way the numbers are displayed in the worksheet but don't actually change the way the numbers are stored in Excel. The entire number is still used in all calculations. If instead you want to eliminate part or all of a number's decimal portion, you can use the ROUND and INT functions described on these pages.

TIP SHEET

► Using a negative number to specify the number of decimal places in the ROUND function rounds the number to the left of the decimal place. For example, =ROUND(12345,–1) returns the result 12350, ROUND(12345,–2) returns 12300, and so on.

► Rounding doesn't necessarily determine how many digits are displayed to the right of the decimal point. It instead determines how many significant digits there are. For example, if you round the number 123.4567 to two decimal places, the number will become 123.46, yet this number may display as 123.4600 if you've selected a number format that shows four decimal places or as 123 if your number format shows no decimal places.

► You can increase or reduce the number of displayed decimal places by altering a number format via the Number tab of the Format Cells dialog box (see Chapter 8). But a quicker way to do this is to use the Decrease Decimal and Increase Decimal toolbar buttons. Click these buttons as often as you need to remove or add decimal places. But don't forget that this doesn't change the way the numbers are stored in Excel.

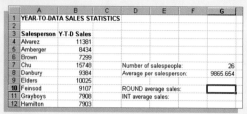

1 Click in the cell that will contain the rounded value and then click the Paste Function toolbar button to display the Paste Function dialog box. (If you prefer, you can type in the ROUND and INT functions, without using the Paste Function dialog box.)

8 Click OK to place the results in your worksheet. The INT function drops everything to the right of the decimal point, leaving just the integer portion of the number. In some cases—such as this one—you can get different results with INT than with ROUND.

This is the value as it will appear in your worksheet and *as it will be used in calculations*.

This is the number for which the decimal portion is being dropped.

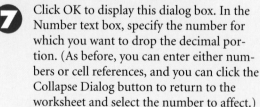

7 Click OK to display this dialog box. In the Number text box, specify the number for which you want to drop the decimal portion. (As before, you can enter either numbers or cell references, and you can click the Collapse Dialog button to return to the worksheet and select the number to affect.)

2 If you see the name of the function you need in the Function Name list box, click on it to select it. Otherwise, choose the appropriate category from the Function Category list. If you don't already see the ROUND function, choose Math & Trig and then choose ROUND from the Function Name list box.

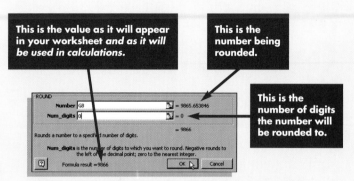

This is the value as it will appear in your worksheet *and as it will be used in calculations.*

This is the number being rounded.

This is the number of digits the number will be rounded to.

3 Click OK. In the resulting dialog box, enter the number to be rounded in the Number text box and enter the number of digits to round to in the Num_digits text box. (In both cases you can enter either numbers or cell references.) If you like, click the appropriate Collapse Dialog button to return to the worksheet and select the numbers in question.

COMPARING THE ROUND AND INT FUNCTIONS

Number	INT	Rounded to Three Decimals	Rounded to One Decimal	Rounded to No Decimals
12.3456	12	12.346	12.3	12
23.4567	23	23.457	23.5	23
34.56789	34	34.568	34.6	35
45.6789	45	45.679	45.7	46
56.78	56	56.78	56.8	57

Number of salespeople:	26
Average per salesperson:	9865.654
ROUND average sales:	9866
INT average sales:	

4 Click OK. Excel deposits the results into your worksheet. The ROUND function rounds a number to the specified number of digits. If you choose 0 digits, the number is rounded to the nearest integer, as shown here. If you chose 1 digit, you'd see one digit after the decimal place.

5 To use the INT function to display only the integer portion of a number, click in the cell to contain the value, and then click the Paste Function toolbar button.

6 If the INT function is not displayed in the list of most recently used functions, click on Math & Trig and then choose INT from the Function Name list box.

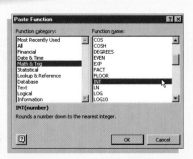

How to Sum Numbers Conditionally

In Chapter 2 you learned a number of ways of summing numbers. In all cases—whether you were typing formulas or using the AutoSum button to speed up the process—you were using Excel's SUM function. This function adds up all the values in the designated cells. If you instead want to add only numbers that meet specified criteria, you can use the SUMIF function, as outlined here.

TIP SHEET

▶ **If you don't specify a range of cells in the Sum_range text box, Excel assumes you want to sum the cells specified in the Range text box. For example, you could check which salaries are over $50,000 and total them all.**

▶ **In this example, you just entered a fixed value in the Criteria text box. But you can also use conditional operators, such as >700 or =<50000, to specify criteria, and you can also specify a text string such as "Johnson" (to find everyone named Johnson) or "M*" (to find everyone with a name that begins with the letter *m*).**

▶ **There's also a COUNTIF function. As you can probably guess, this function operates much like the COUNT function, which you learned about in Chapter 9, but it lets you count up the number of cells that contain values meeting the specified criteria. (For example, you could count how many of your employees earn under $40,000.) If this thought sparks your interest, you can look up the function through the Office Assistant or the Help Contents screen.**

	A	B	C	D	E	F
5					Projected	Projected
6	Last Name	First Name	Emp. #	1998 Base	% Increase	1999 Base
7	Eng	Stephanie	3	$51,935.50	4%	$54,012.92
8	Savage-Hill	Terry	6	$59,100.00	4%	$61,464.00
9	Martin	Samantha	9	$46,092.83	7%	$49,319.33
10	Bernard	James	8	$36,700.00	7%	$39,269.00
11	Blochner	Hobart	7	$53,082.48	4%	$55,205.78
12	Fuentes	Carla	1	$68,945.03	4%	$71,702.83
13	Lambert	Charles	5	$38,935.49	7%	$41,660.97
14	Rothstein	Jay	2	$42,412.43	7%	$45,381.30
15	Tashjian	Doris	4	$40,095.83	7%	$42,902.54
16						
17						
18				Sum of 4% raise salaries:		
19				Sum of 7% raise salaries:		
20						

1 Click in the cell that will contain the sum value and then click the Paste Function toolbar button.

=SUMIF(E7:E15,4%,F7:F15)

C	D	E	F
		Projected	Projected
Emp. #	1998 Base	% Increase	1999 Base
3	$51,935.50	4%	$54,012.92
6	$59,100.00	4%	$61,464.00
9	$46,092.83	7%	$49,319.33
8	$36,700.00	7%	$39,269.00
7	$53,082.48	4%	$55,205.78
1	$68,945.03	4%	$71,702.83
5	$38,935.49	7%	$41,660.97
2	$42,412.43	7%	$45,381.30
4	$40,095.83	7%	$42,902.54
	Sum of 4% raise salaries:	$242,385.53	
	Sum of 7% raise salaries:		

7 Click OK. The dialog box will close and you'll see your results—the sum of all projected salaries based on a percentage increase of 4 percent. Now you could easily generate another SUMIF function to total the projected salaries for those slated for 7 percent raises. Simply repeat steps 1 through 7 but specify 7% in the Criteria text box.

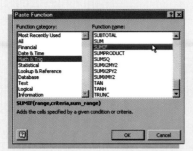

2 If you see the SUMIF function in the Function Name box, click on it. Otherwise, choose Math & Trig under Function Category and then choose the SUMIF function.

3 Click OK. In the dialog box that comes up, you need to specify which cells to evaluate (the Range text box), what criteria to use to evaluate those cells (the Criteria text box), and which range of cells to sum (the Sum_range text box).

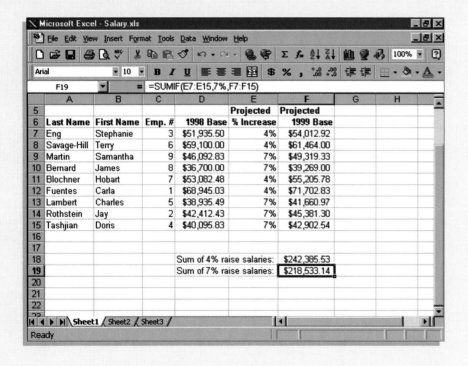

4 Click the Collapse Dialog button to the right of the Range text box. Drag across the range of cells you want to evaluate. (Here the cells containing the raise percentages are selected; these values will be evaluated to determine which projected 1999 salaries will be summed.) Then press Enter or click the Collapse Dialog button again.

6 Click the Collapse Dialog button to the right of the Sum_range text box. Drag across the range of cells you want to sum. (Here the cells containing the projected 1999 salaries are selected; these values will be summed if they are based on a projected percent increase of 4 percent.) Press Enter or click the Collapse Dialog button again.

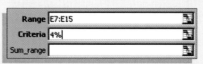

5 Next, enter the criteria in the Criteria text box. In this case, 4% tells Excel to consider only those earning a 4 percent raise.

How to Calculate a Loan Payment

Excel can speedily carry out a number of fairly simple calculations, such as summing a batch of numbers or calculating an average value. In addition, it can perform a wide range of financial functions. As just one example, you can use the PMT function to determine your monthly loan payments if you plug in values for the interest rate, the number of periods (total number of payments), and the present value of the loan (that is, the principal).

TIP SHEET

▶ **To calculate the total amount of interest paid over the life of the loan, you can simply subtract the amount of the loan from the total amount paid. (Since Total Paid is expressed as a negative number in this example, you can use the formula =B10+B6 to determine the total interest, expressed as a negative number.) If you do this, you'll notice that you pay almost twice as much interest with the longer-term loan!**

▶ **With the example worksheet shown on these pages, you could easily check the monthly mortgage payments for loans of different amounts and with different interest rates and terms just by plugging those values into the existing worksheet.**

▶ **If you know a loan's interest rate, the loan amount (present value), and the amount of the monthly payment, you can use the NPER function to determine how long it will take you to pay off the loan. (In other words, you know the amount of the monthly payments instead of the term of the loan, as with PMT.) See the Help system for more information on the NPER function.**

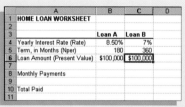

▶ **1** In your worksheet, enter the amount of the loan (the present value, or pv), the interest rate, and the term (length) of the loan (also called the number of periods, or nper). Here's a comparison between two $100,000 loans, one at 8.5 percent yearly interest for 15 years (180 months) and another at 7 percent yearly interest for 30 years.

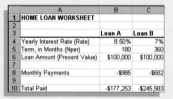

8 To determine how much you'll shell out over the life of the loan, you can multiply the monthly payment by the number of periods, or months, as shown here. Notice that while monthly payments are significantly lower for the longer-term loan, the total amount paid is much higher. In other words, the shorter-term loan is a better deal in the long run, in spite of the higher interest rate and higher payments.

7 In this example, you could drag the fill handle one cell to the right to duplicate the formula for Loan B. Notice that the monthly payments at the lower interest rate are significantly lower.

2 Select the cell to contain the monthly payment amount and click the Paste Function Wizard toolbar button. Choose Financial under Function Category, select the PMT function under Function Name, and click OK.

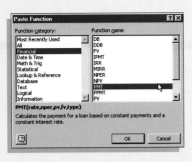

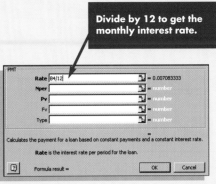

Divide by 12 to get the monthly interest rate.

3 In the Rate text box, enter the rate **8.5%** (or use the Collapse Dialog button and select the worksheet cell containing that rate) and then type **/12**. You must divide this yearly rate by 12 to get a monthly interest rate that corresponds to the monthly loan term. (Using months lets you determine the monthly, not yearly, mortgage payments.)

4 In the Nper (number of periods) text box, enter the number of periods—that is, the term, or length of the loan. (Again, you want this in months.) You can also use the Collapse Dialog button and select the worksheet cell containing the number of periods.

HOME LOAN WORKSHEET

	Loan A	Loan B
Yearly Interest Rate (Rate)	8.5%	7%
Term, in Months (Nper)	180	360
Loan Amount (Present Value)	$100,000	$100,000
Monthly Payments	-$985	-$682
Total Paid	-$177,253	-$245,583

Once you plug in all the needed values, the results (the mortgage payment) show up here.

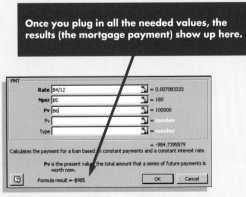

6 Click OK. You'll see the monthly mortgage payments in your worksheet. Note that they're displayed as negative numbers since they're considered an outlay.

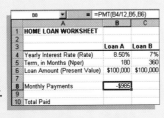

5 In the Pv (present value, or loan amount) text box, enter the present value of the loan or select the worksheet cell containing the loan amount. (Fv and Type are optional arguments that you don't need to worry about in this case.)

How to Make Decisions with the IF Function

Frequently you'll want to do one thing in one situation and another thing in another situation. If so, the IF function could be just what you need. IF lets you evaluate a specified condition, performing one action if the condition is true and another if the condition is false. For example, you could use this function to calculate one commission rate for employees with sales of over $10,000 and another rate for those with sales of $10,000 and under. As you'll see, the IF function includes three arguments: the condition to be evaluated, the value to return if the condition is true, and the value to return if the condition is false.

TIP SHEET

▶ When setting up an IF function, you can also use text values for the second and third arguments. For example, you could have Excel display the text "OVER BUDGET" if the value in a field went over a specified amount or "UNDER BUDGET" if the value didn't exceed that amount. When you do this, you have to include the arguments within double quotation marks.

▶ If you leave the Value_if_false text box blank, Excel doesn't return a value if the condition evaluates to false, but instead displays the word *FALSE*.

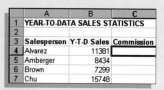

	A	B	C
1	YEAR-TO-DATA SALES STATISTICS		
2			
3	Salesperson	Y-T-D Sales	Commission
4	Alvarez	11381	
5	Amberger	8434	
6	Brown	7299	
7	Chu	15748	

 1 Select the cell in which you want to place the function results.

C29 = =IF(B29>10000,B29*0.06,B29*0.05)

	A	B	C	D	E
20	O'Ryan	9356	467.80		
21	Prasher	8215	410.75		
22	Quinonez	7556	377.80		
23	Ramirez	10264	615.84		
24	Sabella	12359	741.54		
25	Thompson	9991	499.55		
26	Urbaniak	7652	382.60		
27	Vargas	9182	459.10		
28	Williams	13247	794.82		
29	Zadeh	4628	231.40		

 7 If you want to copy the function, you can do so using any of the techniques you're already familiar with. Here, you could calculate commissions for all other employees simply by dragging on the fill handle to duplicate the function you created in steps 2 through 6.

C4 = =IF(B4>10000,B4*0.06,B4*0.05)

	A	B	C	D	E
1	YEAR-TO-DATA SALES STATISTICS				
2					
3	Salesperson	Y-T-D Sales	Commission		
4	Alvarez	11381	682.86		
5	Amberger	8434			

 6 Click OK. Excel places your function into the worksheet, displaying its results in the selected cell.

2 Select the cell to contain the monthly payment amount and click the Paste Function Wizard toolbar button. Choose Financial under Function Category, select the PMT function under Function Name, and click OK.

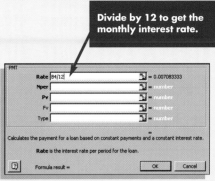

Divide by 12 to get the monthly interest rate.

3 In the Rate text box, enter the rate **8.5%** (or use the Collapse Dialog button and select the worksheet cell containing that rate) and then type **/12**. You must divide this yearly rate by 12 to get a monthly interest rate that corresponds to the monthly loan term. (Using months lets you determine the monthly, not yearly, mortgage payments.)

HOME LOAN WORKSHEET

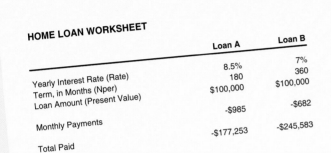

	Loan A	Loan B
Yearly Interest Rate (Rate)	8.5%	7%
Term, in Months (Nper)	180	360
Loan Amount (Present Value)	$100,000	$100,000
Monthly Payments	-$985	-$682
Total Paid	-$177,253	-$245,583

4 In the Nper (number of periods) text box, enter the number of periods—that is, the term, or length of the loan. (Again, you want this in months.) You can also use the Collapse Dialog button and select the worksheet cell containing the number of periods.

Once you plug in all the needed values, the results (the mortgage payment) show up here.

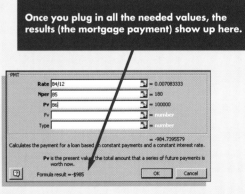

5 In the Pv (present value, or loan amount) text box, enter the present value of the loan or select the worksheet cell containing the loan amount. (Fv and Type are optional arguments that you don't need to worry about in this case.)

6 Click OK. You'll see the monthly mortgage payments in your worksheet. Note that they're displayed as negative numbers since they're considered an outlay.

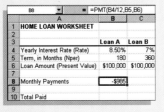

How to Make Decisions with the IF Function

F requently you'll want to do one thing in one situation and another thing in another situation. If so, the IF function could be just what you need. IF lets you evaluate a specified condition, performing one action if the condition is true and another if the condition is false. For example, you could use this function to calculate one commission rate for employees with sales of over $10,000 and another rate for those with sales of $10,000 and under. As you'll see, the IF function includes three arguments: the condition to be evaluated, the value to return if the condition is true, and the value to return if the condition is false.

TIP SHEET

▶ When setting up an IF function, you can also use text values for the second and third arguments. For example, you could have Excel display the text "OVER BUDGET" if the value in a field went over a specified amount or "UNDER BUDGET" if the value didn't exceed that amount. When you do this, you have to include the arguments within double quotation marks.

▶ If you leave the Value_if_false text box blank, Excel doesn't return a value if the condition evaluates to false, but instead displays the word *FALSE*.

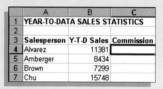

	A	B	C
1	YEAR-TO-DATA SALES STATISTICS		
2			
3	Salesperson	Y-T-D Sales	Commission
4	Alvarez	11381	
5	Amberger	8434	
6	Brown	7299	
7	Chu	15748	

▶ **1** Select the cell in which you want to place the function results.

C29 = =IF(B29>10000,B29*0.06,B29*0.05)

	A	B	C	D	E
20	O'Ryan	9356	467.80		
21	Prasher	8215	410.75		
22	Quinonez	7556	377.80		
23	Ramirez	10264	615.84		
24	Sabella	12359	741.54		
25	Thompson	9991	499.55		
26	Urbaniak	7652	382.60		
27	Vargas	9182	459.10		
28	Williams	13247	794.82		
29	Zadeh	4628	231.40		

7 If you want to copy the function, you can do so using any of the techniques you're already familiar with. Here, you could calculate commissions for all other employees simply by dragging on the fill handle to duplicate the function you created in steps 2 through 6.

C4 = =IF(B4>10000,B4*0.06,B4*0.05)

	A	B	C	D	E
1	YEAR-TO-DATA SALES STATISTICS				
2					
3	Salesperson	Y-T-D Sales	Commission		
4	Alvarez	11381	682.86		
5	Amberger	8434			

6 Click OK. Excel places your function into the worksheet, displaying its results in the selected cell.

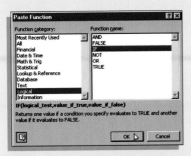

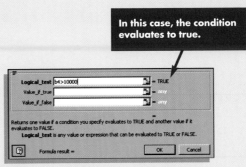

In this case, the condition evaluates to true.

2 Click the Paste Function toolbar button, choose Logical under Function Category, choose IF under Function Name, and click OK.

3 In the dialog box that appears, enter a condition in the Logical_test text box. For example, if you wanted to give one commission to salespeople with over $10,000 in sales and another to those with $10,000 or under, you could enter the condition **b4>10000** in this text box, assuming cell B4 contains the sales amount.

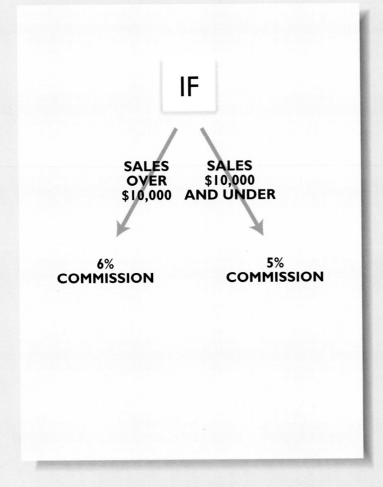

This is the commission for the selected cell if the condition evaluates to true.

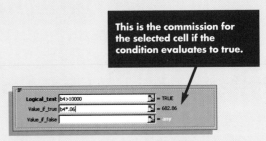

4 In the Value_if_true text box, enter a value to be returned if the condition being evaluated turns out to be true. For example, if you wanted to give a 6 percent commission to those who brought in over $10,000, you could enter **b4*.06** in this text box, again assuming cell B4 contains the relevant sales amount.

Because the condition is true for the selected cell, the formula result will be the Value_if_true value.

This is the commission for the selected cell if the condition evaluates to false.

5 In the Value_if_false text box, enter a value to be returned if the condition being evaluated turns out to be false. For example, if you wanted to give a 5 percent commission to those who brought in $10,000 or under, you could enter **b4*.05** in this text box. (Again, this assumes B4 contains the relevant sales amount.)

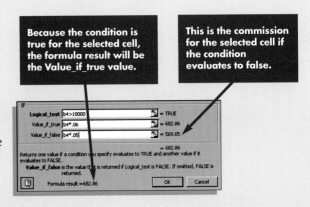

How to Use LOOKUP Functions

Excel's VLOOKUP and HLOOKUP functions let you look up specific values in *lookup tables* of data. For example, you could look up prices in an inventory price list or tax rates in a tax table. VLOOKUP looks for a value in the leftmost column of your table, returning a value from a specified column in the same row. (It might find your income level in the leftmost column and hunt down your associated tax rate in another column in the table.) HLOOKUP looks for a value in the top row of your table, returning a value from a specified row of the same column.

TIP SHEET

- ▶ LOOKUP functions can also refer to tables in other workbooks.

- ▶ Excel can pick the nearest value as opposed to a matching value. For example, when assigning bonuses based on salaries, you'd want to list the bonus associated with a *range* of salaries. Here's what you'd do: Sort the values in the leftmost column in ascending order. Enter true in the Range_lookup text box. Suppose the leftmost column lists salaries of $25,000, $30,000, and so on, and a bonus of $4,000 is associated with salaries of $25,000 and a bonus of $3,500 is associated with salaries of $30,000. If you look up the bonus for $27,350, Excel determines that this salary is less than $30,000 and looks down to find the next applicable bonus, which turns out to be the $4,000 bonus associated with $25,000. (If you're feeling befuddled, read up on the HLOOKUP and VLOOKUP functions in the online help system.)

 1 Your first task is to create a lookup table containing the data you want to be able to look up. This table includes item numbers and corresponding descriptions and prices for film at a photography supply store. Because the values you'll be looking up—the item numbers—fall in the leftmost column of the table, you'll be using the VLOOKUP function.

8 Choose OK. Excel places the function results in your worksheet. As you can see, it had no trouble finding the correct price for the designated film. (Although the LOOKUP function in this example lives on the same worksheet as the data table, you could just as easily place your function on a different worksheet.)

 7 In the Range_lookup text box, enter **false** to have Excel search for exact matches only. (The Tip Sheet explains what happens if you enter **true** instead. It also describes how to search for a range of values—someone's tax bracket, for instance—rather than matching one specific value.)

7	G-962	Ilford HP5 -- 120	$3.23
8	H-443	Ilford HP5 -- 35mm, 24	$4.78
9	I-321	Ilford HP5 -- 35mm, 36	$5.75
10			
11			
12		Item Number:	E-223
13		Price:	

2 Now you can construct a lookup function that uses the table to track down values. For example, you can look up the price for a given type of film based on its item number. Start by selecting the cell to contain the formula and clicking the Paste Function toolbar button.

3 In the Paste Function dialog box, choose Lookup & Reference under Function Category, choose VLOOKUP under Function Name, and then click OK.

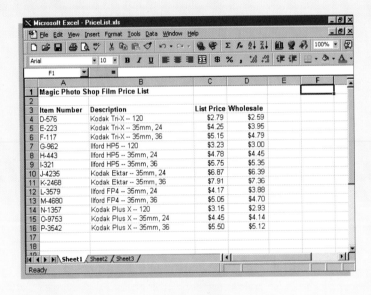

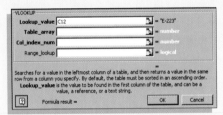

4 In the Lookup_value text box, specify the value you want Excel to look up in the leftmost column of your table. Here you want to find the item number for a particular type of film. (As usual, you can type in the value or you can click the Collapse Dialog button and select it from the worksheet.)

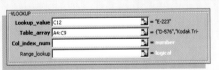

5 In the Table_array text box, enter the range containing the lookup table. In this case, it's A4:C9—the item numbers, descriptions, and prices. (Note that you don't include the column headings.)

6 In the Col_index_num text box, enter the number of the column Excel should look in to find a value to return. Here you want to look for prices in column 3. If you specified column 2 instead, Excel would return a description of the film for which you entered the item number in the Lookup_value text box. If your table included a fourth column with wholesale as opposed to list prices, as in the center of these pages, you could look up wholesale prices by entering 4.

How to Do Arithmetic with Dates

Y ou can enter dates into Excel in a variety of formats. In addition, Excel lets you perform various operations with dates. You can change date formats (use the Number tab of the Format Cells dialog box) and sort dates into ascending or descending order. You can also perform arithmetic involving dates. For example, you can add a specified number of days to a date to determine a future date. Or you can subtract one date from another to determine the number of days in between the two.

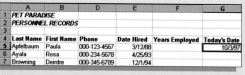

1 To determine how long employees have worked for the company, you need to subtract their dates of hire from today's date. If the worksheet already includes the dates of hire, you can add today's date, as shown here. (A handy shortcut for entering today's date is the Ctrl+; key combination.)

TIP SHEET

▸ **To change the way dates are displayed in your worksheet, select the cells in question and choose Cells from the Format menu. From the Number tab, you can select Date under Category and choose from a wide range of date formats under Type. This doesn't change the way the date is stored in Excel; it just changes the way the date is displayed within the worksheet.**

▸ **In addition to performing date arithmetic, you can use date functions that Excel provides. For the details, look up "date functions" in the Index tab of the Help Topics dialog box.**

▸ **The example on these pages shows how to subtract one date from another. You can also add a number to a date to determine a future date. For instance, you could add 30 to today's date to find out the date 30 days from today. This type of date arithmetic is invaluable for determining whether bills are past due, as just one example.**

▸ **To enter a date directly into a formula—as opposed to entering a reference for a cell containing a date—enclose the date within double quotes.**

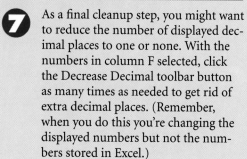

7 As a final cleanup step, you might want to reduce the number of displayed decimal places to one or none. With the numbers in column F selected, click the Decrease Decimal toolbar button as many times as needed to get rid of extra decimal places. (Remember, when you do this you're changing the displayed numbers but not the numbers stored in Excel.)

Date Hired	Years Employed	Today's Date
3/12/88		10/3/97
4/25/93		

2 Activate the cell that will show how long the employee has been with the company.

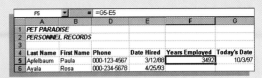

3 Subtract the date hired from the current date. In this example, you could first try the formula =G5–E5. Notice the results! They're so high because the formula calculates the number of days (not years) of employment.

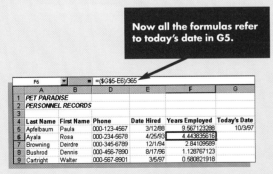

AUGUST calendar

4 Divide the results by 365 to get a yearly figure. In this case, the formula would be =(G5-E5)/365. Now you can see that the first Pet Paradise employee has been with the company for nine plus years.

Cell G6 is a blank cell!

These results are off because the reference to today's date was not an absolute reference.

Now all the formulas refer to today's date in G5.

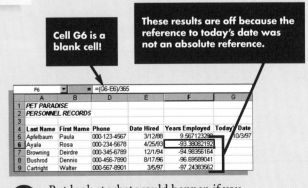

6 If you change the formula to =(G5–E5)/365 and copy it down column F, you get the correct results, as shown here. Having today's date in a single cell like this is handy because it allows you to recalculate all formulas at once just by changing the value in that cell.

5 But look at what would happen if you copied the formula down column F. Can you figure out what went wrong? Since today's date is housed in a single cell (G5), the reference to that cell must be absolute so it doesn't change when copied. As is, the reference to G5 changed to G6, G7, and so on—and these are all blank cells!

CHAPTER 17

Automating Your Work with Macros and Templates

You'll undoubtedly find yourself doing the same things over and over in Excel. You'll repeatedly type the same sets of column and row headings, frequently issue identical command sequences, and regularly apply similar formatting combinations. Fortunately, Excel provides shortcuts for speeding up these kinds of repetitive chores, as you'll discover here.

First you'll learn how to take advantage of macros. A *macro* is a series of automated steps that you can play back all at once, kind of like speed dialing on a telephone: When speed dialing, you press a single button to dial the entire telephone number automatically. Similarly, when running a macro, you issue a single command and Excel "plays back" the entire sequence of actions.

Working with macros is a two-step process: You "record" the macro, carrying out the steps you want Excel to perform automatically. Then you can run the macro, having Excel repeat all the steps automatically so you don't have to carry them out one by one.

This chapter also discusses templates. *Templates* are like blueprints that you can use as the basis for similar workbooks. For example, if you regularly build workbooks with four sheets of quarterly sales information, the same column and row headings, similar titles, identical formulas, and so on, you can create a template that includes all of this common information. Then you can base workbooks on this template—adding specific sales information as needed—instead of repeatedly having to enter the entire workbook from scratch.

How to Record Macros

As mentioned, you can create macros to streamline your work when you repeatedly carry out the same sequence of steps. The easiest way to create a macro is to record it—literally telling Excel to make a record of your actions and then carrying out the steps you want the macro to perform automatically. Before you record a macro, it's smart to plan ahead, even running through the sequence of steps once or twice before you actually record it. Otherwise, there's a good chance you'll record some mistakes, and there's no quick and easy way to fix them, short of rerecording the macro under the same name.

TIP SHEET

▶ Shortcut keys you assign to macros override any existing Excel shortcut keys when the workbook containing the macro is open. For example, if you give your macro the shortcut key Ctrl+P, you won't be able to use Ctrl+P for printing if the workbook that includes your macro is open. For this reason, it's a good idea to use Ctrl+Shift shortcut keys where possible; they're less likely to conflict with existing shortcuts.

▶ You can't use the Undo command to reverse the effects of macros. In other words, run macros with care. If you're feeling extra cautious or if you're trying a new macro for the first time, save your workbook before running the macro. That way you can revert to the previous version of the workbook (by closing without saving and then reopening) if the macro runs amuck.

▶ If you select the Personal Macro Workbook option, it remains selected until you choose one of the other available options. For this reason, it's a good idea to get back into the Record New Macro dialog box and select This Workbook unless you want to record all subsequent macros in the Personal Macro Workbook.

▶ **1** Open the workbook in which you want to record the macro. Choose the worksheet to be affected, and, if applicable, select a range to operate on.

8 Perform the series of actions you want to record. When you're done recording, click the Stop Recording button or choose Macro from the Tools menu and then choose Stop Recording.

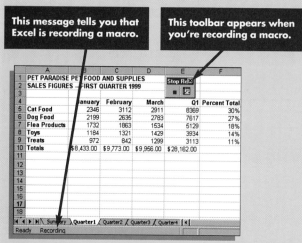

This message tells you that Excel is recording a macro.

This toolbar appears when you're recording a macro.

7 Click OK to start recording the macro. You'll return to the worksheet and see the "Recording" indicator on the left side of the status bar, as well as a mini-toolbar that includes a Stop Recording button on the left. (If you've lost your toolbar, choose View, Toolbars, Stop Recording to bring it back into view.) At this point, all actions you take—even mistakes—are included in the macro. (That's why it's good to figure out ahead of time exactly what you want to do.)

2 Choose Macro from the Tools menu and choose Record New Macro from the submenu that appears.

3 Type a name for your macro in the Macro Name box. (Although Excel suggests a name such as Macro1 or Macro2, it's better to enter a descriptive name that will help you remember the purpose of the macro.) Names can be up to 62 characters; must begin with a letter; and can include letters, numbers, and the underscore.

1. Choose Page Setup from the File menu.

2. Click on the Page tab.

3. Choose Landscape orientation.

4. Click on the Margins tab.

5. Select Horizontally and Vertically under Center on Page.

6. Click on the Header/Footer tab.

7. Select the header that lists the Workbook name.

8. Select the footer that lists your name, the page number, and today's date.

9. Click OK.

4 To create a macro you can run quickly with a shortcut key that consists of Ctrl plus a letter, enter a letter in the Shortcut Key text box. (You can also hold down Shift while typing a letter to create a keyboard shortcut that you issue by pressing Ctrl+Shift plus a letter.) Check the Tip Sheet for an important caution on this one.

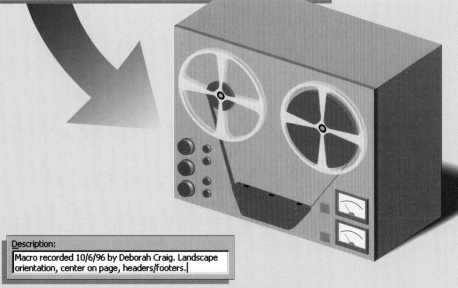

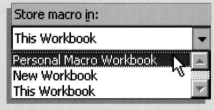

5 By default, macros are stored in, and available in, the current workbook only. To record a macro that's available in all workbooks instead of just the current one, choose Personal Macro Workbook from the Store Macro In drop-down list. (The Personal Macro Workbook is a special, hidden workbook; the macros stored here are always available.) Another option is to store the macro in a new workbook.

Description:
Macro recorded 10/6/96 by Deborah Craig. Landscape orientation, center on page, headers/footers.

6 If you want, enter a description of your macro in the Description text box. (Excel automatically enters a brief description that most likely lists your name and the date.) This description shows up again when you choose a macro to run, as explained on the next set of pages.

How to Run Macros

Once you've recorded a macro, it's an easy matter to run it, playing back the entire sequence of actions with a single command or keystroke. You can run any macro you've recorded, provided that the workbook it's stored in is open. There are actually two ways to run macros: You can run any macro by using the Macro command on the Tools menu. In addition, if you assigned the macro a shortcut key, you just need to press that keystroke combination to carry out all the commands stored in the macro.

TIP SHEET

▶ **To assign a shortcut key to a macro after you've recorded it, choose Tools, Macro, Macros, select the macro in question, choose the Options button, and choose a shortcut key as described on the preceding pages. (You can also add or modify a description from here.)**

▶ **Editing macros is a fairly complex process that involves knowing something about the programming language macros are written in. (Macros are essentially little computer programs.) If you accidentally click the Edit or Step Into button in the Macros dialog box, you may be confronted with a screenful of incomprehensible computer code. Don't panic. Instead just take a deep breath and click the Close button in the upper-right corner of the screen to go back where you came from.**

▶ **You can't delete macros stored in the Personal Macro Workbook by selecting their names in the Macro dialog box and clicking the Delete button. Instead you have to "unhide" the Personal workbook these macros are stored in by choosing Unhide from the Window menu, choosing the Personal workbook, and clicking OK. Then you can delete the macro in the normal fashion, after which you should rehide the Personal workbook by choosing Hide from the Window menu.**

▶ **1** If necessary, open the workbook you want to affect, activate the desired worksheet, and select any cells you want to operate on.

6 To delete a macro you no longer use, choose Tools, Macro, Macros, click on the name of the macro you want to delete, and click the Delete button. Click on Yes when asked to confirm the deletion.

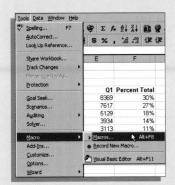

2 Choose Tools, Macro, Macros.

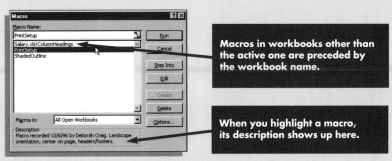

Macros in workbooks other than the active one are preceded by the workbook name.

When you highlight a macro, its description shows up here.

3 You'll see the Macro dialog box, which by default lists the macros in all open workbooks. (You can make another selection from the Macros In drop-down list to view macros from any one of the open workbooks.) The Personal Macro Workbook is always open, so its macros are always available when you're working in Excel. Click on the name of the macro you want to run; its description appears at the bottom of the dialog box.

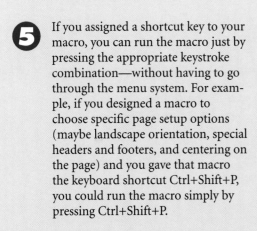

1. Choose Page Setup from the File menu.

2. Click on the Page tab.

3. Choose Landscape orientation.

4. Click on the Margins tab.

5. Select Horizontally and Vertically under Center on Page.

6. Click on the Header/Footer tab.

7. Select the header that lists the Workbook name.

8. Select the footer that lists your name, the page number, and today's date.

9. Click OK.

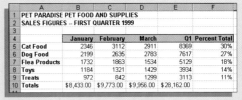

4 Click the Run button to run your macro. (You can also double-click on a macro name to run the macro.) All the actions stored in the macro will be carried out automatically. For example, if the macro is designed to place a shaded outline around the selected cells, it does so, as shown here.

5 If you assigned a shortcut key to your macro, you can run the macro just by pressing the appropriate keystroke combination—without having to go through the menu system. For example, if you designed a macro to choose specific page setup options (maybe landscape orientation, special headers and footers, and centering on the page) and you gave that macro the keyboard shortcut Ctrl+Shift+P, you could run the macro simply by pressing Ctrl+Shift+P.

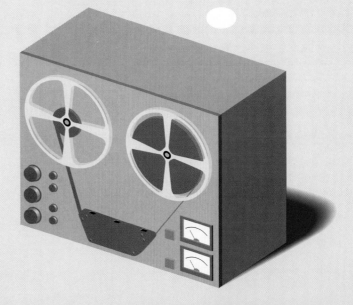

How to Set Up a Template

When you frequently construct workbooks that have a similar look and layout, you can create a template to speed up your work. Templates are special files that contain all the information—including text, formatting, page layout instructions, formulas, macros, and graphics—that doesn't change from one workbook to the next. You can use the template as a starting point for a workbook instead of having to build it from the ground up. Here you learn how to build templates, and on the next set of pages you learn how to use them as the basis for new workbooks.

TIP SHEET

▶ It's perfectly possible to use existing workbooks as the basis for templates. Just open the workbook, delete any specific data that won't be the same from workbook to workbook, keep any generic information that won't change, and save the revised file as a template, as described in steps 2 through 7 on these pages.

▶ You can also create templates that Excel uses by default when you create new workbooks, worksheets, and so on. For example, if you create a default workbook template, Excel automatically opens a copy of it each time you create a new workbook file by clicking the New toolbar button or pressing Ctrl+N. To create such a template, construct the file that will serve as the default workbook, choose Save As from the File menu, enter Book as the file name, choose Template from the Save as Type drop-down list, choose the Xlstart folder from the Save In list (it should be a subfolder of the Program Files\Microsoft Office\Office folder), and click the Save button.

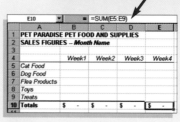

This template will include formulas, even though it won't include specific data.

① First build a workbook that contains the worksheets, text (including titles, row headings, and column headings), formulas, formatting, and so forth that you want to include in all workbooks based on the template. Make sure the template does not include information—such as sales data—that will be specific to particular workbooks.

⑦ Choose Close from the File menu to close the template file and protect it from further changes.

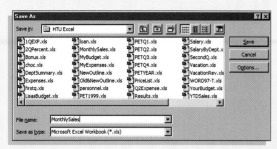

2 Choose Save As from the File menu. In the File Name text box of the Save As dialog box, type a name for the template. (See Chapter 3 if you need to remind yourself how the Save feature works.)

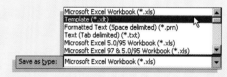

3 Choose Template from the Save As Type list box.

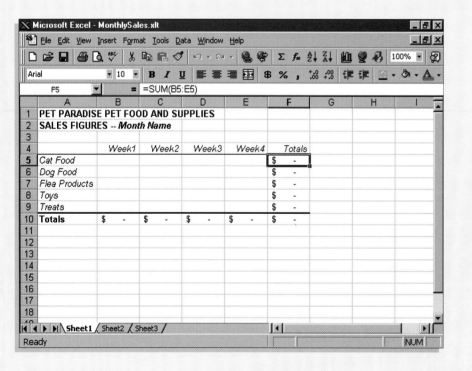

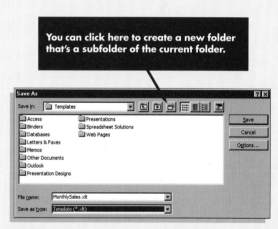

> You can click here to create a new folder that's a subfolder of the current folder.

4 Excel suggests using the Templates folder in the Save In box. (If you like, you can also save the template in one of the existing subfolders of the Template folder, or you can create a subfolder of your own by clicking the Create New Folder button.)

6 Double-check the template carefully for accuracy. If you find any mistakes, correct them and click the Save toolbar button or choose Save from the File menu.

5 Click the Save button. (On the off chance that a Properties dialog box appears, you can either fill it out or skip this step and just click OK.)

How to Use a Template

Once you've constructed a template, it's easy to build workbooks based on it. Although you could theoretically use regular workbook files as the basis for new workbooks, you'd run the risk of overwriting the originals. But when you base a workbook on a template, Excel creates a copy of the file, leaving the original safely intact for the next time you want to create a workbook based on it.

TIP SHEET

▶ **If you want to modify the original template rather than just create a new workbook based upon it, here's what you do: Choose Open from the File menu, choose the folder containing the template, and open the template to be modified. Then make the desired changes and click the Save toolbar button or choose File, Save. Now all new workbooks you base on the modified template will reflect these changes.**

▶ **These pages describe how to use regular templates stored in the Templates folder or its subfolders. If you or someone else has set up default templates in Excel, you don't have to do anything special to use them. Just clicking the New toolbar button opens a copy of the default workbook template. (You can also choose New from the File menu and choose Workbook from the General tab of the New dialog box.) To open a copy of a default worksheet template, simply choose Worksheet from the Insert menu.**

▶ **Excel provides a few ready-made templates. They're in the Spreadsheet Solutions tab of the New dialog box, in case you want to test them out.**

▶ **To delete a template, right-click on its name in the New dialog box and choose Delete from the shortcut menu that appears. (You can't delete the default workbook template this way, however.)**

1 Choose New from the File menu. (Despite what it says on the File menu, you can't use the New toolbar button or the Ctrl+N keyboard shortcut in this case. Both of these commands open a new, default workbook automatically, without giving you any say as to which template you use.)

6 When you're done making changes to the workbook, click the Save toolbar button or choose Save from the File menu, and then save the file using either the name Excel assigned to it or some other name that suits it better.

2 In the New dialog box, display the General tab if you stored your template in the Templates folder. Otherwise, click on the tab representing the sub-folder you stored the template in. (For example, click on the Spreadsheet Solutions tab if you stored your template in that subfolder of the Template folder. By the way, folders show up here only if they contain Excel templates.)

3 Click on your template and then click OK. (You can also just double-click on the template you want to use.)

The workbook name consists of the template name plus a number.

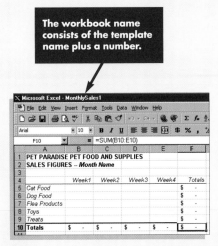

4 Excel creates a workbook based on the template, as shown here. Notice that the workbook name is a variation on the template name. (It's the name of the template plus a number that's incremented each time you open a new workbook file based on the template.) This is so you won't overwrite the original template when you save.

PET PARADISE PET FOOD AND SUPPLIES			
SALES FIGURES -- *Month Name*			
	Week1	Week2	Week3
Cat Food			
Dog Food			
Flea Products			
Toys			
Treats			
Totals	$ -	$ -	$ -

PET PARADISE PET FOOD AND SUPPLIES					
SALES FIGURES -- January					
	Week1	Week2	Week3	Week4	Totals
Cat Food	542	579	448	625	$ 2,194.00
Dog Food	473	499	475	598	$ 2,045.00
Flea Products	301	295	324	406	$ 1,326.00
Toys	326	294	382	223	$ 1,225.00
Treats	205	274	231	327	$ 1,037.00
Totals	$ 1,847	$ 1,941	$ 1,860	$ 2,179	$ 7,827.00

5 Now you can enter data into your workbook and make any changes you like. (Here, for example, you'd not only enter the monthly data but substitute the actual month name for the *Month Name* placeholder.)

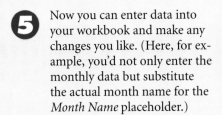

CHAPTER 18

Excel and the Internet

 The Internet (aka "the Net") is a worldwide collection of computer networks, connected so they can communicate. The Internet lets literally millions of people around the globe share information and carry on electronic conversations.

A crucial piece of the Internet is the World Wide Web—"the Web" for short. The Web lets you navigate the Internet using an intuitive graphical interface. (Web documents are often called *Web sites*; because the Web uses a protocol called HTTP to transfer documents, Web site addresses begin with the letters *http*.) If you're shaky about what the Internet or the Web is, or if you just want to soak up some Internet basics, read a good beginning book on the Internet. *How to Use the Internet* by Heidi Steele (Ziff-Davis Press, 1996) is an excellent place to start.

What do Excel and the Internet have in common? More and more applications—Excel among them—are tapping the Internet's potential. Excel now includes a number of features that let you use the Internet. Among other things, you can insert hyperlinks into your workbooks that let you quickly hop to other files on your system, on your network or company intranet, and even on the Internet. (An *intranet* is a private network that supports the HTTP protocol.) In addition, you can use Excel to build a Web page—a special type of electronic document you can make available to others via the Web—that includes data from your workbooks. And you can view files not just on your local hard drive or your network drive, but also on the Internet.

To use Excel's Internet-related features, you need an Internet connection and a Web browser such as Netscape Navigator or Internet Explorer. To create a Web page in Excel, you also need to have installed the Office 97 Web page authoring tools.

How to Insert Hyperlinks

Excel now lets you insert hyperlinks into your workbooks. *Hyperlinks* are simply elements, whether text or graphics, you can click on to jump to other documents. The documents you're jumping to (the *destination files)* can be Excel workbooks, word processing documents, graphics, and even Web pages. These files can live on your system, on your network, or on the Internet. Hyperlinks let you quickly open files without having to remember what their names are or where they're located.

TIP SHEET

► **You can follow the steps here to transform a graphic into a hyperlink.**

► **A URL, or Uniform Resource Locator, is an address for a location on the Internet. URLs typically begin with http://, but they can begin with ftp:// and other mysterious sets of characters. *http* stands for Web or intranet sites. *ftp* stands for FTP sites, either on your own network or on the Internet; FTP is another protocol used to transfer files on the Internet. For additional information on this topic, check a book such as *How to Use the Internet.***

► **To get rid of a hyperlink, right-click on it, choose Hyperlink, select Hyperlink, and then press Del. To change a hyperlink destination, right-click on the link, choose Hyperlink, Edit Hyperlink, enter a new file or URL in the Edit Hyperlink dialog box, and click OK.**

► **To edit link text (as opposed to the hyperlink destination), first select the cell by using the arrow keys. (Don't click on the cell or you'll jump to the destination file.) Then edit the cell contents as usual.**

This text will become a hyperlink.

1 To create a text hyperlink, first enter the text that will make up the hyperlink. (If you already have some suitable text, skip to the next step.) It's best to give users a clue where this link will take them.

8 To get back where you came from, you may be able to click the Back button on the Web toolbar. If you're in an Office program such as Excel or Word but this toolbar hasn't put in an appearance, choose View, Toolbars, Web or click the Web Toolbar button. If you jumped to a location where the Web toolbar isn't available, you can return to Excel by clicking the Microsoft Excel button in the Windows taskbar.

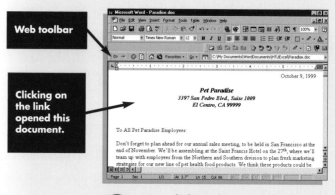

Web toolbar

Clicking on the link opened this document.

7 Now click on this text to "jump" to the specified document or location. If the destination is another Excel workbook file, it's opened. If the destination is a file from another application, such as Word, that application launches and the file is opened. If the destination is a URL—that is, a location on the Internet—you have to connect to your service provider, your Web browser launches, and you're deposited in the specified location.

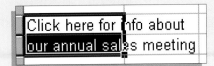

2 Select the text to be used for the hyperlink; you can use the text from one or more cells.

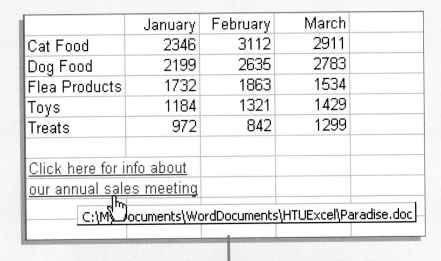

	January	February	March
Cat Food	2346	3112	2911
Dog Food	2199	2635	2783
Flea Products	1732	1863	1534
Toys	1184	1321	1429
Treats	972	842	1299

Click here for info about
our annual sales meeting

C:\My Documents\WordDocuments\HTUExcel\Paradise.doc

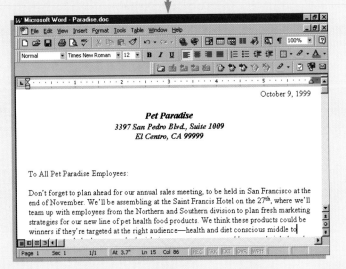

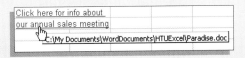

6 Click OK to insert the hyperlink. The text you selected in step 2 becomes blue and underlined. When you place your mouse pointer over this hyperlink, it turns into a hand with the index finger extended, and a ScreenTip lists the destination file or URL.

3 Click the Insert Hyperlink toolbar button or choose Hyperlink from the Insert menu.

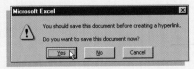

4 Save the workbook if you're asked to do so. (Excel asks whether you want to save your workbook if you haven't saved it before.)

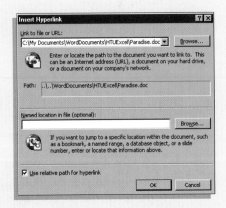

5 In the Insert Hyperlink dialog box, enter the address of the destination file in the Link to File or URL text box. (The Tip Sheet says more about URLs.) Remember, the destination can be a file on your hard drive, a file on a network drive, or even an address on the Internet. The Browse button is a convenient way to locate a file on your network you want to link to. (You can use the Named Location in File text box to make the hyperlink jump to a particular spot in the destination file. For example, you can jump to a named range in an Excel workbook file or a bookmark in a Word document. For additional details, consult the help system for the program in question.)

How to Create Web Pages within Excel

You can use a special Excel Wizard to create Web pages that contain Excel data and/or charts. This is an excellent strategy if you want to make your data widely available, either to those within your company or to the cyber-public at large. Keep in mind that Excel lets you create special files you can place on the Web but doesn't help out with the job of actually installing those files so others can gain access to them. For more details on how to actually "publish" your pages on the Web or your intranet via the FTP protocol, refer to a guide such as *How to Use the Internet.*

TIP SHEET

▶ If you don't have a Save As HTML command on your File menu, you have to install the Web page authoring tools. Check the Excel help system for details on how to go about it. (If you're brave enough to strike out on your own, start by choosing Settings from the Windows Start menu, choosing Control Panel, and double-clicking the Add/Remove Programs button.)

▶ A Web browser is a special program that lets you view files on the Web. Netscape Navigator is currently one of the most widely used browsers; Microsoft's Internet Explorer is another big one. For information about how to acquire and install a browser, as well as to gain access to the Internet, consult a good beginning book on the Internet.

▶ HTML stands for Hypertext Markup Language; it's the language used to create Web pages. Don't be intimidated; HTML is surprisingly straightforward. It consists of text with "markup codes" inserted to tell browsers how to format the page. Some of the "obscure" codes it includes are <B> for boldfacing and <I> for italic. If you'd like to learn more about HTML, refer to a good book on HTML.

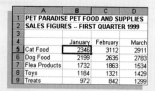

 1 Select the range of data that you want to include in the Web page, or select one of the cells containing data if you want to include all the worksheet's data in a Web page.

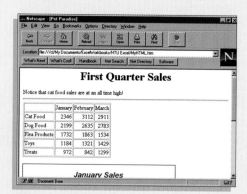

7 Excel saves the file in the specified location. At this point you can look at your Web page by using your Web browser to open the HTML file. Here, for example, is the newly created Web page viewed in Netscape Navigator, one of the most popular Web browsers on the market. The figure in the center of these pages shows the graph from that Web page.

② Choose Save As HTML from the File menu. This brings up the Internet Assistant Wizard, which converts your data into HTML, the format used for Web pages. (Don't press your panic button if you can't track down this menu option. Skip to the Tip Sheet for details.)

③ The first Internet Assistant Wizard dialog box asks you which data ranges and charts to include in the Web page. All charts are listed automatically. To exclude any charts or data ranges, select them and click Remove. To add a data range, click the Add button and then select the range in the worksheet. To change the order in which data ranges or charts appear on the Web page, use the Move buttons. When you're done, click Next.

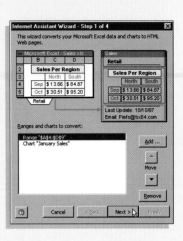

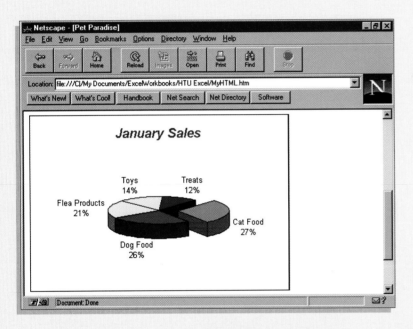

④ In the second Internet Assistant dialog box, you decide whether to create a brand-new Web page or to add data to an existing page. (You're better off creating a new page unless you're acquainted with HTML.) Again click Next once you've made your selection.

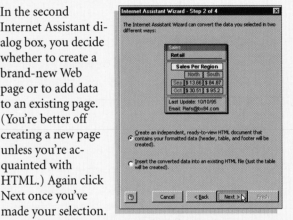

⑥ In the final Wizard dialog box, you enter the code page to use. (If you're not sure what this option is for, leave it as is.) Also, make sure Save the Result as an HTML File is selected and enter a file path and name, including the .htm extension, in the File Path text box. (Excel uses the current path and suggests the name MyHTML.htm by default.) Click on Finish when you're done.

⑤ In the third Wizard dialog box, you enter the information that will appear on your Web page alongside your data. Among other things, you can generate a title (it will appear on the title bar), a header that becomes the first line within the Web page window, and horizontal rules above and/or below your data to set it off from the text. It's a nice touch to enter your e-mail address in the Email text box. This way people viewing your Web page can easily e-mail you just by clicking on your e-mail address. As usual, click Next when you're ready to move on.

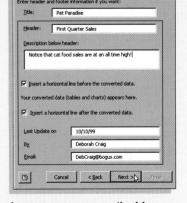

How to View Files on the Web or an Intranet

Assuming you have a connection to the Internet and a Web browser, Excel lets you view workbook files and Web pages located on Web sites or on your company intranet. Excel files are displayed in your Excel window. However, when you view a Web page—that is, an HTML file—you can launch your browser from Excel to display the page. This feature literally makes Excel a doorway to the wide world of the Internet. (Although you can open Web pages within the Excel window, often much of the formatting and graphics is lost; the pages look much better when viewed with a Web browser such as Netscape Navigator or Internet Explorer.)

TIP SHEET

▶ The techniques described here work for files on the Web or on an intranet—that is, files with URLs that begin with http://. Viewing files on FTP sites (files with URLs that begin with ftp://) involves a completely different strategy. For the inside scoop, check the online help or a more advanced book on Excel.

▶ When you click the Search the Web button, you land on the default search page. You can also set a new search page. To do so, display the Web page or file to use as a search page. (You must display the file or Web page *within Excel*—not within your browser—by entering the URL in the File Name text box of the Open dialog box.) Then choose Set Search Page from the Go menu on the Web toolbar and click Yes in the resulting dialog box.

▶ Clicking the Start Page button on the Web toolbar takes you to Microsoft's home page. To set up a new start page, display that page *within Excel*. Then choose Set Start Page from the Go menu on the Web toolbar and choose Yes in the dialog box that appears.

▶ **1** If the Web toolbar is not already displayed, bring it into view by clicking the Web Toolbar button. (It looks like a globe with one rightward and one leftward pointing arrow.)

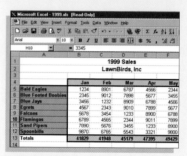

8 Excel loads the worksheet, displaying "Read-Only" in the title bar to indicate that you cannot edit the file. If you need to make changes to the file, first save it onto your computer's drive or a network drive. (You can view but not modify files you open on an intranet or a Web site. You may, however, be able to modify files at FTP sites. See the Tip Sheet for additional details.)

Here's the URL for a file on the company intranet.

7 You can also view workbook files—located either on your intranet or at a Web site—within an Excel window. Click the Open toolbar button (or choose Open from the File menu). Type the URL in the File Name text box and then click the Open button. For instance, here's the URL for a file of 1999 sales data on the company intranet.

2 Type a Web page URL in the Address box at the right end of the Web toolbar. For example, you could type **http://www.pridefund.com** to go to a Web site that provides information about socially responsible investing. (To speed things up, you can actually skip the http:// part of the address; Excel assumes that bit.) If you don't specify a particular file (Web page files have the .htm or .html extension), your browser finds the default page at the designated site.

3 Press Enter. Your Web browser loads and, in a moment, deposits you at the specified Web site. (If you weren't already connected to the Internet, you are first asked to supply your user name and password.)

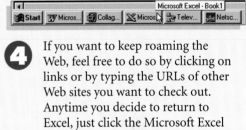

4 If you want to keep roaming the Web, feel free to do so by clicking on links or by typing the URLs of other Web sites you want to check out. Anytime you decide to return to Excel, just click the Microsoft Excel button in the Windows taskbar. (If you're done using your browser, you should close that program and disconnect so you don't unintentionally stay online, potentially racking up online charges.)

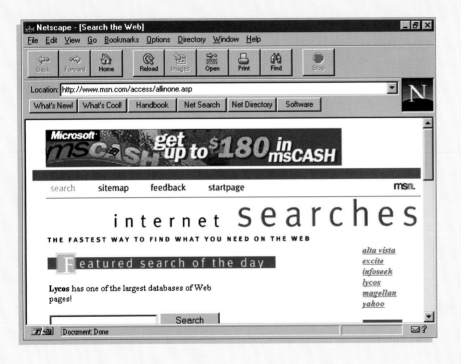

6 This method of opening Web pages works fine if you know what their names are. In some cases, however, you'll need to do a bit of sleuthing to track down the Web sites you need. Click the Search the Web toolbar button. (If you're not already online, you'll be asked to log in and your browser will start up.) You'll see a search page something like the one in the center of these pages. From this particular site, you can choose one of several search services and then begin entering keywords that indicate the types of topics you're searching for. (Check a beginning book on the Internet for more information about how to search the Internet. It's fun and easy, but be careful: You might get hooked!)

5 If your browser is already open and you want to jump to a new Web site, switch from Excel to your browser before doing so. (Click the browser's taskbar button.) Otherwise, Excel may decide to load a new copy of your browser each time you type a URL in the Address box.

INDEX